"*American Wolf* races along
like a predator on the hunt."
—TEXAS OBSERVER

"Ambitious."
**—NEW YORK TIMES
BOOK REVIEW**

"Startlingly intimate."
—ERIK LARSON

"Wild, poignant,
and compelling."
—SUSAN ORLEAN

"Transcendent."
—S. C. GWYNNE

"Vibrant."
**—ENTERTAINMENT
WEEKLY**

"Masterful and
elegant."
—ASSOCIATED PRESS

"Beautiful."
**—PUBLISHERS
WEEKLY (STARRED)**

"Jack London—like."
—NICHOLAS LEMANN

"Intimate and
riveting."
—JOHN VAILLANT

"Stunning."
—MICHAEL FINKEL

"Shakespearean."
—J. B. MACKINNON

"A must-read."
—SCIENCE

Praise for *American Wolf*

"Blakeslee draws O-Six in novelistic . . . detail, using the conflicting insight and perspective of biologists, politicians, ranchers, environmentalists, lawyers, other animals, and hunters. . . . Seeing a wolf is exceptionally rare, and this book is as close as most readers will come."

—*The New Yorker*

"A matriarch overthrown in what seems fairly described as a 'putsch,' marauding gangs running attacks into neighboring territory, an hours-long standoff with a grizzly, a discarded water bottle—a rarity in the wilderness of a national park— tossed around and protected like a prized new toy. The lives of the wolves in Yellowstone are often dramatic, but are full of touching, tender moments too, as Nate Blakeslee vividly writes in *American Wolf*."

—*Los Angeles Times*

"The story of one wolf's struggle to survive in the majestic Yellowstone National Park offers an ambitious look through the eyes of an endangered animal."

—*New York Times Book Review*

"*American Wolf* takes its place in a long lineage of wolf books. . . . [T]here are cherished, striking images here . . . testament to the ever-flowing life force that is the wolf."

—Rick Bass, *New York Times Book Review*

"[*American Wolf*] is a startlingly intimate portrait of the intricate, loving, human-like interrelationships that govern wolves in the wild, as observed in real time by a cadre of dedicated wolf-watchers—in the end, a drama of lupine love, care, and grief."

—Erik Larson, author of
The Devil in the White City and *Dead Wake*

"Wild, poignant, and compelling, *American Wolf* is an important, beautifully wrought book about animals, about values, and about living on this earth."

—Susan Orlean, author of
The Orchid Thief and *Rin Tin Tin*

"A transcendent tale of the American West."

—S. C. Gwynne, author of
Empire of the Summer Moon and *Rebel Yell*

"Gripping and fascinating! Wolf versus wolf, wolf versus man, man versus man."

—Margaret Atwood, author of
The Handmaid's Tale and *Hag-Seed* (via Twitter)

"[A] vibrant work of nonfiction."

—*Entertainment Weekly*

"[*American Wolf*] reads like a novel . . . a testament to the genius of Blakeslee's tautly constructed narrative."

—*Outside*

"A genuinely human tale told with the energy and verve of a bestselling thriller . . . *American Wolf* races along like a predator on the hunt."

—*Texas Observer*

"A masterful and elegant tale."

—Associated Press

"This is a must-read for anyone interested in the passions that wolves arouse."

—*BBC Wildlife*

"Beautiful, detailed."

—*Publishers Weekly* (starred review)

"O-Six's story [is] told with great immediacy and empathy in a tale that reads like fiction."

—*Booklist* (starred review)

"Deeply informed yet fast-paced and deftly structured . . . [*American Wolf*] is as much an account of the deep divisions within contemporary America as it is a tale about the world's most enduring carnivore."

—*New Statesman*

"Utterly compelling . . . Blakeslee's masterly use of fiction writing techniques to ratchet up the tension will hook a wide swath of readers."

—*Library Journal* (starred review)

AMERICAN WOLF

A True Story of
Survival and Obsession
in the West

NATE BLAKESLEE

B \ D \ W \ Y

BROADWAY BOOKS

NEW YORK

For Manny and June

It would be so lovely to not have to follow the scents of the politics, the laws, the cattle, the humans, the hunters, the roads. It would be so lovely to just stay in the dark woods and concentrate only on pure unencumbered biology: foot sizes and body weights, diets, range and distribution. It would also be fiction.

—Rick Bass, *The Ninemile Wolves*

No beast so fierce but knows some touch of pity.
But I know none, and therefore am no beast.

—*Richard III*

All stories are about wolves. All worth repeating, that is. Anything else is sentimental drivel. . . . Think about it. There's escaping from the wolves, fighting the wolves, capturing the wolves, taming the wolves. Being thrown to the wolves, or throwing others to the wolves so the wolves will eat them instead of you. Running with the wolf pack. Turning into a wolf. Best of all, turning into the head wolf. No other decent stories exist.

—Margaret Atwood, *The Blind Assassin*

CONTENTS

AUTHOR'S NOTE

Every scene depicting wolves in this book was drawn from contemporaneous observations. I could not have accomplished this without the generous cooperation of Laurie Lyman, who lent me her notes—some twenty-five hundred pages—on the wolves of Yellowstone's Northern Range. Laurie's daily observations, supplemented on the occasions when she was absent from the park with notes she collected from friends, allowed me to get to know the Lamar Canyon Pack, and they form the basis for my descriptions of the life of O-Six and her family.

Rick McIntyre graciously provided me copies of his own notes from key moments in the life of the pack, which, along with my interviews with other observers, allowed me to draw those scenes more fully.

Rick and Laurie's cooperation should not be construed as an endorsement of the ideas—about wolves or people—found in these pages. Those are my own.

Finally, the names and identifying characteristics of two individuals, referred to in this account as Steven and Wayne Turnbull, have been changed to protect their privacy.

O-Six Lineage

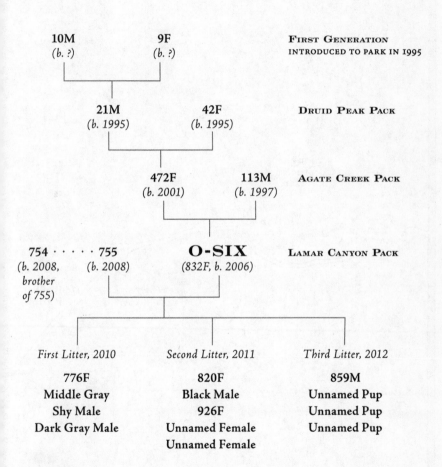

10M *(b. ?)*	**9F** *(b. ?)*	**First Generation** **introduced to park in 1995**
21M *(b. 1995)*	**42F** *(b. 1995)*	**Druid Peak Pack**
472F *(b. 2001)*	**113M** *(b. 1997)*	**Agate Creek Pack**

754 · · · · · 755   **O-SIX**   **Lamar Canyon Pack**
(b. 2008, brother of 755)   *(b. 2008)*   *(832F, b. 2006)*

First Litter, 2010	*Second Litter, 2011*	*Third Litter, 2012*
776F	**820F**	**859M**
Middle Gray	Black Male	Unnamed Pup
Shy Male	926F	Unnamed Pup
Dark Gray Male	Unnamed Female	Unnamed Pup
	Unnamed Female	

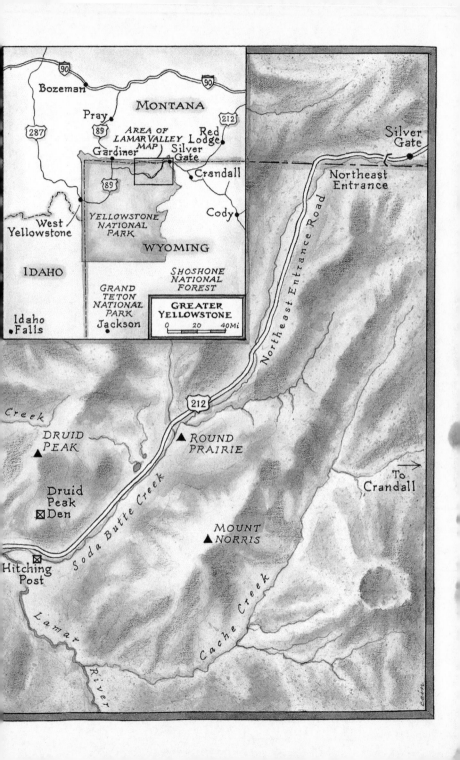

PROLOGUE

December 6, 2012

The hunter left his truck at the end of the gravel road and trudged into the fresh December snow. He was a broad-chested, clear-eyed man of middle age, wearing a brown Carhartt sweatshirt and heavy winter boots. The snow before him, tinted blue by the soft early-morning light, was crisscrossed with wolf tracks, and he followed them to the edge of an open field. Beyond it, perhaps a quarter of a mile away, was a steep, heavily forested ridge, and to his right another peak loomed, blocking out the morning sun.

On a cord around the hunter's thick neck hung a brown plastic whistle, shaped like a chess pawn. He put it to his lips and blew a series of short bursts, covering and uncovering the small fluted horn on the end, mimicking the wail of a dying cottontail rabbit. It resembled nothing so much as the cry of a colicky baby, a noise he had not heard in twenty-five years. He waited half a minute, then sent another call floating through the thin mountain air—shrill and defiant at first, then tapering off into whimpering acceptance.

You had to make it sound real, that was what most people didn't understand. Just blasting away on the call like a kazoo would get you nowhere; the trick was to imagine what it would be like to be eaten alive by a coyote, the horror and pain of that kind of death.

And you had to be patient. He'd been stalking the pack for weeks, sighting a wolf or two here and there but never getting close enough for a shot. He'd howled them the night before, using nothing more than his cupped hands and his own voice, and had eventually heard a response. They hadn't been far, and they weren't far now. He waited.

His name was Steven Turnbull, and he was in a valley known as Crandall, deep in the Absaroka Mountains northwest of Cody, Wyoming. The Clark's Fork of the Yellowstone River flowed through a narrow canyon at the western end of the valley, opening up into a wide, flat basin ringed with lodgepole pine, where it was joined by Crandall Creek, cascading down from the mountains bordering Yellowstone National Park. The creek was named for a gold prospector who was killed by Indians while making his way to a promising placer mine near the headwaters of the Clark's Fork in the spring of 1870. With the nearest settlement at least twenty miles away, the bodies of Marvin J. Crandall and his partner were not found until the following spring, when a search party came upon their severed heads, said to have been mounted on their own picks, on the banks of the creek.

Crandall was still a difficult place to reach, especially in winter. It was served only by a single road, the two-lane Chief Joseph Highway. In summer, the winding road provided a scenic route from Cody through the Shoshone National Forest to Yellowstone, which lay about twenty miles west of the basin as the crow flies, over some of the most rugged terrain in the Northern Rockies. In winter, the snowplows went no farther than Crandall's western edge; travel to Yellowstone required a snowmobile.

No more than fifty people lived in the valley year-round, raising cattle or running one of a handful of guest ranches or hunting outfitters. A single store, known as the Painter Outpost, sold breakfast and beer, catering in winter mostly to snowmobilers and hunters, and in summer to the few Yellowstone-bound tourists determined enough to take the less-traveled route to the park.

Yellowstone became a national park—the nation's first—shortly after Marvin Crandall and his fellow prospectors arrived, which theoretically protected its resources from the great wave of western migration that washed over the Rocky Mountains by the end of the nineteenth century. In reality, the fur traders who inundated the park ignored the designation, along with almost everything else that originated in Washington, D.C. Now Yellowstone was overrun with tourists, at least in summer. Turnbull seldom spent time there. The park was for visitors; Crandall—especially in winter, covered with three feet of snow—was the real Wyoming.

Yellowstone did have one thing he loved, however, and that was elk. Every winter massive herds migrated out of the park, leaving the high country for lower, less snowy pastures. Some of them followed the Clark's Fork drainage east as it wound its way down into Crandall, which became a game highway for months at a time. Turnbull had lost track of how many elk he had taken in this valley over the years.

But it wasn't like it used to be, not since the wolves had come back to Yellowstone. The elk had once paraded down into the basin every winter, some years as many as a thousand. You could pick the animal you wanted to shoot, almost like ordering from a catalog. Now you were lucky to see two hundred in the valley all winter, and the State of Wyoming had begun rationing elk tags by lottery. The wolves took the rest.

Over the last fifteen years, the wolves had spread—well beyond the borders of the park, where the first few packs were reintroduced by federal wildlife officials back in the mid-1990s. Like most people he knew, Turnbull had been against the plan from the beginning, and he thought there were now far too many wolves in Wyoming. But, of course, nobody had asked him for his opinion.

It was the same with grizzlies. When he was a kid, he could throw down a bedroll and sleep on the ground anywhere in Crandall. He would never do that now. After decades of federal protection, the woods were full of bears—so many that you didn't even have to be in the backcountry to spot them. You saw them from the road; people saw them right outside their cabins when they stepped onto their porches in the morning. To be safe, Turnbull always carried a .44 Magnum pistol with him in the woods (even in hunting season, when you weren't really supposed to).

The grizzlies claimed their share of game, too, especially newborn elk and moose—but nothing like what the wolves took. The wildlife experts in Yellowstone claimed game numbers were down because of drought more than anything else, but Turnbull didn't buy it. It was the wolves. He'd seen the chewed-up carcasses in the woods with his own eyes.

HUNTING BIG GAME WAS WHAT LIFE IN WYOMING WAS ALL ABOUT, as far as Turnbull was concerned. He couldn't remember the last time he'd bought beef at a grocery store. He might pick up a little suet from time to time, to help make lean elk meat into good burger. But meat to him meant elk. Even though hardwood was difficult to come by in his part of the world, he always found what he needed to smoke his own jerky every winter. With a healthy dose of coarse black pepper and a little garlic, there was nothing like it. He bagged it up and gave it to his friends, at least those who didn't already have sacks full of it themselves.

He wasn't in the woods every fall just for the meat. He loved the elk, and he loved the mountains they called home. He had a house about an hour's drive east, in a small farming town, but he spent most of his time at his cabin in Crandall, supporting himself with any work he could find nearby: painting cabins in the summer, acting as a caretaker for those same places in the winter, cutting firewood—manual labor of various kinds.

His grandfather had started taking him hunting for rabbit and duck in the backcountry around Cody when he was five years old. When he was a teenager, he'd hunted with his mother's old .30-40 Krag, the rifle of choice for the U.S. Army before World War I. He wasn't sure how old the gun was, but it had been given as a wedding present to his maternal grandfather, who then handed it down to his daughter on the occasion of her own wedding. It was reliable only up to a hundred yards or so, with a muzzle speed so slow you could practically see the bullet coming out of the barrel. Turnbull's sister had asked for it after their parents died, and he hadn't argued. He had a much better rifle slung over his shoulder now, but he didn't use it that much. He was mainly a bow hunter these days. He'd killed moose, black bear, eight-hundred-pound bull elk— any kind of big game you could find in these mountains—with his bow.

He loved the elegance of the bow, the same weapon (albeit greatly refined) that Indians had used to hunt elk in these very woods for hundreds of years. He'd always been taught to get as close to an animal as you could before you took your shot, and leaving your rifle at home ensured that your stalking skills would be tested. He watched all the hunting shows and read all the magazines, and he'd noticed that these days the emphasis seemed to be on long-range shooting. A manufacturer in Cody made a rifle that could supposedly kill an elk at a thousand yards. To Turnbull, that wasn't ethical. For him, fair chase, the notion that a hunter should eschew any technique that gave him or her an improper advantage over game, was more than just an empty slogan.

The other good thing about bow hunting was that the archery season for elk began in September, a month before the general rifle hunt, which meant you could get out in the woods when they were still relatively devoid of other hunters. Crandall had become increasingly popular with out-of-towners in recent years, and there were guide services in the area catering to wealthy clients—though not as many as there once were, when the elk were more plentiful. Private ranches along the Clark's Fork were world famous for their lightly hunted herds and their enormous bulls. He couldn't afford to hunt at those places, and he didn't care. Most of Crandall was National Forest land, where anybody could hunt for the price of a fifty-dollar elk tag—assuming you could get one.

The start of bow hunting season was his favorite time to be in the woods. The weather in September was still beautiful, with warm days and nights chilly enough to bring out the fall color in the aspens, cottonwoods, and willows. The bulls were rutting then, bugling to the cows in their harems and butting heads with their rivals. You had to get the meat out fast, as temperatures were warm enough to be a concern—though you couldn't really leave your kill out overnight anyway because of the bears. When you got back the next morning, there'd be nothing left of your elk, or worse, you'd find a seven-hundred-pound grizzly lying on top of it.

October meant the rifle hunt for bulls, followed by antlerless elk, usually beginning in mid-November. By the end of December, the season was over, but Turnbull still found excuses to get out into the woods. He'd stalk elk with his video camera, filming the big bulls in his favorite spots, getting to know them by their racks. In late winter, he'd go out and collect shed antlers, occasionally trying to match them with the bulls on his recordings. The woods were full of sheds, and he'd fill his pickup and sell them by the pound in town. They usually ended up as meal for animal feed. Black bear season came in the spring, and in the summer he kept himself sharp with archery practice, fletching his own arrows. It was the only time of year you could shoot at targets without losing arrows in the snow.

You couldn't shoot a grizzly—not legally, anyway. But now you could, at long last, shoot a wolf. He wasn't sure why it had taken so long for the bureaucrats in Cheyenne and Washington to see what had long been obvious to him. It wasn't that he minded seeing wolves in Crandall. Unlike some of his cowboy friends, who given the opportunity would have killed every last one of them to protect their stock, he believed they had a place on the landscape. But they needed to be controlled. When Wyoming's first legal wolf-hunting season in more than fifty years was announced that fall, game officials had set a limit of eight in this part of the Shoshone National Forest, and Turnbull had been among the first in Crandall to pay the twelve dollars for a wolf tag. Now, twelve weeks into the hunt, seven wolves had already been taken, and the tag was still in his pocket, unfilled. He planned on getting the last wolf.

IT WAS GETTING CLOSE TO SEVEN O'CLOCK WHEN TWO WOLVES stepped out of the willows along the edge of the field. They were perhaps two hundred yards away, moving in tandem across the virgin snow. One was all black and so large he could only be a male in his prime. The other—his mate, Turnbull guessed—was a gray. She was smaller but still a good-size wolf. Her thick winter pelage was white underneath, darkening to gray along the flanks. The long guard hairs on her back and shoulders were stippled with black, like a cape. At this distance, the gray might have been mistaken for somebody's lost malamute, had she not been standing next to her dark companion, who resembled nothing else under the sun but what he clearly was.

The wolves spotted the hunter immediately, but didn't run. He slowly raised his rifle to his shoulder and sighted through the scope.

He had time to choose between them.

1

RETURN OF THE WOLF

The wolves drove an elk down the side of a steep, snow-covered butte under a sky close and gray. There were three wolves. The one in the lead was almost pure white. She was followed closely by her sister, a good-size gray. Several yards back and struggling to keep up was a mature black male, his snout and withers gone silver with age.

The elk had been one of many cows atop the butte; now she was alone, hurtling pell-mell toward the broad valley below, dodging the lichen-covered glacial erratics—some the size of small cabins— that dotted the hillside, leaping over what she could, and exploding straight through the sage and juniper. It was early winter, and the snow was not yet deep, offering the kind of footing that favored the elk. For such an enormous animal—at least five times heavier than any of her pursuers—she was surprisingly fast and nimble. Her chocolate ears laid back against her head, her bouncing, ovoid rump the same shade of buff as the sedge poking up through the snow, she seemed an impossible quarry.

The cow headed for the river, as her kind often did when the wolves came. The deep water offered long-legged animals an advantage: a swimming wolf has no leverage for biting and pulling. Chases often ended in stalemate this way, with an elk standing in hip-deep water, warily eyeing a pack of wolves lounging on the nearby bank as they patiently waited to see if the frigid water would force the elk back onto dry land. The refuge the cow sought was the Lamar River, not far from where it joined the Yellowstone, and on this winter morning it was frozen solid. Perhaps she didn't know that, or perhaps in her panic she could think of nowhere else to go.

It was only five hundred yards or so from the base of the butte to the river, but once the chase reached level ground, the wolves began to close the gap. The four animals were now in single file, running flat out, pounding the snow into a fine powdery spray, like the dust under a racehorse's hooves. The contest had become purely a matter of speed, and the canines—the primordial ancestors of the greyhound, unsullied by the inbreeding that stripped away the tiger-muscled shoulders, the massive head, the powerful jaws—ran with a raw and joyous energy that the ungulate could not match.

As the race neared its climax, it was the gray who stood out. Her body seemed to stretch and elongate as the ground swept beneath her. Her legs were long—much longer than a dog's—and her hips narrow, like a cheetah's. She held her tail straight out, and her head was a flattened triangle. She was an arrow, and by comparison the elk suddenly seemed not only clumsy but also excessively— sadly, fatally—upright. Every time the cow missed a step, stumbling slightly in a pocket of deep snow, she had less time to recover, until finally there was no time at all.

The wolves pulled her down in a frozen marsh between two icy ponds.

· · · ·

ABOUT A QUARTER OF A MILE AWAY, A MAN STOOD ON THE SIDE OF a road watching the wolves eat. His name was Rick McIntyre, and he worked for the National Park Service. Bundled in a heavy black down coat that extended past his waist, only the familiar forest green of his pants marked him as a park employee. He was in an area of Yellowstone known as Little America, where the Lamar River swept through a series of low hills and rocky knolls in the park's mountainous Northern Range. Rick was sixty years old, though with his ramrod posture and tall, lean frame, his age was hard to guess, especially with a stocking cap covering his thinning red hair.

He was surveying the scene through a spotting scope, a kind of tripod-mounted telescope used for watching wildlife. Every so often he reached inside his coat and pulled a microcassette recorder from the breast pocket of his uniform and described what he was seeing. Just a few words, economical and to the point. Then the recorder disappeared back into the coat. For the most part, he stood motionless behind his scope, silently watching. It was nine a.m. on December 12, 2009, and it was the 3,467th day in a row that he had spent in the park, looking for wolves. It was getting close to lunchtime for Rick, who had been awake since about four that morning. The wolves were often active at dawn, and he liked to be in place when the landscape first became visible, about a half hour before actual sunrise.

Both the male and the white female in his scope, a mated pair, wore thick leather collars with radio transmitters attached, which was how he'd found them. Every pack in Yellowstone had at least one wolf that had been darted from a helicopter, collared, and assigned a number by the park's small team of wolf biologists. Each morning Rick drove until the antenna on the roof of his yellow

Nissan SUV picked up a wolf's unique signal, and then he stepped out into the darkness to scan the nearby landscape with his hand-held receiver.

As he watched the trio of wolves tugging at the elk carcass, Rick found his eye drawn back to the gray female. She had no collar, which meant she had not been given a number, but she did have a nickname: O-Six, for the year in which she had been born. At this range, his scope revealed every detail; she might as well have been sitting at his feet. She was a wonderful specimen, with a dense coat and a heavier physique than most females, who averaged around ninety pounds.

Not much usually distinguished one black wolf from another, but every gray was different. O-Six had unusually attractive markings—a faint black oval around each eye, offset by twin wedges of white along the bridge of her nose. Her cheeks were also white, and an unbroken streak of gray ran from the tip of her head to the end of her nose, tapering off into buff along the sides of her snout. The overall effect was of a vaguely owl-like mask, which gave her a look of quiet concentration.

She had been born a member of the Agate Creek Pack, in a den about five miles to the south, not far from where Agate Creek spilled into the chossy, sulfurous canyon that held the Yellowstone River. After leaving her pack as a yearling, she had been more or less on the run for the last two years, looking for a mate and a territory of her own.

So far she had been unsuccessful. Rick had observed her mating with five different males the previous winter without settling down with any of them, which was unusual behavior for a lone female. It was also hazardous. Young wolves had to leave their natal packs in order to find a mate, but outside their home territory, alone, they were in constant danger. Almost every part of

Yellowstone's landscape belonged to one pack or another, and the various tribes patrolled their holdings relentlessly. Lone wolves caught trespassing could count on being chased, and entire packs occasionally clashed with one another, especially along the borders of adjoining territories. Territorial conflict was the most common cause of death for the park's wolves, most of whom didn't live beyond four or five years. Life for wolves was an adventure, but it was usually not a long one.

At three and a half, O-Six had already reached middle age. Unless she found a mate soon, her prospects for survival were not good. Had she been a male, it might have been different; young males unable to find a mate were sometimes accepted into other packs. Such subordinate males were generally not allowed to breed—only the alpha male had that privilege—but they at least had a chance to take over from an aging alpha one day. Packs usually had just a single breeding female, the alpha, who tended to reject any newcomer who might bear pups of her own. Few lone wolves of either gender ever found what they were seeking: they either returned to their natal pack or died alone far from home.

Yet O-Six had a knack for not getting caught, and her moxie had made her one of Rick's favorites. In recent months, she'd been tagging along with the collared pair in his scope—one of whom was her older sister and the other an unrelated male—as they hunted the outer reaches of Agate territory, pushing farther and farther north in search of unclaimed habitat.

It was an arrangement unlikely to last. O-Six was an outstanding hunter, which made her an asset to her companions, but there wasn't much in the deal for her. Once her sister had pups with her new mate in the spring, she would be the alpha female of their new pack. O-Six would have to defer to her in every regard for as long as she remained healthy and fit to breed. Rick couldn't imagine it. O-Six simply didn't fit the mold of the beta female, content to wait her turn for a chance to lead and to have pups of her own. She didn't have the temperament for it.

O-SIX'S GREAT-GRANDMOTHER HAD BEEN ONE OF THE FIRST wolves reintroduced to the park, captured on the plains of western Canada, eight hundred miles to the north, and ferried south by plane and truck in the winter of 1995. By that time, Yellowstone had been essentially devoid of wolves for almost seven decades. Once found in virtually every habitat between the Arctic Circle and present-day Mexico City, gray wolves had been the target of a centuries-long campaign of trapping and poisoning—a war waged both for their valuable pelts and to protect livestock. They were all but eliminated by the 1920s across the vast majority of the Lower 48.

The last wolves believed to have been born in Yellowstone—a pair of pups discovered near Soda Butte Creek, about fifteen miles east of where Rick was now standing—were shot in 1926. They were killed not by poachers, but by park rangers. Almost from the time the park was created, in 1872, early superintendents had pursued a rigorous predator-control program, aimed chiefly at protecting the big game animals—elk, antelope, moose, and bighorn sheep—that were considered Yellowstone's prime attractions. Rangers patrolling on horseback finished the job the trappers had started: finding active dens, destroying the pups, and then trapping or tracking the returning adults so they could be killed as well.

As a science, wildlife management was still in its infancy, and park officials genuinely believed that predators would eventually decimate the park's prey population if left to their own devices. They didn't realize that wolves and elk had coexisted in Yellowstone for thousands of years, that the two species had in fact evolved in tandem with each other—which explained why the elk could run just as fast as the wolf but no faster. Wolves were the driving force behind the evolution of a wide variety of prey species in North America after the last ice age, literally molding the natural world around them. The massive size of the moose, the nimbleness of the white-tailed deer, the uncanny balance of the bighorn sheep—the architect of these and countless other marvels was the wolf.

Nor did Yellowstone's early managers understand what would happen to an ecosystem without predators. Once the wolves were gone, the ungulate population in the park exploded, and the quality of the range quickly began to deteriorate. Overgrazed hillsides eroded, and stream banks denuded of woody shrubs began to crumble, damaging prime trout habitat. Elk browsing at their leisure, undisturbed by predators, decimated stands of young aspen and willow. Too many animals on the landscape brought starvation and disease, and the elk population followed a boom-and-bust cycle.

By the 1930s, Yellowstone officials had no choice but to do what they had done with the wolves. They started quietly culling the park's enormous elk herds, shooting thousands of animals in an average year (usually in the winter, when few visitors were around to see the carnage). This continued until the 1960s, when hunters in areas adjacent to the park pressured their elected officials to intervene. Fewer elk in Yellowstone, they knew, meant fewer elk migrating out of the park in winter, which in turn meant fewer hunting opportunities. The elk population was once again allowed to grow untrammeled.

The idea that wolves might be the solution to Yellowstone's problems surfaced as early as 1940, though it wasn't until the 1970s that the federal government began seriously considering reintroduction. Elected officials in Idaho, Wyoming, and Montana (the states surrounding the park) were adamantly opposed to the idea, in deference to two constituencies that exercised an out-size influence on local politics: ranchers and hunters. Ranchers, whose own ancestors had helped rid the mountains of predators in the first place, feared they'd lose livestock once the reintroduced wolves began spreading beyond the park's boundaries. Elk-hunters, meanwhile, knew the wolves would be subsisting on the same game they cherished—and they'd only just won the fight to keep rangers from reducing elk numbers. From the hunters' perspective, every elk taken by a wolf was a lost opportunity, and wolves ate a lot of elk.

Hunting was big business in the Northern Rockies—not just for the professional hunting guides who relied on a steady stream of clients to earn a living, but also for the restaurants and motels that hosted the influx of out-of-town hunters who arrived every fall. As an endangered species, wolves would be protected even when they weren't in Yellowstone, but in order to get the states on board, the U.S. Fish and Wildlife Service had made a promise: as soon as the reintroduced wolf population was sufficiently numerous and stable, the wolf would be taken off the endangered species list, and the states could manage their respective populations however they wished. It was understood that this would eventually mean an annual hunting season for wolves. Still, opponents of reintroduction fought literally to the very last minute, delaying the opening of the wolves' cages as a federal judge considered their final pleadings.

In the end, proponents of reintroduction won, and the wolves were released in the park with great fanfare. Interior Secretary Bruce Babbitt and Fish and Wildlife Service director Mollie Beattie personally helped carry the cages the final stretch through the deep January snow to the release point. The Yellowstone wolves were fitted with radio collars and initially set loose into three acclimation pens, each about an acre in size. Project leaders hoped the period of adjustment afforded by the pens would make it less likely that the wolves would take off for home once they were set free. The truth was, nobody really knew what would happen. No one had ever tried this before.

WITHIN A MONTH OF OPENING THE PENS IN MARCH 1995, THE project lost its first wolf. Known as 10, he was by far the most stunning animal brought down from Canada, the very epitome of an alpha male. Just getting him sedated so that he could be collared was a challenge; he grabbed the jab stick holding the needle and snapped it in his jaws, not once, but twice. Most of the other captured wolves were scared senseless when humans approached, but 10 had the unsettling habit of staring his captors in the eyes. The project biologists placed him in an acclimation pen with wolf 9, a mature female, and her adult daughter, wolf 7, though whether the trio would bond under such artificial circumstances was far from certain. To the researchers' surprise, 9 and 10 mated even before leaving the pen. The trio, now a nascent pack, was released with high hopes that as the wolves settled into the park, a new litter— the first born in Yellowstone in decades—would soon follow.

But 10 and his pregnant companion struck out north over Druid Peak, heading out of Yellowstone and into the heart of the Absaroka-Beartooth Wilderness, with 7 in tow. Two days later Doug Smith, the project's chief biologist, picked up their signal from a small plane. They were high above the tree line in the rugged Absaroka Mountains, headed for the even higher Beartooth Plateau. It was the kind of place only a wolf could reach in winter—a ten-thousand-foot-high treeless, craggy wasteland—but it was unlikely these wolves, hailing as they did from the plains of western Canada, had ever encountered anything like it.

The long-term goal of the reintroduction project was that dispersing wolves would gradually recolonize the wilderness

surrounding the park, a twenty-million-acre expanse known as the
Greater Yellowstone Ecosystem. But not in the first week, and not
before the national park itself—free from poachers, livestock, and
busy highways—had been repopulated. Eventually the trio came
back to the park, but immediately after their return bad weather
prevented Smith from flying for eleven agonizing days. The pack's
whereabouts were unknown.

When the wolves were finally located, 7 hadn't gone far, but
it seemed that the alphas had traveled out of the park once more,
forty miles northeast, to where the Absarokas end and Montana's
central plains begin, near a town called Red Lodge. The signal
from 9's collar suggested she was in a reasonably accessible spot on
the side of a peak known as Mount Maurice. But 10's transmitter
was beeping twice as fast as normal—mortality mode.

When Smith and his team hiked to 9's last known location,
they discovered that she had denned—nothing more than a hastily
dug depression in the earth—and apparently given birth, though
she and the pups were nowhere to be found. It was as disastrous a
turn of events as Smith could have imagined, but he wasn't easily
deterred. Tall, lean, and handsome, with a thick head of unruly
brown hair and a handlebar mustache, he was not just a wildlife
biologist but a mountain man as well—someone who could design
a study and turn out a well-written paper, yet was equally in his
element hunting elk or hanging out the side of a helicopter buzzing
just over the treetops with a tranquilizer gun in his hands.

Smith called in Carter Niemeyer, the best tracker he knew, to
lead the search for the pups. Niemeyer was very familiar with 9 and
10; he was the one who had brought them down from Canada in
the first place. Prior to joining the Yellowstone Wolf Project, as the
reintroduction effort was known, he'd spent his career as a government trapper killing "nuisance" animals for farmers and ranchers,
and as a professional taxidermist. He had been a curious hire for

a program designed to bring predators back to the landscape, but Fish and Wildlife had needed someone who could gain the trust of the local trappers in the remote backcountry of western Alberta. Niemeyer, who had skinned thousands of coyotes in his lifetime— along with the occasional wolf—was the man for the job.

Not that it was easy. Suspicious of anyone who wanted a live wolf, the trappers challenged Niemeyer, then forty-eight years old and an imposing six foot five, to prove his backwoods credentials. He found himself on the floor of a trapper's cabin on the edge of the woods, knife in hand, as he and one of the locals, both drunk on homemade chokecherry wine, raced to see who could skin a freshly killed wolf the fastest. Niemeyer won the contest and came back with the wolves the project needed.

Now, scrambling across the side of Mount Maurice, grunting like a mother wolf looking for her pups, Niemeyer at last heard the whimpering and squeaks he was seeking, deep under a pile of talus. The search party pulled eight puppies out of the rocks and returned them, along with their mother, to the park, where they became known as the Rose Creek Pack.

As his collar indicated, 10 was indeed dead. He had been shot by a local man named Chad McKittrick, who, after being arrested and charged with a federal offense for shooting an endangered animal, claimed he had thought he was shooting a feral dog. It wasn't the perfect crime; a friend of McKittrick's had disposed of 10's collar in a culvert filled with spring runoff, not realizing that it was, of course, perfectly waterproof and still transmitting. The defendant was anything but repentant; while out on bail, he rode his horse down the middle of Red Lodge in the annual Fourth of July parade wearing a T-shirt that read NORTHERN ROCKIES WOLF REDUCTION PROJECT.

McKittrick's defiance made him a bit of a local hero to some. When a federal judge sentenced him to six months in prison, it

only reinforced what many in the area thought about wolf reintroduction and about the federal government in general: overreaching bureaucrats in Washington had rammed wolves down their
throats, and people weren't going to just stand by and do nothing.

IN THE YEARS THAT FOLLOWED REINTRODUCTION, THE PROJECT
spawned a great many papers in academic journals, though Rick
himself had never written one. Born and raised in rural Massachusetts, he had joined the Park Service shortly after graduating from
college with a degree in forestry—but he was an interpretive ranger
by training, not a biologist. That meant he'd spent his thirty-year
career talking to park visitors and helping them understand what
they were seeing. He'd started work as a seasonal ranger in 1976,
spending most winters in west Texas at Big Bend National Park
and summers in Denali National Park in Alaska.

Life as a seasonal ranger meant being satisfied with less. You
couldn't have much in the way of possessions, since you had no
permanent residence; nor could you make commitments or form
long-term relationships. Not that there were many people around
to get close to anyway—both parks operated with minimal staff.
Even getting news from the Lower 48 was difficult in Denali,
which covered two million acres but was serviced by only one road.
Rick lived by himself in the basement of the visitor center, sixty-
six miles from the nearest highway. It wasn't for everyone, but it
suited Rick's temperament perfectly; he had always preferred his
own company.

By the early 1990s, when Yellowstone's reintroduction plan
was beginning to take shape, Rick had already spent countless
hours watching wolves in Denali. He'd seen his first wolf deep in
the park's roadless backcountry and become obsessed, spending
all his free time watching and photographing them. In 1993 he

published a book of his wolf photos, pairing them with essays he had written about the prospects for wolf reintroduction at various national parks. He was following the progress of the Yellowstone project from afar, as it slowly moved through the federal bureaucracy. After the park had gone nearly seventy years without wolves, Rick knew that Yellowstone's naturalist division didn't have any interpretive rangers with relevant experience. He convinced Yellowstone's brass that he should be their first-ever wolf interpreter, and after fifteen seasons in Denali, Yellowstone became his new summer home.

Rick arrived in May 1994, less than a year before the first wolves were scheduled to be released, and found a community deeply divided about the wisdom of reintroduction. Over time he came to know which gas stations, restaurants, motels, and curio shops were run by pro-wolf proprietors, and which were anti-wolf. The downstairs gift shop at the airport in Bozeman, Montana, where most Yellowstone visitors landed, stocked all things wolf—stuffed animals, knickknacks, calendars, posters—while the upstairs shop near the gates had nothing. A wolf-loving friend of Rick's had once asked the woman at the upstairs counter why. After some hedging, she finally put her cards on the table. "Because we don't like wolves, that's why," she said.

In some cases, entire communities were considered to be on one side or the other. Rick rarely drove into the mountains just east of the park, for example, even though he knew Yellowstone wolves often ranged as far as Crandall. He knew Crandall was elk-hunting and cattle-ranching country, and wolves weren't popular there. Rick's yellow SUV with its telltale antenna was easy to spot, and he worried that locals might follow his movements in hopes of getting a shot at a wolf. In its early years, the project had lost at least three wolves to poachers in Crandall; it had become known as a place where Yellowstone wolves ventured and did not return.

Rick himself lived in a cabin about twenty miles northwest of Crandall, in the tiny mountain town of Silver Gate. The town was just outside the park's northeast entrance, the one least used by tourists. In the summer, it had perhaps twenty-five full-time residents. Most of them headed for lower elevations before the onset of winter, which began in mid-October and lasted at least five months.

Rick had seen his share of snow in New England, but winter in Silver Gate was different. Situated in a narrow valley at seventy-five hundred feet, the town averaged about seventeen feet of snow per year, and it wasn't unusual for Rick to wake up to temperatures of thirty below. He never quite got used to it, but he had learned to make accommodations. Each of his gloves had a pocket near the wrist that held a nine-volt battery, which powered tiny electric filaments to warm his fingers and stave off frostbite. He flattened the snow in front of his cabin with his SUV on a daily basis, lest so much accumulate that he couldn't get out at all. Plows kept the road westbound from Silver Gate into the park open, but the road eastbound was closed beyond the neighboring hamlet of Cooke City. Silver Gate in winter was the kind of place you really had to want to be.

If you loved wolves, though, nowhere else even compared. When wolves were first brought back to the park, the leaders of the Wolf Project chose a broad river valley in the northeast section of the park called the Lamar Valley as one of their release points. The valley was almost always filled with elk, making it prime wolf habitat. It was also relatively treeless, offering researchers a good chance to observe wolves hunting prey on open land, something that had rarely been seen in the wild.

The Lamar Valley had a road running through the middle of it and was popular with park visitors, and researchers figured the wolves might quickly disappear into the park's vast interior, where regular observation would require a lengthy horseback ride or, more likely, a plane. Some of the wolves did leave the valley, but to everyone's delight, a few stayed put. They didn't seem to mind the road or the people. And Yellowstone's wolves multiplied just as fast as Smith and his team had hoped they would. By the winter of 2003, the 15 wolves released in 1995, along with an additional 17 introduced a year later, had become a population of 174, divided into fourteen packs spread throughout the park.

As anticipated, scores of others had left Yellowstone to colonize the surrounding mountains, including Grand Teton National Park to the south and protected wilderness and national forest land in eastern Idaho and southwestern Montana, areas that had been wolf-free for decades. As part of the same project, wolves had also been returned to a wilderness area in central Idaho, and that population was flourishing and dispersing as well. Wolves dispersing south from Canada, meanwhile, had recolonized a wide swath of northwestern Montana, centered around Glacier National Park. Now, just fourteen years after the first pens were opened in the Lamar Valley, the wolf population in the Northern Rockies had grown to over seventeen hundred animals.

Catching a glimpse of a wolf in the wild anywhere else, even for a biologist engaged in full-time fieldwork, was rare, but in Yellowstone the possibilities for groundbreaking research were endless. Rick had once hosted a visiting researcher from Wisconsin who studied wolves in the thick forests of the Upper Midwest, the one area in the Lower 48 where gray wolves were never fully extirpated. His method was essentially the same as Rick's: following radio-collared wolves all day using telemetry and trying to observe them through a spotting scope. After a week of amazing viewing in the Lamar Valley, Rick asked his excited visitor how often he saw wolves back home. The researcher thought for a moment. "Last year I saw wolves maybe five or six days," he said. The rest of his time was filled with following tracks and collecting scat. Things weren't like that in Yellowstone. It had been almost nine years since a day had passed without someone spotting a wolf somewhere in the park. Yellowstone was a wolf-watching mecca.

AS RICK WATCHED O-SIX AND HER COMPANIONS EAT, THEIR MUZzles bright red in his scope, he noticed a pair of skittish coyotes eyeing the carcass warily. The coyotes were less than half the size of the wolves and not nearly as fast. But they were hungry, and one of them eventually edged closer to the feeding wolves. The male wolf leaped to his feet and lunged at the coyote, which ran tuck-tailed and panicked across the snow. When he was satisfied it would not return, the wolf made his way back to his meal.

Rick made a note of it on his recorder and went back to watching. His field notes, which he typed up on his computer in his cabin every evening, were nothing if not meticulous. Each day's report began with a summary of the weather, followed by brief descriptions of behavior observed throughout the day, each labeled with the time of day and the exact duration. He considered his research to be in the tradition of the great naturalist Adolph Murie, the first biologist to undertake a steady observation of wolf behavior in the wild. Murie carefully documented the activities of a Denali pack for two consecutive denning seasons and reported his findings in a 1944 book that was now considered a classic. During the fifteen summers Rick spent in Denali as a seasonal ranger, he came to know the descendants of the same pack that had been watched by Murie decades before.

Rick, who had once gone 891 consecutive days with at least one wolf sighting, had in essence turned his life into a field study. He had more than eight thousand single-spaced pages of notes—his life's work—saved on his computer. He had never printed out the entire thing; his ancient printer likely wouldn't survive the task. But he did have a couple of years' worth of notes compiled in red three-ring binders that he sometimes got out to show visitors. When he had enough notes, he would start his own book, about Yellowstone's wolves.

SUDDENLY ALL THREE WOLVES BOLTED FROM THE ELK CARCASS, O-Six sprinting across the snow as though she were a spooked coyote herself. Rick scanned the landscape with his scope and spotted five black wolves approaching from the north.

It was the Druids.

The carcass was on the west end of Little America, which was more or less Agate territory, but the Druid Peak Pack made regular forays into the area from their stronghold, the Lamar Valley, five miles to the east. Now the Druids had arrived in force, and O-Six had to surrender her prize—which would have lasted the three wolves a couple of days at least—after only an hour of feeding. Rick recognized the white muzzle of the Druid alpha male, known as 480, along with White Line, the uncollared alpha female. Eventually the entire pack came in to feed: Black Bar, Dull Bar, Thin Female, Triangle Blaze, 691, and 690.

Rick was happy to see them. He had spent more time watching the Druids, one of the original packs brought down from Canada, than any other pack. Everyone had. Ensconced in the sparsely wooded Lamar Valley since the early days of reintroduction, the Druids were the easiest pack to spot for researchers and park visitors alike, making them the face of the reintroduction program for over a decade. And there were lots of them. In their heyday, the Druids had numbered thirty-seven wolves, one of the largest packs ever recorded anywhere in the world.

As the stars of the show, the Druids did not disappoint: defending the valley against invading packs, running down countless elk, raising litter after litter in their den on Druid Peak, all within view of an audience of visitors that grew bigger every year. Rick began taking notes on the pack when they were first brought to the park, and he never stopped.

Rick leaned into his scope and hunched his shoulders against the biting wind. O-Six was now long gone, but he zeroed in on the carcass, and his scope was soon filled with familiar faces. Every wolf in the pack was like an old friend, just as their parents had once been, and their parents' parents. Watching from the roadside in the Lamar Valley, he'd seen generation after generation of Druid pups leave the den, follow adults on the hunt, find their place in the pack, learn how to be wolves. As always, he found himself absorbed by the tableaux on the other side of his eyepiece, drawn into the world where nothing mattered but the welfare of the pack. He was hungry, his feet were freezing, and he was more than a little worried that O-Six wouldn't survive the winter. But at least there were wolves in his scope.

2

IN THE VALLEY OF THE DRUIDS

Rick had been tracking O-Six for only a short time, but he knew her lineage well. Her grandmother had been one of the park's most celebrated wolves, the Druid alpha female known as 42, which made her a descendant of Yellowstone's canine royalty. Over the years, at least a half-dozen of 42's female pups had become alphas in their own right, in packs spread across the park. Rick had seen them all come of age, each rising to the top in her own time and place, and he saw the same potential in O-Six, despite the perilous circumstances in which she currently found herself.

O-Six's story began where all good Yellowstone wolf stories began: in the Lamar Valley. The Druid Peak Pack had held the territory for so long that it was hard to imagine one without the other. But for those longtime observers, like Rick, who could remember the pack's beginnings, nothing about their rise had seemed inevitable.

The Druids were among the second group of wolves brought

to the park from Canada, in 1996. The original pack consisted of a large gray male, known as 38, his mate, and three yearling daughters. When they were released into the Lamar Valley, it was already home to the Crystal Creek Pack, which had been introduced to the valley the year before and had never strayed far. The park had millions of acres of unoccupied habitat, and the hope was that the newcomers would roam until they eventually found their place alongside the handful of other packs that had established themselves in the Northern Range, the fifty-seven-mile-long mountainous stretch between Gardiner, near the park's northwest entrance, and Silver Gate.

But the Druid alphas preferred to stay in the valley and fight. One morning in May, scarcely three weeks after the Druids had been released from their acclimation pen, project biologists detected a mortality signal from the collar of the Crystal alpha male. Nobody witnessed the battle, but the dead wolf's bloodied carcass told the tale well enough—the Druids had killed him. The Crystal pups were missing as well, presumably killed or scattered. The alpha female, injured and desperate, retreated into the park's interior with what remained of her pack.

Another conflict soon followed. Exploring the western edge of their new territory, the Druids encountered the Rose Creek wolves. Once again the bold new pack attacked. This time Rick was present for the melee, and he watched as the Rose Creek alpha male defeated 38 in single combat, driving the Druid alpha and his pack back into the Lamar Valley. The Druids had emerged unscathed, however, and managed to kill a Rose Creek yearling in the process.

The Druids' early battles, the first territorial conflicts witnessed since reintroduction, made Rick and his colleagues see Yellowstone's landscape in a new light. From a wolf's perspective, the Lamar Valley was a territory worth fighting for.

Doug Smith had assumed there would be a certain amount

of friction as the newly introduced wolves sorted out their various territories, but actually witnessing the conflicts—thrilling to
see but chastening in their sudden violence—was more than project biologists could have hoped for. Although it was hard to lose
wolves they had invested so much time and money into relocating,
the conflicts served to divide Yellowstone's untapped wolf habitat
into discrete units, each big enough to support one pack. Wolves
fighting other wolves was part of the natural order of things.

In early December 1997 the pack, which now included five
nearly full-grown pups and an unrelated male who had recently
joined, journeyed up over snowy Mount Norris at the eastern end
of their territory and into the high country that divided Yellowstone from the Shoshone National Forest. They were far beyond
the range of telemetry equipment, and following them through
that country—ridge after heavily wooded ridge, riven by plunging
valleys lined with frozen creeks—was unthinkable in winter. Coming down the other side, the wolves followed Crandall Creek as it
wound its way toward the Clark's Fork of the Yellowstone River.

It was elk-hunting season, and hunters on horseback, rifles
slung over their shoulders, patrolled the trail that followed the
lower reaches of the creek, studying the snowy ground for the
tracks of last night's passing game. Both pursuing elk, the wolves
and the hunters instead found each other.

On December 3, Doug Smith got a call from the Wyoming
Game and Fish Department, which regulated hunting in the state.
An outfitter had found a dead wolf along Crandall Creek and
packed him out. His collar identified him as the Druids' beta male,
and he'd been illegally shot. When Smith took the plane up over
Norris and into Crandall, he picked up the signal for 38, the alpha
male. He seemed to be holed up at the bottom of a deep gorge that

held one of the creek's tributaries. He wasn't dead, but he wasn't moving much, either. Most likely he'd been shot, too.

Smith and his colleagues debated whether to hike down to the injured wolf, tend his wounds, and relocate him to the park. Ordinarily they'd let a wolf fend for himself—they weren't zookeepers, after all—but it wasn't natural causes that had endangered 38, and this made the decision less clear-cut. They ultimately decided not to interfere, though Smith flew over the gorge once a day to track the wolf's progress. After a few days, 38 had scarcely moved from his original location, though the collar indicated that he was still alive. Unable to hunt and isolated from his pack, he was in all likelihood beginning to starve to death. It was bad enough to lose a wolf to some elk-hunter's fleeting impulse; 38 alone, at the bottom of that ravine, slowly dying was too much for Smith. He took a helicopter up and dropped meat into the gorge, hoping 38 would find it.

It took eleven days for the wolf to die. When Smith retrieved his body, the Druids' former leader—a hefty 122 pounds when he was introduced into the park—weighed just 88. The perpetrator was never found, though suspicion fell on a local hunter.

NOT LONG AFTER THE DRUIDS RETURNED TO THE LAMAR VALLEY, a veteran wildlife cinematographer named Bob Landis spotted a young black wolf moving cautiously toward the pack. Taciturn and endlessly patient, Landis had spent nearly as much time in the Lamar Valley as Rick, whom he had known since his Denali days and often relied on to find the wolves he filmed. The visitor was 21, a two-year-old from the Rose Creek Pack. He'd been roaming in recent months, eager to leave his natal pack and begin a family of his own, but his appearance in Druid territory was a surprise. The

Rose Creek yearling that the Druids had killed just a year before had been one of 21's own littermates.

But fortune had always been kind to 21. The fact that he had lived to adulthood at all was something of a miracle. He was one of the eight rescued offspring of the ill-fated 9 and 10 recovered from the makeshift den near Red Lodge and returned to the park by Doug Smith. Although he could never be sure, Smith had always suspected that lucky 21 was the last pup found on that unforgettable day, when he'd returned for one last look to the talus pile in which the pups had holed up. Groping blindly on his knees, shoulder-deep in a crevice, he had felt something soft just beyond his grasp. The pliers on his pilot's Leatherman gave him the extra inch of reach and the purchase he needed to pull the squirming, yelping pup from the hole.

Now 21 was a robust and adventuresome adult, the very picture of an alpha, if he could find a place in the Northern Range where such a wolf was needed. The Druids had lost 38 and their beta male only a few days earlier, but something—perhaps the family's collective howl, diminished as it now was—had told 21 that the pack's adult males were gone.

That didn't mean the remaining Druids weren't dangerous. This was especially true of 40, the alpha female, who ran to meet 21 on a snowy hillside not far from the river as Landis watched through his camera's viewfinder. She was a slender gray, unimpressive in stature—especially nose to nose with the hulking black intruder—but notorious for her ill temper. She had risen to leadership in a putsch of her own design, driving out her mother, the former alpha female, who had been reduced to forlornly following her brood, scavenging at whatever scraps she could find. 40 was equally hard on her two sisters, constantly reminding them of their inferior status. Largely symbolic in most packs, pinning an underling was an activity that the snarling 40 undertook with uncommon enthusiasm.

Now she advanced on 21, with her sisters in tow. The male retreated, but not far. When he turned to face the females, it was with his tail raised high—he didn't want to fight, but he wasn't afraid, either. With his camera rolling, Landis watched from the roadside in quiet fascination as 40 and her sisters chased him across the hillside for hours, seemingly on the verge of attacking but always stopping short. The five pups, anxious and unnerved, looked on from a distance. The confrontation had shifted from a territorial challenge to a ritual of sorts, one seldom observed in the wild and never before filmed. The new male was being tested, Doug Smith would say later, to see if he possessed that ineffable combination of qualities that make an alpha an alpha.

Had 21 been found wanting, he would have been lucky to escape without injury. As it happened, the choreography of the encounter gradually took on the trappings of play. The male bowed, his forelegs spread wide and his head near the ground, and the sisters leaped forward. He hopped aside, and they turned with him in delight, nearly skipping as they took off running together, like a pack. Eventually one of the females put a paw across 21's back, and he allowed it to remain, his lips split wide in a canine grin. When the pups finally joined in, they jostled one another for a chance to lick at 21's jaw from below, wagging their tails as they had for 38, as though they had known the newcomer all their short lives.

THUS BEGAN 21'S TENURE AS ALPHA MALE OF THE DRUIDS. His reign lasted six and a half years, though his partnership with 40 didn't survive nearly that long. The problem lay in the delicate politics of breeding. A wolf pack is essentially a family, typically consisting of a breeding male and female, known as the alpha pair, along with yearlings from the previous spring's litter, and a few two- or even three-year-old offspring who have yet to leave home. Wolves breed only once a year and are reluctant to do so with their own offspring, which means that usually only the alpha pair will mate. When an unrelated male joins a pack, however, other combinations become possible, and 21 showed interest not only in 40 but in her two sisters.

For the first three years after 21's arrival, 40 prevented her sisters from breeding as best she could, savaging them at every opportunity. They rarely if ever fought back, submitting to her attacks by rolling over and showing their stomachs. If any pups were born to 40's sisters, they didn't survive. (It was possible that the alpha had killed her rivals' litters, though project biologists couldn't be sure.) Meanwhile, 40 produced few pups of her own, and the pack's numbers grew only modestly.

That changed in the spring of 2000, when 21 managed to impregnate a sister known as 42, along with her adult daughter, even as he sired pups with 40 herself. He divided his time between three dens spread across the valley, each about three to four miles apart. One evening in May, while away from her den on a hunt, 40 came upon 42, who was also out hunting with another female for company. As Rick watched through his scope, 40 delivered a vicious attack, forcing both the wolves to submit. She then followed the pair back toward 42's den, where her pups, barely a month old and still defenseless, were being watched by a third female. Rick and his colleagues feared the worst. The next morning he spotted a female wolf near the road, so wounded she was barely moving.

But to his surprise it wasn't 42. It was 40. She was bleeding from bite wounds, including one that had severed her jugular artery, and she died shortly after she was found. On closer examination, project biologists found that she had been bitten all over, almost certainly by multiple attackers. The savagery of the attack was startling; Doug Smith discovered a hole in the back of 40's neck deep enough to sink his index finger all the way to the knuckle. Sometime during the night, the long-suffering Druid females had apparently decided they'd had enough. It was the first documented instance of a pack's subordinate members killing their own alpha. 40's pups were now motherless, and their future was in doubt. Would they be killed along with their mother?

As Rick and his colleagues looked on in amazement, 21 supervised the relocation of the far-flung litters, consolidating the pups—twenty-one in all—into one massive brood. 42 rose to become the new alpha female, and suddenly harmony reigned in the pack, as all the females worked together to raise the enormous litter. Even under normal circumstances, keeping pups fed, healthy, and safe from predators is a struggle, and mortality rates of 50 percent are not uncommon. Yet an astounding twenty of the Druid pups survived to adulthood, ushering in a golden era for the pack.

21 continued to breed with multiple females, and by August 2001 the pack had grown to thirty-seven wolves, roughly three times the size of the next-largest pack in Yellowstone. The Druids became the dominant force in the Northern Range, expanding their territory and winning battle after battle with neighboring packs. 21 had become a kind of Abraham of Yellowstone wolves, siring more pups than any alpha before or since.

The entire Druid saga played out in the wide-open landscape of the Lamar Valley, and some of the most astonishing action happened in full view of the park road, to the delight of both researchers and visitors. Wolves had already been among the world's most studied animals prior to the reintroduction, yet there was so much more to learn. This was especially true of predation: in the project's first decade, researchers in Yellowstone witnessed an unprecedented one hundred wolf kills. Employees who lived in the park watched wolves run down elk in their own front yards. Yellowstone had become a place where you might see something out your kitchen window that researchers elsewhere waited years to observe.

THE YELLOWSTONE WOLF PROJECT'S OFFICES WERE IN THE PARK headquarters in Mammoth, not far from the northwest entrance near Gardiner. When he was first hired, Rick's job was to organize talks at the Mammoth visitor center. But every chance he got, he drove thirty miles east to the Lamar Valley to look for wolves—usually the Druids—with the project biologists. He knew he was supposed to be talking to visitors, but the excitement of following wolves around the valley as they made their first kills and established their territories was irresistible. As a sort of compromise, he began approaching any visitor he happened to see in one of the park road's various pullouts, as he was scanning the mountainsides with his scope. "Hello, my name is Rick McIntyre," he told them. "Would you like to see a wolf?"

With only a few dozen wolves in the park in these early years, visitors had virtually no chance of seeing one on their own. But with Rick's help, they could. Soon word got out, and Yellowstone's traffic enforcement rangers found themselves dealing with overflowing parking lots in spots where normally there would be only a handful of cars. Park management was not pleased. Wolf reintroduction was about making an ecosystem whole; it was never really supposed to be a tourist attraction, and everyone had assumed the wolves would be too difficult to spot in any case. Now, thanks to Rick, visitors were trampling the sage to get a better view of history in the making. Rules were being broken, and wolves, from the perspective of some park employees, were becoming a hassle. Rick's supervisor urged him to stick to his assigned duties, but nothing he told his new charge seemed to deter him.

It wasn't Rick's first conflict with Park Service management. With over twenty thousand employees, the service was as bureaucratic and hierarchical as any agency of the federal government, though Rick found that some bosses were more hidebound than others. A few would have been right at home in the U.S. Army. Rick once sat in the back row at a meeting of interpretive rangers while a supervisor demonstrated in surprising detail how pens were to be carried while on duty.

Rick himself was not a stickler for rules. He had been issued a green clip-on tie, though he never wore it. The Park Service gave rangers a yearly allotment to spend on uniforms, but Rick tended to wear his until they were threadbare—and sometimes beyond. He had repaired the crotch of a particularly comfortable pair of green government-issue jeans with dental floss.

In an effort to rein him in, the Park Service assigned Rick to the visitor center near Old Faithful, seventy miles from the Lamar Valley. The main attraction in that part of the park, of course, was the geyser itself. It could be counted on to go off every ninety minutes or so, and the park kept visitors apprised of the estimated time of the next eruption on a chalkboard in the viewing area. If they had a little time to kill, families might get ice cream or wander into the auditorium during Rick's slideshow on wolves. The pictures were interesting, but there would be a great deal of watch checking in the audience, and periodically a mass exodus would occur to get a good spot to watch the eruption. It was like trying to do stand-up comedy at a nightclub with the Super Bowl playing on the TV above the bar. Rick could have had slides of an alpha female giving birth in a den while her mate wrestled grizzlies outside in an ice storm, and it wouldn't have made a difference. Old Faithful was Old Faithful.

He was also required to conduct "wolf walks" through the woods near the visitor center, in which he discussed the role wolves played in Yellowstone's ecosystem. To his frustration, there were no wolves in those woods nor anywhere else in the vicinity of Old Faithful; they were all still in the Northern Range. In the calculus of the Park Service, that was of little consequence. Old Faithful was where the visitors were, so this was where Rick needed to be.

One afternoon a boy asked him, "Are we going to see wolves on this walk?" Rick had to admit that they would not. "Why not?" the boy wanted to know.

"Because there aren't any wolves in this part of the park," Rick replied.

"Then why are we doing a wolf walk here?" the boy asked.

Someday, Rick wanted to tell him, *you'll have a boss, and you'll know the answer to that question.*

What tortured him wasn't just that the Druids were so far away. It was the knowledge that if he had been conducting his talks in the Lamar Valley, his audience wouldn't have to be content with mere slides—they might actually see wolves. Still, he wasn't going to let the distance keep him from seeing the animals himself. Rising long before dawn, he made the tiresome drive—an hour and a half each way on the park's roads, where the speed limit was only forty-five—to the Lamar Valley and back every day, returning in time to do his talks at Old Faithful. Sometimes he arrived in the evening instead and slept in his car, so he would be in the valley at first light. Eventually, after four summers of frustration, Rick's superiors in the naturalist division gave up and transferred him to the biology department. His new boss was Doug Smith.

IMMEDIATELY AFTER RICK'S TRANSFER, SMITH RECEIVED A WARN-ing from his own boss. Ranger McIntyre, he said, was essentially unsupervisable. But he was Smith's problem now, and the boss made it clear he considered the matter closed. "If I hear the name 'Rick McIntyre' again," he said, "you're in trouble."

Rick liked and admired Smith, and he was happy to leave the crowds at Old Faithful behind. His new job was to help the Wolf Project keep tabs on the wolves in the Northern Range, mostly in the Lamar Valley. He became a key spotter for the annual winter study, in which teams of researchers—often graduate students—were brought in to follow each pack intensively for thirty days, documenting the wolves' daily movements and hiking out to investigate every kill after the wolves had finished eating.

Smith was impressed with Rick's fieldwork and his encyclopedic knowledge of wolves and their habits, but he wanted Rick to keep talking to park visitors, too. Now that it was clear that wolves weren't going to leave the valley, visitors inevitably were going to interact with them, especially as their numbers grew. Smith needed someone to help manage that interaction, to make sure visitors didn't approach wolves, or disturb dens, or park along the road in areas where wolves were likely to cross. If Rick could help people understand wolves in the process, and help shape the new and rapidly growing phenomenon of Yellowstone wolf-watching, Smith figured, all the better. He hired Rick on as a permanent employee in the spring of 1999; for the first time in twenty-four years, Rick spent a summer and a winter in the same place.

ONCE HE BECAME A FULL-TIME YELLOWSTONE RESIDENT AND SETtled into his daily routine of watching the Druids, Rick found that he didn't want to do anything else. Strictly speaking, he worked only forty hours a week, but he came to the park every morning regardless of whether he was on the clock. When he wasn't officially on duty, he didn't wear his uniform—otherwise there was no difference in his daily routine. He didn't take vacations, and he rarely got sick. He would occasionally get offers to speak on wolves at various conferences around the country, but he always turned them down. His work in the park was too important.

In June 2000 he took a short trip to Massachusetts for his mother's funeral. Although he didn't realize it at the time, it would be the last time he ever traveled any real distance from Yellowstone. It wasn't that he'd made a conscious decision not to leave again; it just sort of happened that way. His father, an engineer at AT&T, had died of a heart attack when Rick was ten, and his mother, a homemaker, had never remarried. His only sibling, Alan, was six years older, and the two were not close. For the next fifteen years, the farthest Rick ever ventured from the park was an occasional evening trip to the nearest movie theater, seventy-five miles away in Cody. He never missed another day watching wolves.

If he did skip a day, who knew what he might miss? The celebrated primate researcher Jane Goodall didn't even have a college degree when she was assigned to watch chimpanzees in Tanzania, Rick liked to remind people, yet she was the first to record them using twigs as tools for fishing termites out of the ground, a discovery that upended the conventional understanding of primate intelligence. She had been in the field for months, much longer than any other observer, before she witnessed that startling behavior. And yet if you had approached her the day *before* she made that discovery and asked her if a chimp was smart enough to use a tool to get what it wanted, she would have said no.

It was all about showing up.

IN THE PARK, MEANWHILE, THE WOLVES OF THE LAMAR VALLEY were putting on a never-ending show that as many as thirty thousand visitors per year were witnessing. Guide services catering to wolf-watchers sprang up in Gardiner, near the northwest entrance, and cabins and motels near the park saw increased bookings even in the low seasons. Wolf tourism was booming. In 2003 the National Geographic channel aired Bob Landis's documentary on the saga of 21 and 42. The film, which won an Emmy, was so popular that Landis eventually made two more about the pack. President Bill Clinton came to see the wolves, as did a string of celebrities, whom Doug Smith dutifully shepherded around the park, relying on Rick to make sure everyone got to see a wolf. Rick's favorite such occasion was a visit from Cameron Diaz and the rapper DMX for an environmentally themed MTV show. DMX, who was raised in Yonkers, had trouble adjusting to the scale of Yellowstone. "I had no idea any of this was even here," he marveled.

By then, wolf reintroduction was being called the greatest wildlife conservation success story of the last fifty years. The men and women who made it happen had become celebrated figures in the insular world of wildlife biology. Mike Phillips, the original project leader, had been hired away from the Park Service by Ted Turner to head the Turner Endangered Species Fund in Bozeman and was eventually elected to a seat in the Montana state legislature. Doug Smith, who succeeded Phillips as director, published a pair of books about the project and was in considerable demand as a speaker at conferences around the country. Perhaps the unlikeliest hero was Carter Niemeyer, who had come to admire the animals despite his decades-long career as a government trapper. His wolf-skinning story had become a treasured part of the lore of reintroduction, and he'd since gone on to become the head of Fish and Wildlife's wolf office in Idaho.

As the years went by and Yellowstone wolf-watching became a full-blown phenomenon, Rick became something of a celebrated figure himself, with all the perks—and headaches—that appertained. Visitors interested in seeing wolves learned by word of mouth that their best course of action was to look for Rick's yellow

Nissan Xterra. He wasn't hard to find: only one road transected the park's Northern Range, where viewing was generally best and where he spent most of his time. "That's the wolf guy," people would whisper as they spotted him standing near his scope.

Rick never quite got used to being followed, but he grew resigned to the routine: if he so much as paused in a pullout or parking lot, it was just a matter of time before one car would stop, then another. Soon a dozen cars would be squeezing in. Like a grizzly or a bald eagle or any of the park's traffic-jam-inspiring attractions, he had been sighted.

ONCE HE BEGAN STAYING IN YELLOWSTONE YEAR-ROUND, RICK came to know the Druids' homeland intimately. The pack routinely covered twenty miles in a day, and Rick learned to move with them, methodically making his way across the Lamar Valley until he'd located their signals. On the eastern end of the valley was massive Mount Norris, beyond which lay the park boundary and, farther still, Crandall. At the foot of Norris was a wide, flat alluvial plain, where the Lamar River dropped down from a high plateau in the park's interior and was joined by a trout stream known as Soda Butte Creek, tumbling in from the northeast. Druid Peak, the mountain for which the pack was named, overlooked the confluence of the two streams from the north side of the valley. Moving downstream, the river flowed through a classic U-shaped glacial valley, dotted here and there with boulders and small ponds left behind by the retreating ice. Heavily wooded Specimen Ridge, named for the abundance of petrified wood found on its flanks, stretched along the entire southern side of the valley. The ridge dropped down toward the river in a series of broad grassy benches—the largest of which, called Jasper Bench, was a favorite hunting ground for the Druids. A series of more or less treeless

ridges formed the opposite side of the valley, which narrowed at its
western end to a modest gorge, known as Lamar Canyon, before
opening back up again as the river flowed through Little America.
About halfway down the valley's length on the northern side was a
small cluster of buildings known as Buffalo Ranch, which included
a ranger station and a classroom where wildlife classes were taught.
All this was Druid country.

Rick grew accustomed to the natural rhythms of the wolves'
existence. Winter was a time for roaming, as the Druids patrolled
the full width and breadth of their territory, scent-marking the
borders with urine and following the various elk herds that didn't
migrate out of the park. The pack was at its most cohesive in these
months, traveling and hunting together as a group. In the spring,
21 and 42 became inseparable, and Rick learned to watch for the
telltale signs of another litter on the way. 42 would begin visiting
the pack's den in a thickly wooded dale on a shoulder of Druid
Peak, preparing it for an extended stay. In early summer would
come the first sightings of the pups, and the excitement of counting
how many had been born and the parsing of coat color and gender,
so difficult to determine through a spotting scope.

Around midsummer the alphas would move the family from
the mountain down onto a favorite spot on the valley floor. It was at
the base of Specimen Ridge, about a mile south of the river, where
a minor creek came down amid a large fan of boulders and other
detritus, evidence of what was once a larger watercourse. Such
gathering points, known as rendezvous sites, are typically used by
packs whose pups have grown large enough to leave the den area
but not yet quite sturdy enough for the endless roaming that comes
with winter. With secrecy no longer quite so essential to the pups'
survival, the alphas usually choose a more open area with better
access to prey.

Watching the Druid alphas move their pups from the den

to the rendezvous became a favorite summertime ritual for wolf-watchers, who took advantage of a parking lot near the base of the mountain to observe the action. Since the den was on the north side of the park road, and the rendezvous site was on the south, the journey included a highly visible crossing of the blacktop—usually the pups' first—which in turn meant that everyone was able to get a close look at the youngsters for the first time.

Though the annual relocation was a distance of only perhaps two and a half miles, it was a major undertaking. Besides the road, the pups also had to cross Soda Butte Creek. Especially if the previous winter's snowpack had been high, the creek could be dangerously deep and fast-moving. Getting across alive was a rite of passage for every Druid pup and a moment of high drama for the watchers, complete with cheers every time a drenched youngster dragged himself up, spooked and bedraggled, onto the far bank.

By the fall, the pups were almost as big as the adults and beginning to accompany them on short hunting excursions, until winter came and the pack was free to roam en masse once more. The composition of the pack was constantly in flux. Pups became yearlings; yearlings became adults and wandered off to seek their fate, some to eventually return, others never to be seen again. The one constant was 21 and 42. Rick never tired of watching the alpha pair, especially 21, who was unlike any wolf he had ever seen.

Even before 21 left his natal pack, Rick had known he was unusual. One morning in the spring of 1997, two years after Doug Smith and Carter Niemeyer rescued 21 following the death of his father, Rick watched the handsome young wolf returning from a hunt. With him was the big male who had become the pack's new alpha when 21 was still a tiny pup. The pair had killed an elk, and 21, already an outstanding provider, had brought a massive piece of meat back to the den, where a new litter of pups had been born.

The pups, his new brothers and sisters, showered him with

affection, but 21 seemed tense, pacing back and forth across Rick's scope. Finally the wolf found what he was looking for: a troubled pup that he had recently taken an interest in. There was usually one pup who held the lowest rank in a litter's pecking order, but this pup was different; he had some physical problem that held him back. Rick couldn't tell exactly what was wrong with him, though his littermates clearly recognized that he was different and shunned him. But 21 seemed to have empathy for the pup, the way a dog seems to know when his owner is feeling depressed or lonely. As Rick looked on, the strapping 21 played with the tiny wolf as though he were still a pup himself, giving him the attention he so seldom enjoyed from his siblings.

This capacity for empathy was one of the qualities Rick loved most about wolves. As a pup, 21 had been reared by a father who was unrelated to him but still felt compelled to provide for him and his siblings; in turn, 21 found himself caring for pups who were not his own when he stepped into 38's place as the leader of the Druids. It was very unusual in the animal world, except among canines (and humans). Wolves had an evolutionary imperative to become attuned to the emotions of others because they lived in packs, where cooperation—for hunting, for protection from rivals—was paramount. Sociability enhanced the chances for survival.

Over years of watching wolves, Rick had become convinced that empathy was the single most important trait that an alpha could have, and 21's capacity for it continued to amaze him. After 21 became the leader of the Druids, Rick watched him win many territorial battles—he'd once fought off five intruders single-handedly—but he'd never seen him actually kill a wolf. His mate was the same way. Unlike that of the sister she had helped depose, 42's rule was a benevolent one.

In 2002 the enormous pack split apart, with the various factions forming at least three new packs in areas south and west of the

Lamar Valley, while 21 and 42 maintained control of their original territory. Alpha wolves with Druid lineage were now spread throughout the Northern Range, including the female who would eventually lead the Agate Creek Pack and give birth to O-Six. To Rick, the Druids were like the Kennedys, American royalty.

BY THE END OF THE FIRST DECADE AFTER REINTRODUCTION, DIS-persing wolves were showing up in far-flung wilderness areas where they hadn't been seen in generations, making headlines on a regular basis. The project even had its first celebrity wolf, a Druid whose remarkable ramblings were reported in newspapers nationwide. He was part of the enormous brood of twenty-one pups that enthralled watchers in the spring of 2000. Although his official collar number was 253, everyone called him Limpy, thanks to an injury to his left hind leg he'd sustained as a puppy. Even with his bad leg, he thrived, growing up to become a barrel-chested black wolf with a dark mask across his eyes and a distinctive hopping gait that made him instantly recognizable through a scope and endeared him to watchers.

Had any misfortune befallen his father, 21, Limpy would have been a likely candidate to replace him as alpha male. But 21's reign never faltered, and that meant Limpy had to leave the Lamar Valley to have a chance to establish his own pack. In mid-October 2002, Rick noticed that Limpy's signal hadn't been detected for several days running. He had finally made his move.

Six weeks later a coyote trapper checking his snares in the hills outside a town in Utah found he'd caught something far too large to be a coyote. There hadn't been a confirmed wolf sighting in the state in over seventy years, but the trapper knew one when he saw one, even if the rancher he was working for initially didn't believe him. The wolf he'd caught was still alive and wearing a research collar. Word quickly reached Yellowstone: Limpy had been found—almost three hundred miles from the Lamar Valley.

Rather than carry him all the way back to Yellowstone, officials with the Fish and Wildlife Service decided to release him in Grand Teton National Park, about 125 miles north of where he was captured. A few packs had already been established in Grand Teton by dispersing Yellowstone wolves, but it still offered plenty of opportunities for an ambitious young wolf looking for his own territory. Limpy, however, had his own agenda. Eleven days after he was dropped off in the far northern end of the park, his signal was picked up east of Yellowstone Lake, some forty miles away. He was headed home. On December 20, Limpy was back with his clan in the Lamar Valley. In a little over two months, he had completed a remarkable round-trip of more than a thousand miles.

It was the kind of story newspaper editors loved, and Limpy's homecoming saga was reported far and wide. But he didn't stay in the park for long. He spent the next few years roaming southwestern Wyoming, until researchers eventually lost track of him.

Rick thought of Limpy often over the years and told his story to countless park visitors. It was fun to imagine him out there, somewhere in the West, following his nose wherever it might lead him. It was still a world hostile to wolves—over the years the project had lost so many to poachers, to traffic, to ranchers protecting livestock—but Limpy seemed blessed.

42'S TENURE AS THE MATRIARCH OF THE WORLD'S MOST CELEBRATED pack ended on February 1, 2004. She was killed on top of Specimen Ridge by invading wolves from the same pack the Druids had driven out of the Lamar Valley eight years before, when she was just a pup. Now known as the Mollies Pack, the wolves had flourished after their exile to the park's interior, though they made periodic forays north when the snows got too deep and the game too scarce in their home territory. This time they had caught 42 wandering alone. At nearly nine years of age, she was no match for them. She'd been the last of the park's remaining Canadian-born wolves. Her death, if not peaceful, had at least been a natural one, and for that Rick was grateful.

In the weeks that followed, he watched as 21 roamed the valley, howling for his missing mate. He had become an old wolf, his black coat gone almost completely silver with age. He found another mate that spring, a young female in the pack who was unrelated to him, and sired one last litter. One day in June, Rick watched as 21 lounged in the pack's summer rendezvous, surrounded by several generations of his offspring. Suddenly a bull elk appeared in the meadow, and a number of the younger wolves leaped up to give chase. The old male stood, too, but declined to join the pursuit.

It was the last time Rick saw 21 alive. Over the next few weeks, he searched in vain for him as the Druids moved through the valley. Old alphas sometimes wandered off when they were no longer up to the task, ceding their duties to younger males. The battery in 21's collar had died long ago, however, so there was no way to know where he'd gone. Then, one afternoon in July, an outfitter who guided horseback tours in the valley turned in a radio collar to park rangers. He'd found a dead wolf high up on Specimen Ridge, he said. The collar was old and worn, but the serial number on the inside confirmed it had belonged to 21.

The next morning Rick and Doug Smith set out on horseback up the Specimen Ridge trail to retrieve his body. Following the outfitter's directions, they found him lying under a copse of pines, not far from a tree that he and his longtime mate had scent-marked hundreds of times together over the years. There he was, the wolf who had begun the Druid story. It was the first time Rick had ever actually touched 21's fur or seen him at such close range.

Rick mourned 21's death for a long time. In the years he'd watched the wolf, he felt he'd learned everything there was to know about him—his quirks, his moods, his strengths and weaknesses. He could guess what 21 would do before he did it. Rick liked to tell visitors that "21 never lost a fight, and he never killed a vanquished rival." In fact, Rick sometimes called him "Superman," because he'd always felt that 21, of all the wolves he'd known, had the perfect blend of valor and nobility. He hung a poster-size print of the enormous silver male on the wall above his writing desk in his cabin. Captured at full sprint, he appeared to be flying.

3

A Star Is Born

O-Six had been howling for days, and at last it had paid off. Atop a partially forested knoll on the western edge of Little America, she stood nose to nose with two young black wolves, a pair of roaming brothers who had only recently made a tentative stab at joining the ranks of the Druids. They were both yearlings, though one was noticeably larger, already over a hundred pounds, with room on his lanky frame for more if he continued to eat well. The bigger brother had a salt-and-pepper muzzle and a white blaze on his breast shaped like a cross. He was acutely interested in O-Six, sniffing her as she stood still, tail held high, and allowed herself to be inspected.

But it was the smaller of the brothers who was clearly in charge, and he was the one O-Six wanted. This wolf's jaw was stippled with gray, as were his withers and chest, making him look older and more weathered than his brother, though in reality neither had much experience being away from their natal pack. His eyes were a light tan color, almost yellow.

As he stood motionless, transfixed by the female in front of him, the jilted brother approached his sibling at a crawl, first reaching up to lick at his chin, then turning on his back in the snow to gently paw at his face. He looked like an overgrown pup, which wasn't far from the truth. O-Six laid her chin across the smaller brother's back. The three of them lingered there on the hilltop under a cobalt-blue sky, three interlopers far from home, and considered one another.

It was late January 2010, six weeks after the Druids had run O-Six off the elk she had brought down not far from where she stood now. In the interim, her fellow travelers, her sister and her mate, had carefully kept their distance from the Druids. They were leery of a clash, but O-Six had been creeping closer and closer to the pack whenever she could find them. No matter how often the Druid females chased her off, she always returned, drawn by the presence of the two new males. When she couldn't see them, she howled for them, and lately they had begun howling back. But so had the female Druids, and their call had been not a welcome but a warning.

The Druids had suffered a reversal of fortune in recent months. In the five years since 21's death, the pack had held its own but never enjoyed the stability it had once known. A succession of alpha pairs came and went, and the pack's size fluctuated. Out of nine pups born to the Druids the previous spring, not a single one had survived. Worse, they had lost their alpha female in the fall—killed by wolves from another pack. White Line, the three-year-old black who had moved in on O-Six's elk, had now assumed the role, but 480, the alpha male, was her father, so they weren't likely to breed. The pack needed fresh blood.

Now an even more immediate problem had emerged: every

wolf in the pack had mange. The disease, which is carried by mites and causes hair loss, is common among wolves and isn't necessarily debilitating, as long as it is confined to a few patches. If it spreads out of control, however, it can become fatal: a wolf deprived of its winter coat can't survive for long in the deep snow of Yellowstone.

Rick had been monitoring the pack's health for weeks, watching as they chased O-Six around Little America. At first he'd been concerned for the intrepid female's welfare. Now, however, he was more worried about the fate of her pursuers, some of whom had lost a good portion of their fur. With more of their energy spent just trying to stay warm, the Druids were getting weaker and weaker, less able to chase prey and feed themselves. A few were already too feeble to hunt, and if their situation didn't improve, they might soon be unable to travel at all.

The females could not afford to lose the two brothers, who had appeared out of nowhere a few weeks before, a pair of black angels in their hour of need. They offered the prospect of an infusion of vitality and, with breeding season approaching, the possibility of a new alpha male and a litter of pups come spring—another generation of hunters and fighters, a chance to hold on to the Lamar Valley for one more year.

O-Six wandered down off the knoll to the west, and the brothers followed. White Line had been lingering just out of sight on the far end of the knoll with two of her sisters, oblivious to the encounter taking place nearby. Suddenly the Druids seemed to realize that they could no longer smell the two males. They began trotting west to investigate.

O-Six was halfway up a neighboring ridge when the trio appeared far below, three black wolves in a line, scent-trailing her and the two males. Hers was a smell they had become very familiar with, and they were never pleased to find it. Now she raced across the face of the ridge and down through the forested slopes on its

far side, heading for a low spot in the Lamar River known as Buffalo Ford. The brothers followed hesitantly. Even in their weakened state, the Druids managed to close the distance, and for a
moment the brothers seemed torn between their new acquaintance
and the pack they had recently adopted as their own. Eventually
the smaller black peeled off and headed back toward the Druid
females. His brother chose instead to follow O-Six as she headed
south across the frozen river.

The Druids had no real chance of catching O-Six, who almost
seemed to be enjoying the chase. The running they had already
done had cost the pursuers energy they couldn't afford to spend.
Having recovered at least one of their males, the three sisters clustered, exhausted, in the lee of a basalt cliff. One of them collapsed
in the snow, while White Line, whose mange was too severe to lie
down on such an icy bed, stood over her, trying to nap standing
up. Before long she tipped over onto the sleeping wolf beneath her.
She managed to right herself, then fell again. Her sister licked her
gently until White Line stood once more, her snout pointed down,
her mangy tail a limp black rope.

O-Six led her remaining prize up to the top of a prominent
butte, and then paused on an exposed ledge, where the pair bedded
down. She had chosen a spot with a commanding view of Little
America, less than a mile from where her pursuers were resting.
Why had she stopped? She had found a willing mate, albeit not
perhaps her first choice, and she was on the far western edge of
Druid territory. She had only to lead the male a bit farther away
from her rivals, and she'd be home free, with the prospect of starting her own pack in a territory relatively unvisited by neighboring
clans. Yet she lingered.

She had been playing hide-and-seek with the Druids for weeks,
gambling with her life on a daily basis for a chance to be near the
two new males. In the meantime, she had eaten reasonably well,

taking down a number of elk, sometimes in tandem with her sister and her sister's mate, sometimes on her own. Killing an elk without the assistance of other pack members was a dicey proposition, one that many lone wolves never managed at all. Even when an entire pack hunted together, most chases didn't end in success, and some ended in disaster—fleeing elk can kick backward with lethal force without breaking stride. Elk that stood their ground—relying on their superior size, and, in the case of bulls, their dangerous antlers, for protection—were seldom taken, either. But O-Six, since leaving her natal pack, had become surprisingly adept at single-handedly bringing down prey. She was an excellent hunter; what she needed was a piece of land where she didn't have to risk her life every time she went looking for a meal. Little America was good habitat, but most of it belonged to the Druids, and the Druids did not tolerate trespassers.

At least that had always been true in the past. The game O-Six had been playing would likely have been fatal during the Druids' heyday, but those days were long gone. In two months of chasing O-Six, this generation of Druids had never come close to catching her. She should have been dead by now, but here she was—not only alive but the healthiest, most vital wolf for miles around.

High on her perch, O-Six seemed to be waiting for the smaller male, bedded far below with the miserable Druid females, to make a decision. She didn't howl, but it seemed she didn't need to. After a brief respite, the male stood up and wandered a short distance away from the resting females, his nose to the ground. He caught the scent he was looking for, and moments later he was gone. The Druids, too exhausted to follow, howled helplessly.

When the black reached his brother and O-Six, there were warm greetings all around, as if the three had been together for years. Shortly thereafter, as the Druids' unanswered howls echoed off Specimen Ridge, the trio set out together once again. O-Six paused to urinate. Instead of squatting, she raised her leg to scent-mark a tree, then scratched the earth nearby, lest her sign be missed somehow. It was the mark of an alpha female, and its message was unmistakable: *This land is mine.*

The two males inspected her mark, then added their own on top. They were hers, too.

EIGHT DAYS LATER DOUG SMITH DARTED THE TWO MALES FROM A helicopter. The larger, puppyish black became known as 754; his dominant brother was now 755. Smith would have liked to collar O-Six, too, but she had an uncanny knack for dodging his efforts. Most wolves seemed to lose their wits when the roaring machine appeared overhead, running flat out with heads down, without re-gard for strategy or cover. But O-Six was different. She watched the chopper as it came around and seemed to anticipate which way the pilot would turn. It wasn't just Rick who considered her to be a special wolf; Smith had noticed her, too.

Over the weeks that followed, the three companions became inseparable, and Smith began referring to the new would-be pack as 755's group. There was no doubt that 755 would become the alpha male. He jealously shepherded his brother away from O-Six, pinning him time and again when he seemed to get too interested. 754 never failed to submit promptly, and the conflict never esca-lated. If the trio stayed together long enough to produce pups, he'd become an uncle but would likely never get to breed O-Six himself. He'd have to leave the pack someday if he wanted a mate of his own, though as Rick watched him rolling on the ground beneath 755 or deferentially squatting to urinate in his presence, it was hard to imagine him as an alpha.

755 might have outranked his brother, but it was clear to Rick that O-Six was very much in charge of the new outfit she had as-

sembled. Now nearly four years old, she had seen a great deal in her time, while the males still had a lot to learn. Hunting was the first lesson. Now that the two males were collared, the group was much easier to locate, and there were many opportunities to watch them chasing elk in both Little America and, increasingly, in daring forays into the Lamar Valley.

O-Six typically took the lead, flushing herds out of the trees and running them back and forth across the hillsides, testing each elk to find the slowest animal. The two males should have been welcome additions to any hunting party; in a typical pack, large males like 754 provided the muscle for the final takedown, grabbing the elk by the throat and crushing the windpipe after the lighter, more fleet-footed females had run their prey to exhaustion. But 754 and 755 seemed unable or unwilling to follow O-Six's cues, running in circles or chasing the wrong animal on too many occasions. They were less partners than trainees. A few of the wolf-watchers had begun calling them "dumb and dumber," a moniker that Rick found offensive. Still, even he had to concede that O-Six's decision to join forces with these two was puzzling. The simple truth was that they were unlikely candidates to be anybody's saviors.

One snowy February afternoon, a few lucky visitors watched as O-Six came thundering down off a ridgeline on the north side of the Lamar Valley in hot pursuit of a bull elk, her two companions sprinting along behind her. The elk bounded across the road near Buffalo Ranch, heading for the Lamar River beyond. O-Six never slowed, but 754 and 755 pulled up when they reached the blacktop, unwilling to cross. O-Six eventually took the bull down herself in the river valley below. Still the two males held back, even after she returned to the road to check on their progress. Only later, under cover of darkness, did they find the courage to cross and join O-Six in a meal.

The same dynamic unfolded time and again as the winter wore

on. O-Six tried to lead her charges to every corner of their new territory, only to be thwarted by the Northern Range's single, solitary road. The males wanted to come with her, but they couldn't conquer their fear of the mysterious surface and its inherent strangeness, oddly elevated and flat, with no cover, smelling like nothing they'd ever known. And, of course, the road was where the cars were, and the people. It seemed that whatever pack the brothers had been born into had seldom encountered humans, and they, too, were alien and threatening.

To O-Six, the road meant nothing. She didn't approach people or cars, but she didn't go out of her way to avoid them, either. To her, a car was like anything else on the landscape that was neither predator nor prey—like a rock or a tree or even a bison. It wouldn't harm her, and she couldn't eat it; it was a nonentity.

It was a phenomenon Rick had encountered many times. In any given population of animals, some will seemingly be up for any challenge—crossing a road, fording a deep stream, attacking a rival or an unusually large prey animal—and some will not. In fighting dogs, the tendency to rise to a challenge is known as gameness, and it has been a highly coveted attribute cultivated through generations of selective breeding. In wolves, the provenance—and the desirability—of the trait is less clear. The same fearlessness that might serve an animal well in Yellowstone, where cars moved very slowly and humans were harmless, might be fatal in the world beyond the park's borders.

BY LATE WINTER O-SIX WAS MOVING BOLDLY THROUGH DRUID territory and encountering little resistance. Sightings of the Druid clan en masse had become less and less frequent; the pack seemed to have splintered. The alpha male was now gone for good. With his mate dead and no unrelated females in the pack to breed, he had finally wandered off in search of better prospects. The members Rick managed to find were now severely afflicted with mange. Their tails were ropy and pink, their fur shaggy around the shoulders and thin across the back and hindquarters. The sick Druids looked more like scrawny, starving hyenas than wolves.

In mid-February a neighboring pack known as the Blacktails killed an elk in Druid territory near Slough Creek, at the far eastern end of Little America. The next day a small group of Druids, starving and unable to take prey of their own, approached the carcass looking to scavenge a meal. They didn't notice that the Blacktails were still in the area, or perhaps they were too desperate to care.

O-Six was nearby, too, and when the Blacktails attacked, she jumped into the melee, singling out White Line, her old nemesis. The Blacktails, meanwhile, ganged up on a Druid known as Thin Female. Even in her weakened state, White Line was still dangerous, but O-Six launched into her with abandon. The two females drove at each other, battling chest to chest, each straining to reach the other's vulnerable neck or flank without exposing her own to counterattack. The parries and counterparries came so quickly that the pair resembled one twisting and lurching mass, half gray and half black. O-Six's muzzle was dark with blood by the time White Line's sisters rallied to her side and drove O-Six away, limping as she retreated, looking back over her shoulder at the scene of the battle. The Druid alpha's flank was bleeding, but she was still upright and moving well.

When the battle was over, Thin Female had gotten the worst of it. Rick, who had witnessed the entire confrontation, watched her slouch away, bloodied and battered, and curl up in the snow with her sisters around her. She had avoided lying down on ice or snow all winter because of her mange; now it seemed she was beyond such considerations. A Wolf Project biologist found her dead the next morning.

. . .

TEN DAYS LATER O-SIX WAS LEADING THE BROTHERS THROUGH
Lamar Canyon, the narrow gorge that connected Little America
and the Lamar Valley, when she came across White Line once
again. This time the Druid female was alone. Uncowed by their
recent clash, she had been tailing O-Six for days, still holding out
hope she could win the two males back. As the highest-ranking
Druid female, she would have been 755's mate had she been able to
hold on to him. Now, as the brothers looked on, O-Six squared off
with White Line for a second time.

The brothers made no move to join in as their leader attacked,
but she didn't need their help. O-Six lunged again and again, as
White Line, weakened by months of poor feeding, struggled to
fend her off. She was losing badly but refused to retreat. Suddenly
she buckled under her attacker, exposing her flank, and O-Six sank
her inch-long canines deep into her opponent's leg. Moments later
White Line, bleeding profusely, simply stopped fighting. As if by
some unspoken agreement, O-Six sensed the contest was over, too,
and stood and watched as her defeated opponent limped off into
the woods alone, looking for a suitable place to die.

The park road ran right through Lamar Canyon, and a dozen
people had been standing near their cars in a pullout when O-Six
attacked White Line. Through their scopes, they watched the
battle in the trees on the side of the canyon above them, until
the warring parties eventually went their separate ways. While the
watchers were still marveling at what they had just witnessed, a
bull elk appeared above the parking area, halfway up the partially
wooded side of the canyon, running full out with O-Six and the
two males just behind. Scopes were frantically swung back and
forth, as the action appeared and disappeared through the gaps in

the trees. Then the watchers lost sight of both predators and prey, and the chase seemed to be over.

Then the bull reappeared. He turned unexpectedly downhill, ran clear of the pines, and barreled straight toward the startled watchers at the roadside. Five feet tall at the shoulder, with an enormous spread of antlers, he was in full flight, panicked and heedless of his surroundings. O-Six was on him again, by herself now, closing the gap in the snow. He veered away from the pavement at the last moment and began running parallel to the road.

The watchers had no need for scopes now—the chase was unfolding only a stone's throw away. O-Six ran right by the lot without a glance at her audience, oblivious to anything but the fleeing bull. These were the moments the most dedicated watchers lived for, the excitement that made the zero-degree mornings, the long cold waits along the roadside in the wind or the driving snow, even the days without a single sighting, all worthwhile.

O-Six reached the bull's heels, close enough to make contact. The elk wheeled and crossed the road, and O-Six suddenly broke off the pursuit. She'd gotten her teeth into his hide in a few places but not enough to slow him down. The bull was big, with plenty of vigor, even this late in winter. If she'd had the two males with her, the trio might have brought him down within two hundred yards of the parking lot, with everyone watching. But the males hadn't been able to keep up with the action—or perhaps quailed when the chase veered toward the road—and had lost track of O-Six and her quarry somewhere in the trees above. The watchers could hear them howling for her as she slowly made her way back in their direction.

· · ·

IT WAS MORE THAN SHEER LUCK THAT LANDED SO MANY WATCHERS in just the right place to catch the stunning action that morning. Spread out along the Northern Range was a small group of aficionados with whom Rick kept in constant radio contact throughout the day, a wolf-spotting network that park biologists and professional guides called "Rick radio" and had come to rely on themselves. Chief among the spotters was a fifty-eight-year-old retired schoolteacher from San Diego named Laurie Lyman, who lived within shouting distance of Rick's cabin in Silver Gate. Laurie had caught the wolf bug in the late 1990s, after observing wolves raised in captivity by a documentary filmmaker in northern Idaho. Fascinated by the complexity of their social interactions, she devoured every wolf-related film or book she could find, and in time almost every piece of art in her third-grade classroom was wolf-themed.

Laurie began visiting Yellowstone whenever she could get away; when she retired, in 2006, she bought a beautiful two-story log house on the edge of Silver Gate. Her husband, also a retired schoolteacher, joined her when he could, but she spent most of her time these days with Rick and a small community of dedicated wolf-watchers from across the country, each of whom lived for the few weeks or months they spent in Yellowstone every year, hauling their scopes from one pullout to another, hoping to see something wonderful.

It was an eclectic group. Many of them were retired, like Sian Jones, a plainspoken former police detective from England, who made the long flight to the park every winter. Kathie Lynch, a biology teacher from northern California, and Marlene Foard, who taught special education in Salt Lake City, were among the many educators who became regulars, taking advantage of long summer and winter breaks. Foard was in her early thirties and hadn't missed a summer in the park since reintroduction. She drove a Toyota

SUV with an enormous decal on the hood depicting a polar bear nosing through a pile of garbage, above the words I'D RATHER BE EATING SEALS.

The youngest regular was Jeremy SunderRaj, whose parents started bringing him to the park when he was six. On one of his first visits, he watched as a pack of wolves defending their den separated two grizzly cubs from their mother and killed them both. He was hooked. Now a teenager, his plan was to study wildlife biology in college. He was working in Silver Gate so he could spend the entire summer in the park, shadowing Rick as he made his rounds every morning.

In between visits, the watchers kept in touch with one another on Facebook and stayed abreast of the latest developments on blogs dedicated to wolves or news from Yellowstone. Laurie stood barely five feet tall, but she had a big personality, by turns assertive and motherly, and she gradually became the hub of the community. She and Rick compared notes on the phone almost every night, and Laurie chronicled what she and her friends had seen in an e-mail she sent out daily to all her wolf-watching contacts. Eventually her updates became so popular that Nathan Varley, a biologist who ran one of the park's most successful wolf-watching guide services, hired her to post them to his website, where hundreds of subscribers around the country could read them every night.

In 2007 Laurie and Rick were joined in Silver Gate by another die-hard wolf-lover named Doug McLaughlin, who ran a boarding service for Thoroughbred horses in rural Washington State. That winter a friend volunteering in Yellowstone had called Doug, who was then sixty and unmarried, to ask if he might be able to fill in for two weeks. He fell into a routine of daily wolf-watching and quickly got to know the regulars in the Lamar Valley, along with their lexicon. The watchers had a name for every pullout along the park road, for landmarks not found on any map—a kind of

shorthand almost indecipherable to the uninitiated. He was mes-
merized by the magic of Yellowstone: the crystal-clear lakes, the
mountains, the endless forests of pine and Douglas fir, and above
all the wolves themselves. After a week he called his three adult
daughters back home in Washington and told them he wasn't sure
when he was coming back. By spring, he had sold his business and
moved to Silver Gate, where he found a job managing resort cabins. He had spent nearly every morning since in the park, watching
wolves.

Doug found he had a knack with a spotting scope and became
so adept that he quickly emerged as Rick's most valuable spotter.
He held the informal record among the watchers for the most distant sighting—eleven miles. He once pinpointed a pack moving
through tall weeds from over a mile away by the pollen cloud bil-
lowing above them as they trotted along. Tall and lanky, with a
quick laugh and an avuncular disposition, Doug was also a natural
salesman; as he became a regular among the watchers, he began
selling spotting scopes to visitors from the back of his truck.

NOTHING COMPARED TO THE SOLITUDE OF A CRISP, COLD YELLOW-
stone morning. And yet wolf-watching was a social experience, too.
It was all about enjoying the camaraderie of your fellow watchers,
with their shared thermoses of hot coffee and stories about grand-
children or home renovations or football or whatever they could
think of to pass the time. You had to cultivate a Zen-like patience
and trust that the sighting would come, somewhere in the park, at
some time, before the sun went down and it was time to go back to
the cabin or the campsite.

Just finding the wolves in the vastness of the park could be an
extremely difficult task. Rick's telemetry readings indicated only

the general direction and distance at which a collared wolf might be found, and sometimes even that information was unreliable. Especially here in Yellowstone's craggy Northern Range, the signals from collared wolves emanating from one direction had an annoying habit of bouncing off the sides of opposing bluffs, such that watchers might spend an entire morning scoping the wrong side of a valley. A bevy of circling ravens might mean wolves on a carcass somewhere nearby, or it might mean nothing at all. A promising signal might be a wolf approaching, or it could be a pack moving away, not to return for hours and hours. There was a lot of standing around, endlessly scanning with scopes set to lowest magnification, listening for howling, fruitlessly checking the radio for reports from the next pullout, and—especially on the coldest days—retreating to the warmth of the car when your fingers or toes became too numb.

Experiencing Yellowstone through a spotting scope was an entirely different experience from seeing the park from a car or even from a hiking trail. Only when you tried scanning the entire length of Specimen Ridge or Druid Peak one two-hundred-yard diameter circle at a time did you get a sense of how big the Lamar Valley really was. Every contour of the land seen with the naked eye from the roadside was really several such folds, each with a dale in between, sometimes visible and sometimes hidden. And each of those dales held countless features of its own—boulder gardens, narrow creek-filled drainages, meadows bound by copses of aspen or fir or lodgepole pine—where a wildlife drama might unfold. You'd follow a creek upstream from the valley floor until its bed became a swale, which in turn became an enormous drainage, big enough to spend an hour exploring through your scope. Then you'd pull your eye away and realize that this miniature landscape you'd just begun to study was only one tiny portion of a vast mountainside.

And beyond that was another valley, and another mountain, and so on, for miles and miles. The fact that wolves were seen at all in Yellowstone was the real miracle.

IN HIS 1944 MONOGRAPH *THE WOLVES OF MOUNT MCKINLEY*, Adolph Murie described the "inexhaustible thrill" of watching wolves, though he conceded somewhat drily that not every minute of every hour was thrilling. "Many hours were spent watching the wolves at the den," he wrote, "and yet when I undertake to write about it there does not seem to be a great deal to relate, certainly not an amount commensurate with the time spent observing these animals." That didn't deter Rick. Wolves tended to run through the night and rest most of the day, and the truth was that he had spent a considerable portion of the last thirty years of his life watching wolves sleep. In recent years, he had begun taking a midday nap himself, since there wasn't much to see in the afternoons anyway. On most evenings, he'd come back out before the sun went down, when the wolves roused themselves for a night of hunting.

Between sightings, the watchers spent much of their time enjoying other species. When wolves were scarce, for example, grizzlies could usually be counted on for a good show, beating the bushes for pronghorn fawns or elk calves every spring, or gorging on berries in the summertime. In time, a dedicated watcher came to know every likely nesting area for eagles and osprey, the carefully hidden locations of coyote dens, the ponds that hosted the park's scattering of beaver colonies, the places where river otters liked to play. And then there were the great herds of elk, pronghorn, and buffalo—the animals that inspired Congress to make Yellowstone the world's first national park. The Lamar Valley boasted the highest prey density of anyplace on earth outside the African Serengeti. The playful bison calves—called "red dogs" for their ruddy fur—cavorting in the spring were a favorite, though the watchers also had to be leery of the bulls in mating season, when surging hormones made them unpredictable and dangerous.

Inevitably they spent a lot of time watching elk, just as the wolves did. It wasn't a bad strategy; wherever there were elk grazing, there was the possibility of a predator sighting, too. As splendid as the elk were, wolf-watchers who had been in the field long enough invariably adopted a kind of morbid humor about their role in the food chain, and the unfortunate but inescapable fact that elk were essentially bait for the animals they were all hoping to see. "Aren't they beautiful?" Doug had been known to comment when he had winter-weakened elk in his scope and no visitors were around. "Maybe if we're lucky, one of them will die!"

Setting up in the darkness every morning, spending countless hours chatting by the roadside, checking in by radio, Rick, Laurie, and Doug became friends. It often fell to the three of them to come up with names for uncollared wolves, so that one could be told from another. It was Laurie who had named O-Six, after she found herself spending so much time chronicling the audacious female's behavior. Rick and Laurie and Doug—between them they knew more about the wolves of the Northern Range than even the Wolf Project biologists. The professionals recorded their subjects' ages and weights, their ranges and diets, their fertility and longevity. But the watchers knew their stories.

LAURIE WROTE UP THE BATTLE BETWEEN O-SIX AND WHITE LINE and the chase of the renegade bull in her update the night of February 20, 2010, and suddenly O-Six and her exploits were all the far-flung community of Yellowstone wolf-watchers were talking about. There was a new star to follow in the Northern Range.

A few days later White Line's carcass was spotted on a wooded ridge not far from Lamar Canyon. Rick volunteered to hike up and remove her remains so the project biologists could examine her. When he reached her, he found that her carcass had been extensively scavenged over the preceding days. Wolves didn't eat other wolves; the most likely culprit was a mountain lion that had been spotted recently in the canyon.

Carrying White Line's remains down to the valley floor, Rick couldn't help but think of the death of 21, the Druid alpha male he had loved so much. Now, nearly six years after 21's death, he was bringing another dead Druid alpha down the mountain. White Line's demise made a difficult truth impossible to ignore: the saga of the Druids—the story of 21 and his descendants—was now all but over.

And it wasn't just the Druid story that had turned sour; things had taken a bad turn for Yellowstone wolves in general. If 21 was the star of the Wolf Project's first decade, the truth was that in the years since his death, the show wasn't quite what it used to be. Dozens of Yellowstone wolves had been lost in recent years to mange and other canine diseases. As the park's surplus population of elk leveled off in response to renewed predation, meanwhile, the wolf population had begun to do the same. From a high of 174 wolves just seven years before, the number of wolves had plummeted to roughly 100.

Project biologists had long suspected that such a drop would occur as a kind of equilibrium was reached between predators and available prey, but it was still hard for veteran watchers to accept. Wolves were now harder to spot than they had been in years, and Rick resigned himself to the inevitability of an occasional day without a sighting.

•   •   •

OUTSIDE THE PARK, MEANWHILE, ANOTHER PROFOUND CHANGE had taken place. As Rick and his friends watched O-Six chase elk across Little America, wolves themselves were being legally hunted for the first time in modern memory. After years of courthouse wrangling, the management of wolves had at last been returned to state control in both Montana and Idaho, though Wyoming's bid to open its first wolf-hunting season was tied up in litigation. Yellowstone wolves were still protected as long as they stayed in the park, where hunting was never allowed, but as soon as they left the park's northern and western borders, they entered woods filled with hunters and were now fair game.

Wolf advocates had fought against this day for years, filing lawsuit after lawsuit to keep wolves on the endangered species list. As employees of the National Park Service, Doug Smith and his fellow Wolf Project members were bound to support the decision made by their colleagues at U.S. Fish and Wildlife to declare the species officially recovered in the Northern Rockies. Unofficially, Smith had long feared losing federal protection, or "delisting," since it would inevitably mean the deaths of wolves his team had followed for years.

It wasn't that Smith believed his wolves were sacred. In fact, almost every year since reintroduction, he had reluctantly approved the shooting of a handful of Yellowstone wolves who had attacked livestock grazing near the park. Such culling wouldn't normally have been allowed under the Endangered Species Act, but a special concession had been made to ranchers in the original reintroduction plan: any reintroduced wolves who preyed on livestock would be shot. The wolves' overall impact on ranching hadn't been severe; around two hundred cattle—out of roughly five million across Montana, Idaho, and Wyoming—were lost to predation in an average year. (By comparison, tens of thousands of cattle were killed every year by winter storms, lightning, floods, or drought.) But some individual operations near the core reintroduction areas were hit hard, and a promise was a promise.

In the spring of 2002, Carter Niemeyer found himself face-to-face with the reality of what that promise meant. After central Idaho's Whitehawk Pack encountered cattle grazing in the Sawtooth National Forest, they began taking livestock on a regular basis, eventually settling near a fenced pasture owned by a local rancher. Government trappers killed several pack members, but still the depredations continued. Niemeyer tried every technique he could think of to drive the remaining wolves off, including installing specially modified speakers along fence lines. Rigged to respond to the presence of radio signals emitted by the wolves' research collars, the speakers blasted the sounds of civilization— gunfire, human voices, car engines—at any collared wolf that came near. Volunteers even camped near the pastures, to ensure a constant human presence between the livestock and the wolves. Nothing seemed to work.

Finally, one morning in April, Niemeyer found himself climbing into a helicopter with a twelve-gauge shotgun, heading out to hunt down the descendants of the very same wolves he had personally brought down from Canada just seven years before. Niemeyer had hoped the day would never come, but he wasn't the type to delegate unpleasant tasks to other people. Over the next five hours, the pilot buzzed the panicked pack as Niemeyer methodically shot every remaining member. It was among the worst days of his life, but if this was the price of having wolves running free in the Northern Rockies again, he was willing to pay it.

· · ·

At least White Line had died the way a wolf was meant to, Rick thought, defending her territory and trying to provide for her family. If the Druid saga really was over, it was equally true that O-Six had helped bring the story to a close. And yet Rick supposed that O-Six was a Druid herself, in a sense. Her mother had been born in the den on Druid Peak, after all, and maybe that gave O-Six as good a claim on the valley as White Line or any other wolf in Yellowstone.

There was something undeniably remarkable about her. If she had pups of her own and stayed in the Northern Range, near the road, the rise of her clan might be a story worth following, too. Even though she had come out on top in her contest with White Line, her odds of survival were not all that good. She was an amazing hunter, a once-in-a-generation hunter. But after she denned, she'd be unable to get food for herself. Her two new running mates would have to do the heavy lifting, and their abilities were far from proven. If they couldn't deliver, the pups might not survive. And O-Six might not, either, for that matter.

But Rick believed she would make it. Druid blood was special.

4

KILLERS

Steven Turnbull parked his truck in front of the Painter Outpost, Crandall's only store—and restaurant, and bar—and stepped out onto the flattened snow in the unpaved parking lot. It was a Monday afternoon in late March 2010, which meant the bar would be full, or as full as it ever got. Mail was delivered to Crandall from the post office in Cody on Mondays and Thursdays, and people up and down the valley drove in around four p.m. to collect their junk mail and bills at the small bank of post office boxes near the store. Afterward a handful of regulars would come inside for a beer.

Crandall wasn't really a town, so its residents had no city hall or library or school or public park, no real center of gravity to gather around. What they had was the store, and sooner or later everyone ended up there. You could pick up a fishing license, along with toilet paper, milk, a few groceries, beer, and the latest gossip.

The Clark's Fork ran behind the store, and beyond loomed Hunter Peak, still dusted with snow, though it was greening up a bit. Across the valley, massive Table Mountain was also beginning to show signs of spring, which meant they would soon be opening the road to Yellowstone. Beautiful as it was, the park had nothing that compared to Crandall's stunning vistas of the heart of the Absarokas.

But they were cruel mountains; you took your chances traveling through Crandall, especially in winter. Tall poles marked the sides of the snow-covered road, which all but disappeared between plowings. Turnbull had pulled more than a few neighbors out of the ditch with his pickup over the years. Occasionally somebody went over the high side on one of the slippery switchbacks and rolled down the mountainside, where they were beyond anybody's help.

The barroom at the Outpost had four or five stools and a few tables, with pine wainscoting running down a back wall covered with beer signs. It was neat and clean and relatively new. The original store had been destroyed in the great 1988 fire that burned nearly half of Yellowstone before sweeping down into Crandall and sending everyone scrambling for their lives.

Turnbull spotted Louie Cary at the bar holding court, as usual. Crandall didn't have a mayor, but Louie was the closest thing to it. He was a small man with narrow cheeks, kind blue eyes, and a thick shock of gray hair, which he habitually combed forward with his fingernails when he was deep in conversation and a word wouldn't come to him. Louie and his wife, Shelley, ran a guest ranch and hunting outfitting service in the shadow of Hunter Peak, about a half-mile up the Clark's Fork from the store, which his family had once owned as well. His grandfather bought the ranch in 1939 to run cattle, and his mother and father converted the property in the 1950s, renovating an old log building raised by one of the valley's original homesteaders and gradually adding cabins and a rustic two-story lodge with a dozen cozy rooms.

For decades, the Cary family had maintained a pair of hunting camps along Crandall Creek: one high up near the headwaters, not too far from the national park boundary, and another lower down. They took clients into the backcountry all fall and winter for a week at a time, heading up the mountain with a string of horses carrying cooks, guides, and horse wranglers. Louie grew up wrangling horses for the crew and later guiding hunts himself. At the camps were tents for everyone and a makeshift kitchen. At dawn, Louie and his dad led the hunters into the timber around the camp in search of an elk. If a client managed to bring one down, Louie dressed it on the spot, gutting and quartering the huge beast and lugging the meat back down the mountain to be cut up and put on ice. The trophy went to the taxidermist.

Outfitting hunters had long been among the most reliable trades in Crandall and the neighboring basin to the east, known as Sunlight; Turnbull's uncle Wayne had been a guide there for years. Like all of Crandall's outfitters, the Carys catered to out-of-town hunters, those who needed someone to help them find an elk. The area was widely known as one of the best elk-hunting spots in Wyoming, if not the nation, and clients came from all over the country. Some had saved up for the opportunity of a lifetime, but most were well heeled; the going rate for a guided elk hunt was five thousand dollars.

In the old days, there had been so many elk up Crandall Creek that clients almost never came back without a quality bull trophy. Louie's dad would put out some salt not far from the camp to encourage the elk—usually a bull and his harem of cows—to gather and linger. Then one of the guides would mimic the warbling mating call of another male—bugling, as it was known—to draw the bull away from the harem, and the client would be invited to take his shot. After a day or two, another bull would find the harem, and the guides would repeat the process for the next client.

Rarely did they have to go into the heavy timber to get a bull. The guides would simply set up on an open ridge with the call and wait for the bull to come out. It was a good way to make a living, and at one time there were nine or ten outfitters working in Crandall and Sunlight. Louie's only son grew up wrangling and guiding, just as he had.

TURNBULL ENJOYED LOUIE'S STORIES ABOUT THE OLD DAYS, THOUGH he was careful not to get him started on the Nez Percé—who famously trekked through the Absarokas in the fall of 1877 with the U.S. Cavalry in hot pursuit—unless he had a solid hour to spare. These days talk at the store inevitably came around to wolves. Louie was among the first in Crandall to spot a wolf wandering over from Yellowstone, and his initial impression was not a positive one. It was the winter of 1997, and he was up Crandall Creek with a couple of clients on an elk hunt. One of them had just shot a bull, and Louie was about to begin field-dressing him. In the meantime, he told the hunters to head up over the next ridge, where he thought he'd seen a second bull. They returned almost immediately, gushing with excitement. They'd seen a wolf, a big black male, just up the trail. *Whatever you do, don't shoot it*, Louie thought. He didn't need that kind of trouble.

But somebody already had. When Louie picked up the wolf's trail in the snow, he could see that he was limping badly and trailing blood. As the trio made their way down the mountain on horseback, he spotted the injured wolf from time to time through the trees. When Louie got back to the lodge, he heard the news: two collared Yellowstone wolves had been illegally shot that morning, a pair of males from the park's Druid Peak Pack. One was dead already. The black he had spotted in the backcountry—the pack's alpha male, it turned out—was now holed up in a gorge on Hoodoo Creek. Officials from Fish and Wildlife had already called the lodge, looking for the guilty party.

Louie had a pretty good idea who might have pulled the trigger, but it wasn't one of his clients, and he kept his mouth shut. The stakes were high. Everybody in Crandall had heard the story of Chad McKittrick, the hell-raiser up in Red Lodge who had gone to jail for shooting a Yellowstone wolf. "Shoot, shovel, and shut up" was a mantra you often heard east of the park, but McKittrick seemed to have forgotten the last part, blabbing to whoever would listen about what he'd done. This time nobody seemed to be talking. Weeks later Louie got a call from the clients, who were back home in Nebraska. It seemed that Fish and Wildlife wanted to ask them some questions, too. Would they have to come back to Wyoming to testify, they wanted to know, just because a wolf got shot? Louie couldn't guarantee they wouldn't. Fish and Wildlife never came right out and accused Louie or one of his clients of shooting the wolves, but he wasn't especially cooperative with the investigators, and he was on their bad side for a long time.

Trouble with the federal government was something he didn't need. His hunting camps were on national forest land, a privilege for which he paid an annual fee, and Fish and Wildlife issued his big game outfitter's license. Doing business with the government meant keeping track of a million rules—you had to have the proper amount of the proper kind of insurance, you had to use your camps a certain number of days every winter or risk losing them—and the regulations always seemed to be changing. Yellowstone was even worse. He and his friends called it "the iron curtain" because of all the rules in the park—which fish you could keep, which you had to release, which lures you could use, what kind of hook—and the zeal with which they were enforced. It was against the rules even to drive through the park with harvested game in the back of your truck, unless it was covered. Visitors didn't want to see dead elk.

Louie had been fighting the government over wolves for a long time. In the early 1990s, he'd represented Crandall on an ad hoc committee formed to oppose wolf reintroduction. Every elk killed by wolves in the summer in Yellowstone, they knew, was one fewer that would be coming down into Crandall in the winter. They'd found a video of wolves demolishing a dairy cow and sent it to a couple of dozen members of Congress. He wondered how many of them had had the stomach to watch the whole thing.

Louie had never lost an animal to a wolf, but he'd seen the aftermath on other people's ranches: calves so thoroughly shredded that they looked like they'd swallowed dynamite, the snow covered in blood. Wolves and sheep were a particularly disastrous combination; stripped of their natural defenses against predators after centuries of domestication, sheep were known for making no attempt to escape when wolves came calling, and the result could be widespread carnage.

Louie and his fellow committee members had made the best case they could; they had even hired a lobbyist. But it all came to nothing. Most of the land in the Northern Rockies belonged to the federal government, and the feds were going to do what the feds were going to do.

The result hadn't surprised anyone. Every year since reintroduction, they'd seen more wolves and fewer elk, as Louie had known they would. In the last count taken before wolves were reintroduced in 1995, over nineteen thousand elk were roaming Yellowstone's Northern Range. By 2010, that number had plummeted to six thousand, roughly what it had been back in the 1960s, before rangers stopped culling the park's herds. Game officials in Montana and Wyoming insisted the drop wasn't entirely due to wolves. Some of the decline was caused by increased hunting in Montana prior to reintroduction, where state biologists had become alarmed at the size of the herd and the amount of damage the elk were doing to the habitat. Regulators had upped the take by extending the elk season and issuing more permits, both popular decisions at the time. A stubborn drought had also taken its toll, they said, as had habitat lost to development. Though still sparsely populated, the Greater Yellowstone area had become one of the fastest-growing regions in the country.

Still, you couldn't deny the impact of the wolves. The problem wasn't just that there were fewer elk. The ones that remained were harder to kill. Prior to reintroduction, generation after generation of elk had lived an essentially predator-free existence, outside the fall hunting season. They had gradually begun to act less and less like wild animals and more like cattle, congregating in large numbers in exposed valleys, moving wherever the forage was best, and feeding at their leisure. Now, after fifteen years of being chased by wolves, the elk in Crandall were much warier. They tended to spend more time in the trees at higher elevations; they were less likely to gather in large numbers. Local hunters like Turnbull who had time to spend in the woods could still get one, if they had the patience and the backcountry skills. Weekend warriors had less luck.

As the elk numbers in Crandall came down, the Wyoming Game and Fish Department issued fewer and fewer licenses, until finally there were no more than twenty for nonresident hunters in any given season. Between the guides, the cooks, the wranglers, the horses, the insurance, and the fees, it cost around $25,000 per year to run a camp. With nine outfitters splitting twenty clients, nobody was making any money, and one by one they closed up shop. These days there were just three working operations. As a business, big game hunting was all but dead in Crandall, and it wasn't coming back.

· · ·

TURNBULL FELT BAD FOR THE OUTFITTERS WHO'D GONE OUT OF business, though the truth was that he'd also come to resent them a bit, or at least the clients they brought in. In 2003 a popular magazine had listed Crandall and Sunlight among the state's top elk-hunting spots, and ever since then the number of out-of-towners seeking permits there had climbed steadily, all while elk numbers continued to drop. Setting aside a certain number of tags every year for hunters from out of state didn't help Turnbull's odds in the annual lottery. The locals complained about the number of non-resident hunters, but Wyoming Game and Fish could charge ten times more for out-of-state permits. Like most state game agencies, the lion's share of the department's budget came from fees paid by hunters and fishermen, so the incentive to keep them coming in was considerable. Turnbull had never failed to draw a tag, but his friends had occasionally come up empty. He knew it was just a matter of time before he was shut out, too.

Turnbull hadn't lost his living to the wolves, but he felt like he had lost something else, something harder to define. Crandall without elk just wasn't Crandall. He had once been one of those hunters who shot the elk closest to the road every season, but now he liked to get out into the woods, to stalk animals, to make a study of their habits. He hunted sometimes with friends or his uncle Wayne, but more often alone, which he preferred. He was a "dawn means dawn" kind of hunter, and not many of his friends were as serious as he was.

He had been that way for a long time. In high school, he once stood up his homecoming date to go hunting with friends. Now he was divorced, with an ex-wife and an adult daughter who lived in rural British Columbia. He had been seeing the same woman for nineteen years, though they had never married. She hunted, too, though not like he did.

Turnbull was what some people might call downwardly mobile. He'd been a trucker, then cashed out and bought a gas station in Cody, which he'd run for a while more or less by himself, until the EPA told him he needed to replace his underground gasoline storage tanks. No leak had been detected, but the federal government had embarked on a nationwide program to eliminate groundwater contamination by forcing gas stations to upgrade their tanks. It was going to cost $160,000 to dig out the old ones and install replacements. With the slim margins he earned on the station, he'd never repay the loan, so he walked away.

Later he'd owned some pool tables and jukeboxes, which he placed in bars around Cody. He'd spent his share of time replacing felt and tinkering with finicky gadgets. That endeavor had started to go south when new Internet-connected jukeboxes became popular; they were more expensive and brought in less money, but customers liked them, so the bars wanted them, too. He hadn't been sorry to see that venture come to an end; it was keeping him in town too much, away from the cabin, away from the woods, away from the hunt. Now he never left Crandall if he could help it, aside from a monthly trip to the Walmart in Cody for groceries, and the odd jobs he found left him mostly free to do what he loved.

IN THE REST OF AMERICA, HUNTING WAS DYING. RATES OF PARTICI-pation had been declining for decades—only 6 percent of Americans still hunted. But in the Northern Rockies, it remained integral to the culture—Montana had the highest number of hunters per capita, and Wyoming wasn't far behind. Women hunted, kids hunted, even wildlife biologists hunted. For some, it was less a sport than a means of supplementing the family food budget. Butchering a five-hundred-pound elk yielded upward of 250 pounds of meat for the freezer, enough to last an average family nearly a year, all for the price of a fifty-dollar hunting permit. When the Yellowstone elk herd was nineteen thousand strong, the animals were so plentiful in the woods adjacent to the park that for most subsistence hunters the driving principle was not fair chase but convenience. The elk closest to the road—and to the back of the pickup, where the carcass had to be lugged—was the right elk. Not every animal shot in the Northern Rockies ended up in a hunter's freezer—many, if not most, bulls were taken purely for the trophy mount—but enough did that the precipitous decline in elk numbers meant at least some families were buying a lot more hamburger than they used to.

Even for those who didn't need the meat or didn't hunt at all, the size and health of the elk herd was a matter of concern, something to talk about at the grocery store or at church, like hay prices or the performance of the local high school football team. The familiar sound of bugling bulls meant another autumn had come; arches made from elk antler sheds marked the entrance to many mountain towns—Afton, Wyoming, was said to have the world's longest, extending all the way across Highway 89. Elk inspired people; they were a symbol of everything that was special about living here.

These days everything seemed to be conspiring against elk and the people who hunted them. The cattle, for example, competed with elk for the best forage. Cattlemen and hunting guides had made common cause against the wolf, but the truth was that they were far from natural allies. There were maybe eight or ten cattle operations in Crandall and Sunlight, almost all of them enormous and well capitalized. Most of the rangeland was unfenced acreage owned by the National Forest Service, which leased huge sections to cattlemen every summer, just as it had for decades on public lands throughout the Northern Rockies. The cattle were brought up into the mountains every spring when the snows melted and the acres and acres of lush green grass came back, then were hauled out in mid-October, before winter really set in.

In the old days, it seemed to Louie, the cattlemen ran their cows higher in the mountains in the spring and summer. They wouldn't bring them down into the valleys, alongside the river and the road, until the first snows came in September. That meant there was still good forage left in the low-lying areas when the cattle were rounded up and hauled off to their winter range, and the elk started coming down into Crandall from Yellowstone, looking for something to eat. Now the Forest Service let the cattlemen run their cows right along the road all summer, taking the best grass for themselves. With the grass gone, the elk had no reason to linger in Crandall. The outfitters had complained about it, but the cattlemen had "more politics," as Louie put it.

The ranchers, meanwhile, begrudged the elk for the grass they ate in the summer, especially when the big beasts left national forest land and came onto private ranches to graze on well-watered alfalfa. A tycoon named Earl Holding, the owner of Sinclair Oil, controlled most of the best leases in Crandall and Sunlight. Holding was the richest of the lot, but almost all the ranchers in the area were wealthy, and they weren't afraid to let everybody know it. Louie had seen drivers stop their trucks on the Chief Joseph Highway, unload their cattle right into the road, and then simply drive off, without even shutting anybody's gate, which was the neighborly thing to do. People would step out of their houses in the morning and find a dozen cows in their yard.

The smart heifers stayed out of the road, but everyone was expected to drive around the dumb ones. Every now and then a visitor on his way to Yellowstone would plow into a black Angus beef at night, and you'd see a game department truck out the next day, hauling off the remains before the road was full of grizzlies looking for an easy meal.

. . .

CRANDALL'S RANCHERS WERE USED TO LOSING CALVES TO GRIZ-
zlies, not to mention mountain lions and coyotes. When you ran
cattle on national forest land, or adjacent to it, it was just the cost
of doing business. But now they were dealing with wolves as well.
Dispersing Yellowstone wolves had established a resident pack in
Crandall by 1999, and though they mostly preyed on the area's
abundant elk, from time to time they killed a calf or a cow.

Unlike Louie and his fellow guides, however, the ranchers
could do something about it. For decades, cattlemen with leases in
Greater Yellowstone had relied on Animal Damage Control, a federal agency that employs professional trappers and hunters in every
western state to remove "problem" wildlife. The agency, a division
of the U.S. Department of Agriculture, kills tens of thousands of
predators annually—mostly coyotes but also bobcats, mountain
lions, black bears, foxes, and red-tailed hawks, among others—to
protect cattle and sheep grazing on both public and private lands.

Once wolves were returned to the Northern Rockies, the pressure on the agency to begin killing them was almost immediate.
Shortly after reintroduction, the owner of a ranch known as the
Diamond G filed suit against U.S. Fish and Wildlife, citing cattle
losses on the seventy thousand acres his stock grazed in the Du-
noir Valley, a remote drainage deep in the Shoshone National Forest, about thirty miles south of Crandall. The ranch managers, Jon
and Debbie Robinett, told reporters wolves first began appearing
on the ranch about a year after they were returned to Yellowstone.

Like every other rancher in Wyoming—at least, those under
the age of eighty or so—they had no experience with wolves. That
spring they lost sixty-one calves. It was difficult to say how many
of those had been killed by wolves and how many were taken by
other predators. Nevertheless, a pro-wolf group called Defenders

of Wildlife, determined to establish goodwill for the reintroduction program, compensated the ranch for the calves from a private fund raised solely for that purpose.

The money helped offset the increased losses, but life on the ranch never felt the same. One night as Debbie was taking her Great Pyrenees, Booger, from the ranch house out to his bed in the barn, a group of wolves appeared out of nowhere. They showed no interest in her, but several of them immediately attacked the dog. Debbie ran to her jeep, jumped in, and flashed the lights and honked the horn. The wolves disappeared, driven off by the commotion. She found Booger the next day, miraculously alive, though covered with bite wounds. "It's very personal to me," Debbie told the Associated Press, speaking of wolves. "I want them eliminated."

Wolves might have been a novel sight on the Diamond G in the 1990s, but the contest Debbie described—dog and shepherd versus wolf, with livestock as the stakes—was as timeless as any in recorded history. Wolves were once the most widely distributed land mammal on earth, and every early pastoral civilization in the northern hemisphere outside of Africa competed with them for land on which to run livestock—and for the livestock themselves. Wolves very rarely attacked people, but a single wolf could ruin a shepherd's livelihood if he developed a taste for cattle, sheep, or goats. For centuries, wolves dominated rural conversation as the weather does today, a legacy reflected in the dozens of wolf metaphors that still color languages around the world, in most cases long after any living memory of seeing a wolf on the landscape remains.

Everywhere human civilization flourished, wolves were routed, until *Homo sapiens*, not *Canis lupus*, became the most widely spread species. Ironically, the dog—a domesticated wolf—became the first line of defense against depredating wolves, which grew more common as wild prey populations declined under pressure from human hunting and loss of habitat. Romans sometimes referred to dawn as *inter lupum et canum*: "between the wolf and the dog." Dogs ruled the day, and wolves owned the night. Humanity's most beloved animal and its most despised were essentially the same creature, but the wolf's threat to the shepherd's livelihood poisoned relations between men and wolves, and the wolf's reputation never recovered. In Western culture, the wolf became an embodiment of wickedness, from the Middle Ages, when the werewolf myth first appeared, to Grimm's fairy tales in the early nineteenth century. Early Christians—"the flock," as believers were called—saw themselves represented in the sheep; their shepherd was God. The wolf that preyed upon the flock was the devil himself.

And now the U.S. Fish and Wildlife Service had brought the devil back to the Northern Rockies. The wolves frequenting the Diamond G weren't eliminated, but Animal Damage Control, in keeping with the bargain made with ranchers prior to reintroduction, shot several of them. In the years that followed, Fish and Wildlife received a steady stream of complaints from ranchers, especially as wolves expanded their territory even further. Losses in Crandall had been minor, though the numbers were trending in the wrong direction, as far as the local ranchers were concerned. They didn't relish learning how to deal with a predator their own ancestors had so decisively defeated long ago.

EVEN BEFORE THE RETURN OF WOLVES, CRANDALL HAD THE FEEL of a world apart, a place that modernity had passed by. Turnbull had never used Google, never sent an e-mail; he was, as he put it, "computer illiterate." His cabin had no landline, and he was too far from the nearest tower to have much luck receiving calls on his cell phone, either, even with a signal booster and a rooftop antenna. He'd never been to a big city (Wyoming, with a total population under 600,000, didn't have any) and rarely ever encountered anyone who didn't look like him; he liked to tell people from out of town that he'd seen far more grizzlies in his life than he had ethnic or racial minorities.

But even Crandall was changing. For the last thirty years at least—ever since *A River Runs Through It* was published—people all over the country had been buying vacation homes in the mountains around Yellowstone, looking to secure their own little piece of heaven. Or not so little. Entire ranches were snapped up, sometimes at outrageous prices. Other times, large spreads were subdivided into ranchettes. High prices accelerated the trend: the more valuable the land became, the less likely the large ranches were to pass intact from one generation to the next. Estate taxes, along with the tremendous incentive to sell, took their toll. The new owners usually kept a few cattle, so they could also keep the generous tax exemption bestowed upon agricultural land, but few of them had any real interest in ranching.

Most of the big ranches in Crandall and Sunlight were still held by traditional cattlemen, unlike the river valleys farther south—such as the prestigious South Fork of the Shoshone, where a five-hundred-acre section of Buffalo Bill's dude ranch, once hunted by Teddy Roosevelt, among other early-twentieth-century celebrities and swells, sold for $3.8 million. But Crandall and Sunlight both had their share of new million-dollar houses owned by vanity ranchers who didn't know an Angus from a Holstein, or a mule deer from an elk. There was the billionaire who cleared a piece of meadow long enough to land a Learjet near his vacation house, for example. Turnbull hadn't even known such a thing was possible. Then there was the private equity fund manager who bought the Switchback Ranch, an 8,200-acre spread situated high above the Sunlight Basin, on a bench so isolated that it could be reached only by a rugged trail barely manageable by an ATV. The new owner didn't seem to mind. He came and went by helicopter, as did all his supplies. Every spring he ferried thousands of pounds of freight—diesel, food, seed to feed the cattle he ran—over the river from a knoll near the highway. Turnbull couldn't even begin to guess what that might cost.

He'd heard some grumbling about the sight of his cabin, which was not the most beautiful structure in Crandall, ruining someone's perfect view of paradise, but he couldn't care less what they thought. As long as he could still get an elk, he wasn't going anywhere.

FOR OUTFITTERS LIKE LOUIE, FEWER WORKING RANCHES MEANT good horses were getting harder to find. Ranch owners traditionally sold off their horses when they reached the age of six or seven years, to force their cowboys to switch to younger animals that needed gentling. That provided local outfitters with a steady stream of horses available for purchase that were calm and predictable—perfect for inexperienced riders. Now there just weren't as many for sale. Louie and his son Casey found themselves holding on to the stock they had for longer and longer, which meant spending more time and money caring for horses with bad knees. Even so, they were increasingly forced to head up the mountain with young and inexperienced horses, which raised the chances of an accident. Panicked horses had been known to throw riders off the side of the mountain or to fall to their deaths themselves.

On one of Casey's final trips up the mountain, he guided a pair of clients on an archery elk hunt. One of them shot a bull, and Casey began to dress him. It was late in the day, and the temperature was dropping. The hunters mounted up to head back to camp, but the smell of fresh blood spooked one of the young horses, and it began galloping down the trail with the client on its back.

"Bail out!" Casey yelled at the man.

The client had the presence of mind to leap to the ground before the horse had gone too far, but he fell awkwardly, and the quiver of arrows on his shoulder wound up beneath him as he landed. When he rolled over, Casey saw a broken arrow shaft sticking out of the man's thigh, its razor-sharp head buried deep in the muscle. They were five miles from camp, and another five from the nearest road. The client pulled the arrow out himself, but he was bleeding badly and couldn't ride. Casey put a tourniquet on the wound, built a fire for the two men, and raced back down the trail on his own horse to get sleeping bags and food, in case the injured man had to spend the night where he lay. When he got within range, he called his mother, who was in camp cooking dinner, on his two-way radio. She found a satellite phone in the client's gear and walked out into a clearing to call the hospital in Cody, which sent a helicopter. Afraid the injured client would sue, Casey didn't charge either man for the hunt.

Not long afterward Casey told his dad he'd had enough. For the amount of money the outfitting business was bringing in, the hassle just wasn't worth it. The Forest Service bureaucracy, the insurance companies, the cattlemen, and now the wolves—it was too much. The family still had the guest ranch, which brought in some revenue, but Shelley and Louie didn't really need Casey to help run it, and he wasn't the type to freeload. He decided to try farming instead. Louie helped set him up on a piece of land the family owned near Powell, Wyoming, about a hundred miles east, out in the arid Bighorn Basin, and Casey, his wife, and their young daughter moved away for good.

It had been a couple of years since they'd left. Now his life was about seed and diesel and irrigation pipe. Once, alone in the Crandall backcountry, he'd shot a charging grizzly with a pistol to save his own life. These days he rode a tractor, cutting and baling alfalfa to sell to the local cattlemen, exposed to nothing more dangerous than sunburn and diesel fumes. Louie and Shelley learned to be satisfied with phone calls and weekend visits as their granddaughter grew up without them.

Casey wasn't happy, either, but he was committed to making a go of it. Since he'd left, Louie hadn't brought many clients up the mountain, and the Forest Service had recently informed him that his big game outfitter license had been suspended for lack of use. He still paid the fees to keep his camps, though he wasn't sure when he'd use them again. He was getting close to seventy, and it was hard to say if anyone would take over the business that had been in his family for generations when he was gone.

TURNBULL'S UNCLE WAYNE HAD LONG SINCE GIVEN UP ON GUIDING, though the two continued to hunt together in Crandall from time to time. Wayne wound up driving a delivery truck through the same mountains where he once guided elk-hunters.

One afternoon at the Painter Outpost, Turnbull overheard a tourist talking to his son about wolves. It seemed the pair had been in Yellowstone and had seen a pack take down an elk calf. "That was something special," Turnbull heard the man tell his son. "We were pretty lucky to be there."

Turnbull couldn't contain himself. "You weren't lucky!" he shouted angrily, as the man listened in stunned silence. He found calves ripped apart by wolves every spring, Turnbull told him.

Wolves weren't special, not in Crandall. Wolves were killers.

5

The King of Currumpaw

The den was in a wide, grassy bowl on the side of the Buffalo Plateau, a flat-topped mountain that formed the northern boundary of Little America, about a mile west of Lamar Canyon. Slough Creek skirted the base of the mountain, collecting snowmelt from a series of shallow, zigzagging drainages that dropped down from the summit. The most prominent of these was so thoroughly carpeted with long grass that it looked like a verdant river cascading down from the den site to the wide, marshy flats of the creek below. The west side of the bowl was cozy and shady, thanks to a small copse of Engelmann spruce and a few aspen. The rest was open to the sky. It was backed by a steep hillside of loose brown earth, dotted with rocks and patches of sage.

The den itself was a hole dug into the side of the slope, about fifteen feet up the hillside. For a wolf, it was a couple of bounds almost straight up from the thick brush below. A narrow tunnel extended from the den's muddy, two-foot-wide mouth back into the hill, where a larger chamber had been hollowed out.

It was a beautiful morning in May 2010, and spring had finally reached the Northern Range. The southern side of the mountain was greening up wonderfully, though snow still clung to the higher reaches. A grizzly sow and two yearling cubs had been working their way across the side of the mountain since dawn. Now they were in the bowl, grazing on the long grass below the den entrance.

One of the yearlings noticed the fresh dirt below the tunnel and began nosing its way up the slope. Attracted by the den's earthy smell—fresh scat, mixed with the lingering scent of O-Six's latest meal—it poked its nose inside. O-Six launched herself from the depths of the tunnel and hit the cub straight on, sending it tumbling down the hillside and into the sage below. A smaller cub she might have killed outright, but this was a yearling, roughly her own size. Even so, the stunned cub was in full retreat, with one hundred pounds of angry snapping wolf pursuing it. The sow was on them in seconds, lunging and slashing at O-Six with her three-inch claws, as the cub scrambled to safety. O-Six retreated toward the den, her lips pulled back to show her teeth, while the grizzly licked her startled cub and the second yearling hovered nearby.

The sow didn't advance on O-Six, but she didn't seem to want to leave, either. Inside the den were four pups, barely two weeks old and completely defenseless. If the bears decided to dig up the hillside to get to them, O-Six could do little about it. The sow was half the size of a mature male grizzly but still capable of killing a careless wolf in an instant with a single swat of her mammoth paw. O-Six had harassed her share of bears over the years, usually when she returned to a kill and found unwelcome visitors. But if it came to actually attacking a mature bear, she would have no hope of killing it and would likely die in the process. O-Six began bark-howling, a high-pitched staccato cry that sounded like a coyote's alarm call, but her mate, 755, and his brother, 754, were away hunting, most likely miles to the west. There was no reply.

This sow wasn't the first bear to wander through the den area. Grizzly numbers had been surging the last few years, and the park was full of them. They were constantly on the move in the spring, grazing like cattle on grasses and tender forbs, always with an eye out for hidden elk calves, hunkered down where their foraging mothers had left them. Grizzlies rarely took an adult elk, but they were capable of startling bursts of speed—more than enough to overtake a fleeing calf.

In the preceding weeks, O-Six had been forced to confront a seemingly endless parade of grizzlies and black bears, keeping them moving until they were a safe distance from the den. Like a mother elk, she was intent on keeping her pups hidden for as long as possible. Some of the intruders had left more willingly than others, but thus far none had seemed to take an interest in the den. This time was different, and O-Six now found herself confronting an enemy she couldn't defeat but couldn't run from, either.

Up until the bears came, the den site had seemed perfect. O-Six's instinct about the weakness of the Druids had been correct. Lacking an alpha male, the pack wasn't denning at all. This made them mobile and, in theory, more dangerous to neighboring packs. Yet none of the handful of remaining Druids had visited the site; they had essentially ceded the Slough Creek drainage to O-Six and her two males, along with neighboring Lamar Canyon.

In fact, everything west of the canyon and north of Specimen Ridge was potentially hers, as far as the Lamar's confluence with the Yellowstone River some four miles from the den. O-Six's own natal pack, the Agates, held the land to the south along the banks of the Yellowstone and made regular forays into Little America to hunt. There had been a few skirmishes; a couple of months before O-Six dug her den, 755 and 754 had been run off a bison carcass by a group of Agates. But they were unlikely to cause serious trouble as long as O-Six's mother still controlled the pack.

The pack to the west, the Blacktails, were more of a concern. They hunted regularly in the western portion of Little America and would be unlikely to give up the area without a fight. The Blacktails weren't an especially large or aggressive pack; still, to defend her land, O-Six needed more wolves. By fall, her pups would be almost fully grown, and her pack of three would be a fully mobile pack of seven—if they survived.

O-Six couldn't nurse the pups, defend the den, and hunt all by herself. She'd been in the den for weeks now, which meant that 754 and 755 had been forced to hunt on their own. The results had been mixed. Without O-Six to lead them, their forays often seemed directionless. Help seemed to arrive one morning in the form of two yearlings, a black and a gray, who unexpectedly joined the brothers on a hunt a few miles west of the den. It was the time of year when young wolves tended to roam alone, and 754 and 755 seemed to know this pair, who might have even been from the brothers' natal pack. The four managed to bring down an elk together and shared it amicably. One of the yearlings even accompanied 754 back to the den, but—suddenly unsure of his welcome in the presence of the formidable O-Six—didn't stay. The new arrivals soon moved on, and the brothers were left to their own devices once more.

They hadn't always been able to keep the few elk they did manage to bring down; grizzlies had driven them away from their kills more than once. Just two weeks earlier, the duo had been lucky enough to find a bison carcass in Slough Creek. It was a free meal, most likely winterkill, as animals who succumbed to the cold were known. Before they could drag it from the water, however, two grizzlies came in to feed. Wading in up to his neck in the swollen creek, the larger of the two took control of the carcass, while the smaller lingered nearby and waited his turn.

Once he had eaten his fill, the bear laid himself down directly on top of it, challenging any creature larger than the ever-present ravens or magpies to come near. A large enough pack might have been able to drive him off, but with only each other to rely on, the brothers didn't even try to dislodge their adversary. Here was a meal for O-Six and the pups, so close she could see it from the den mouth, yet the brothers were powerless to deliver it.

O-Six's standoff with the sow and her yearlings lasted for over seven hours. As the pups cowered unattended in the den, she drove the bears from the bowl, sometimes hundreds of yards away, only to find that the trio had returned before she could make it back to the den mouth. She was forced to lunge at the sow again and again, growing wearier as the hours went by but never losing her poise, lest she put a foot wrong and suffer the consequences. Her barking echoed off the mountain and down into the drainage below, yet still there was no sign of the brothers. The pups needed to nurse four to five times a day, but O-Six couldn't afford to turn her back on the bears long enough to enter the den. Nor could the pups, who had yet to open their eyes, come to her.

After hours of fruitless effort, O-Six tried a new tactic. She charged at the bears, then ran from them, but never very far. When the sow turned away, she darted in again to nip at her retreating rump, then leaped backward to avoid the maw of the spinning bear, like a Camargue matador trying to snatch the ribbon from between a bull's horns. In this way, she eventually managed to draw the bears away from the den, down the mountainside toward the creek below. A kind of stalemate eventually settled in, the sow and cubs grazing with a wary eye on the wolf, while O-Six watched from atop a nearby rock. Finally, with evening coming on, the bears headed west, and an exhausted O-Six turned back toward the den.

BY THE END OF MAY, THE PUPS WERE LEAVING THE DEN AND COMing down into the grassy bowl to explore. There were two males and two females, all grays. The footing around the mouth of the den proved less than ideal for the pups and their caretakers. A pup's first tentative steps out of the den often led to a tumble down into the brush below, while tugging four squirming pups by the scruff of the neck, one at a time, up the fifteen feet of loose dirt when it was time to return tried the patience of mother, father, and uncle.

Whatever 754's shortcomings in other areas, patience with his nieces and nephews was something he seemed to have in abundance. The pups played with bones, bits of hide, and sticks—anything that might be tossed into the air and pounced upon, or that two tiny sets of teeth might tug at the same time. But their favorite game by far was jumping on the adults, and 754 took more than his fair share of these maulings. He seemed to truly delight in the pack's first litter, though like his brother, he sometimes retreated to a secret bedding place that the pups could not find.

Even as 755 and O-Six settled into domestic life, 754 never quite gave up on his furtive efforts to win the female's affection. When 755 was away, he would often nuzzle her jaw or lay his head across her back. She didn't rebuke him, but she didn't give him much encouragement, either, and 755 was rarely gone for long.

755 proved to be an attentive father, poking his head inside the den mouth every time he passed the entrance, obsessively monitoring the pups' location. This got harder as his offspring became more mobile. They especially enjoyed the soggier areas of the bowl, jumping into the water and tackling one another with abandon. He developed the habit, when returning from a hunt, of circling

the perimeter of the den site's broad bowl before visiting the den proper. He nosed his way among the boulders on the mountainside above, down through the copse of trees a few hundred yards east, across the open, grassy meadow below, and back up the sage-covered western edge, sniffing the ground as he went.

By the time he completed his circuit, he had made an inventory of all the creatures that had come and gone in his absence. To him, it was as if the animals, or at least their ghosts, were still present, so visceral was their scent. His nose, at least one hundred times more sensitive than a human's, told him which direction they had come from, how long they had stayed, and where they were headed when they left. Only when he was satisfied that any intruders were gone would he make his way to the den and greet the pups bouncing up to meet him, lean an affectionate shoulder on O-Six, and finally acknowledge his crouching, tail-wagging brother, more often than not with a flash of teeth.

Working in tandem, the brothers became more adept at finding food as the pups grew. There were a surprising number of elk in the immediate vicinity of the den, despite the nearly constant presence of O-Six. They seemed to feel safe there, and to a certain degree they were. The pack was reluctant to kill prey too close to the den, for fear of attracting bears or other wolves.

When the brothers did make kills, the carcasses were often miles from the den site, and getting food to O-Six and the pups that spring kept them busy. One brother would sometimes show up at the den carrying a large piece of elk, such as a leg assembly, but this process was clumsy, involving frequent stops to renew his grip. More commonly the males used their stomachs as grocery bags, swallowing up to twenty pounds of meat and making the long journey back to the den. When they arrived, their sides bulging noticeably, they regurgitated the meat for the pups, like birds feeding chicks in a nest.

As the pups made the switch from milk to meat, the brothers' return from hunting forays set off a frenzy, with all four leaping to lick at their chins—which triggered the regurgitation—then diving headfirst into the meal. Usually the brothers were obliged to repeat the trick for O-Six, after which they wandered off a short distance and coughed up still more, this time burying the meat in a cache to be dug up and consumed later. After a short rest—not too long, lest birds, coyotes, or bears finish off the distant carcass—the delivery team would get up to repeat the whole cycle again.

While the bear problem never went away, it became more manageable, especially with 755's help. He and O-Six developed a kind of tag-team routine, the alpha male driving the intruder away from the den, while his mate wandered off into the brush, luring the bear farther away, before doubling back by an unseen route. Still, the pups could never play on their own without at least one adult nearby, keeping watch, and the site never seemed quite secure enough for O-Six.

One morning she abruptly decided to move the pups to a hole she'd recently enlarged on the eastern side of the bowl. Still covered in mud from her digging, she managed to carry one of her offspring by the nape of the neck the hundred yards or so to the new den, which was somewhat more secluded than the original. But the rest of her brood seemed to think the relocation was a game of hide-and-seek, and she was forced to search the entire bowl before she finally cornered them all. The last to be caught refused to be carried, rolling over on his back, snapping his tiny teeth, and kicking at his mother's open jaws.

Situated high on the mountainside, the den had a clear view of the flats of Slough Creek far below, as well as the Lamar River where it exited Lamar Canyon and, beyond, a long arm of Specimen Ridge. One morning as the pups were playing on a fallen log and 754 and 755 were bedded nearby, O-Six walked to the center of the bowl and sat in a field of luxurious grass, surveying the mountainside that dropped away below her. Suddenly she threw her muzzle into the air and howled. The two males roused themselves and trotted to her side to join in. The pups scampered over, confused and startled, looking everywhere for the danger that had prompted their mother to sound this alarm. But there was no danger. There was just warm sunshine and soft grass and the bounty of an enormous territory that belonged only to them. They tilted their tiny heads back and added their voices to the chorus.

THE LOCATION OF O-SIX'S DEN WAS NOTHING IF NOT STRATEGIC. The plateau itself was only sparsely wooded, and it would have been difficult for roaming wolves to approach the den area unseen. It also happened to be perfectly visible from the Slough Creek campground road, a two-mile dirt track that led from the park road north along the creek toward a popular tent camping area. A short walk from a parking pullout along the road led to a low hill, nicknamed Bob's Knob after filmmaker Bob Landis, that had a perfect view of the entire setting: the den area, the grassy mountainside below, and the broad marshy flats of Slough Creek at the base of the mountain.

Once the pups made their first appearance outside the den mouth, the hill was a mob scene every morning, with tripods for spotting scopes and cameras covering every possible flat surface. The den itself was only about a mile from the viewing area, and the wolves often came even closer, venturing down to the creek just a few hundred yards below the watchers. O-Six's family was now officially known as the Lamar Canyon Pack, though the watchers just called them the Lamars. Every tour guide in the park included a stop to watch the pups, and they put on a show every morning and evening that delighted their audience. By the summer of 2010, O-Six had become the biggest star in Yellowstone.

Bob's Knob became an office of sorts for Rick, who arrived every morning well before dawn and set up his scope, alongside Laurie, Doug, and whoever else happened to be in town. They enjoyed an hour or two to themselves before the crowds arrived. When more cars began to pull in, Laurie and Doug sometimes retreated to a spot high on a hill overlooking the campground road, but Rick almost always stayed to talk to the visitors. It was his job, after all, and he made sure each and every visitor who wanted to see the wolves had a chance to look through his scope.

It had become one of his favorite aspects of wolf-watching— that moment when a visitor saw a wolf for the first time. Somehow the newcomers never quite seemed to believe it was going to happen, despite the chorus of happy murmuring from the watchers, faces glued to their eyepieces, standing all around them. After all, the landscape before them looked like nothing but an empty mountainside, even with the help of the binoculars many visitors kept hanging from their necks. The scope itself was an intimidating tool for the uninitiated, with its multiple knobs and finicky nature, so easily knocked out of focus with the slightest jostle. At Rick's behest, however, they carefully bent forward, hands behind their backs, and looked, and more often than not the exclamation that ensued—in German, Italian, Chinese, Hebrew—was one of pure joy: "I see them!"

Whenever Rick heard a howl, he'd immediately stop talking and urge everyone nearby to be quiet. The veteran watchers treasured every howl. Observing wolves from a mile or two away was like watching a movie without sound; your imagination had to supply the yips you knew you were missing when puppies were at play, or the growl of an alpha wolf pinning a yearling. But howls echoing through the valley were real, and hearing them somehow brought the wolves closer.

As a crowd-pleaser, a good howl never failed to deliver, especially when it was answered by unseen wolves in some far-off part of the landscape. Visitors often wanted to know what the howls meant, and Rick did his best to interpret them. Wolves frequently howl for no evident reason at all, but some sounds do have special significance. A single wolf that has become separated from his pack will sometimes howl for hours in a relatively high pitch that, to human ears, sounds lonesome. An alpha male howling to warn off an intruder will howl at a much lower pitch—a gruff, foreboding sound. The low notes in a howl, coupled with its long duration, help the sound travel farther, making it audible—to other wolves, at any rate—as much as ten miles away in open country.

When an entire pack howls to challenge a nearby rival pack, wolves will join in at different times and will modulate their calls in so many different ways that the chorus becomes a cacophony, making it difficult to determine just how many wolves are howling, which is to say how big a fighting force the pack can muster. Wolves will sometimes howl before setting off for a nightly hunt, apparently as a kind of morale-boosting exercise, or to celebrate returning pack members. This type of howl often follows a "rally," an exuberant display of affection in which wolves leap on one another, forming a furry pile of tail-wagging bodies (a phenomenon many dog owners experience on a daily basis upon returning home from work).

There was a time, centuries ago, when that sound might have been heard almost anywhere in the northern hemisphere. Now it was nothing but fodder for metaphor, like talk of working like a beaver or making hay while the sun shines. Actually experiencing the thing itself, haunting and strange even in the broad daylight, had become one of Yellowstone's signature wonders, and

Rick always enjoyed watching people share the experience for the first time.

AS AN AMBASSADOR TO THE WOLF-WATCHING PUBLIC, RICK WAS IN many ways an unlikely candidate. Outside the stilted setting of nature talks, his interactions with people were often fraught. He could seem oddly formal and even rude at times, though he didn't always realize it. Ending a conversation was a particular challenge for him. He was never quite sure when the other person was finished with him, and he developed the habit of saying "Okay, then" and turning away somewhat abruptly, without the customary wrapping up. As an interpretive ranger, of course, he was surrounded by people all day, listening to him tell stories. But talking at people wasn't the same as talking to people. Communication for Rick was largely a one-way affair, and it was a craft to be perfected.

His first appearance in front of an audience had come about more or less by accident. As a student at the University of Massachusetts, he spent three summers in the backcountry of the White Mountain National Forest in New Hampshire, surveying and re-marking old boundary lines and working on firefighting crews. He had assumed he'd be a backcountry forest ranger after graduation. Then, in his last summer at school, the only job he could find was as an interpretive ranger, giving talks near a campground in the White Mountains. He hated public speaking, and had no idea how to create a presentation. He stumbled his way through it, hiding behind the projector during his first few slideshows.

What he really wanted to do was write. Rick had enjoyed literature classes in high school and dreamed of being a novelist. He grew up only ten miles from Concord, and after reading a selection from Thoreau's *Walden*, he borrowed the family car and visited the replica of Thoreau's cabin on Walden Pond. The solitude appealed to him, as did the notion that there was wisdom to be found in the study of nature. He also liked Thoreau's ideas about work, which aligned nicely with the way a lot of young people saw the world in the late 1960s. The goal was to do as little work as necessary, so that you could maximize the time available to do what you pleased.

After reading Edward Abbey's memoir *Desert Solitaire*, about a couple of seasons the ardent conservationist spent as a ranger in Utah's Arches National Park, Rick decided his future was with the National Park Service. His first assignment was as an interpretive ranger at Denali, where once again his job was to talk to visitors about what they were seeing in the wilderness. He began keeping a journal, though he still wasn't writing much otherwise. In his spare time, however, he began experimenting with wildlife photography and found he had a knack for it. Once he'd mastered the craft, getting good shots was chiefly a matter of patience and dedication, and Rick found he had both in abundance. What began as a pastime quickly grew into an obsession. He published widely, eventually landing his work in *National Geographic*, the holy grail for wildlife photographers worldwide.

He followed a grizzly cub from its early months through adulthood and published a book of photographs documenting the first five years of its life. Eventually his fascination with bears waned, however. They lived a long time, which meant you could follow individuals for years, but they were solitary creatures that seldom interacted with their own kind. That made their behavior, for Rick, somewhat too predictable.

FAR MORE ENGAGING, HE DISCOVERED, WERE THE PARK'S WOLVES. He started spending hours watching a den he had managed to locate, fascinated by the wolves' social dynamics. After several seasons of viewing, he found that he was getting to know individual wolves; just like dogs, they had distinct personalities.

Back in the 1930s, Adolph Murie had been struck more than anything else by what he called the wolves' "friendliness" to one another, a revelation at a time when the popular understanding of wolves still held them to be snarling killers, remorseless and insatiable. Standing alone in the snow behind his scope, watching the wolves feed and care for the pups, Rick understood what Murie had meant. They were indeed friendly, but they could also be cruel, snapping at or even pinning one another to reinforce their relative places in the pack's hierarchy. Inevitably one wolf always found himself at the bottom of the totem pole, living through an endless succession of difficult encounters with his packmates, fraught with fear and the prospect of rejection. And there were others for whom life just seemed easy, who were blessed with the charisma to make others love them and want to follow them.

In time, Rick befriended Gordon Haber, Alaska's best-known wolf biologist. Haber was something of an iconoclast. He was among the first to argue that wolf packs developed their own sets of habits and customs, a constellation of behaviors that changed over time as pack members came and went and that could best be understood, according to Haber, as a kind of culture. Wolf packs continued to use the same den sites for generations, for example, even after the alpha female who dug the original den was long dead. Wolves who grew up mainly chasing elk usually had offspring who did the same; wolves who included deer in their diet passed that tradition down as well. Likewise, packs that frequented cattle and sheep ranches seldom changed their ways unless humans intervened.

When a pack lost its more experienced members, this process of cultural transmission could get derailed. Haber once documented the curious case of a pack that lost its alphas to trappers before any of the yearlings had learned to hunt Denali's mountain sheep, which made difficult prey. The pack survived by learning to catch snowshoe hares, an adaptation that Haber later observed older wolves teaching to pups.

Haber believed that losing even one animal damaged the well-being of the pack as a whole in ways that weren't yet completely understood. He published rarely, but he was very active in local politics, showing up at public meetings to argue with state game managers about hunting and trapping near the park. Alaska's numerous wolves have never had federal protection, and the packs outside Denali are heavily hunted by sportsmen. In an effort to boost caribou herds, the state game department had long controlled wolf numbers through heavy trapping of its own, along with culling from helicopters.

Over the years, dozens of Denali wolves had been lost to trappers, too, when packs ranged out of the park in search of prey. Haber eventually became so frustrated that he gave reporters a disturbing video he'd recorded of a bloodied wolf who had tried to chew himself free from a leg snare set by the game department. The resulting backlash from appalled Alaskans led to a commitment from the state to kill fewer wolves. A hero to some, Haber was widely hated in Alaska's hunting community.

Rick found Haber's take on pack dynamics and the importance of individual wolves convincing. Haber's passion was infectious as well. By the early 1990s, the planned Yellowstone reintroduction was all anybody who cared about wolves was talking about, and Rick channeled his enthusiasm for the idea into what would become his first wolf book, which he called *A Society of Wolves*, a passionate argument for the wolf's return.

In the course of his research, Rick found himself reading everything he could find on the historical treatment of wolves in the United States. The more he read, the more convinced he became that his ancestors had committed a terrible injustice. When the Pilgrims landed on Plymouth Rock, there were perhaps as many as two million wolves on the continent. Most of the early colonial governments, eager to make their settlements safe for livestock, paid bounties for wolf hides; they forced some Native tribes to pay regular tribute in dead wolves. Later, on the Great Plains, wolfers motivated by financial gain—wolf hides were highly valued back east—used poison to devastating effect. The most common practice was to ride for several days in an enormous circle, leaving poisoned buffalo meat all along the route. By the time the wolfer came back around to the beginning of his circuit, dead wolves—along with countless other predators and scavengers, including eagles and other raptors—littered the ground. The wolves were skinned on the spot; the rest of the carcasses were left to rot.

Meanwhile, the elimination of the buffalo removed a key food source for wolves, drastically reducing wolf habitat in the center of the country and making the Mountain West one of the last redoubts of the species. When ranching finally arrived in the Rockies, state-sponsored bounties and government poisoning programs kept the region's woods filled with traps and poison bait. The decades-long campaign was devastatingly effective, though as on the plains, the incidental killing of other woodland creatures was common. Later backcountry-savvy trappers were hired to methodically purge wolves from even the remotest areas in the West. By the 1920s, the wolf had been all but eliminated from the continental United States, except for a small population in northern Minnesota and Michigan's Upper Peninsula.

It was a campaign unprecedented in its scope and thoroughness: one species almost completely wiped out another. The impetus for the killing was clear enough. But as Barry Lopez asked in *Of Wolves and Men*, his seminal meditation on the fraught relationship between the two species, why did the pogrom continue even after the threat to the westerner's way of life was essentially gone? Why did our ancestors feel they had to root out every last wolf, and why were hunters still so eager to shoot them in the few places they remained?

There was hate, Lopez decided, but there was something else, too—something more akin to envy: "Here is an animal capable of killing a man, an animal of legendary endurance and spirit, an animal that embodies marvelous integration with its environment. This is exactly what the frustrated modern hunter would like: the noble qualities imagined; a sense of fitting into the world. The hunter wants to be the wolf."

After Rick finished *A Society of Wolves*, he traveled to western Colorado and spent two days in the land that had been home to one of the last wolves known to have lived in the state. Gazing out over the juniper and sage, he was moved to perform a ceremony of sorts in memory of the wolf, who was known as Rags the Digger. He played a song written by a Blackfoot Indian friend on a portable cassette player, and then offered a silent apology for Rags's death and a prayer that his spirit would one day walk again in the body of another wolf, a belief found in some Native American traditions. Without the wolf, Rick wrote in the book's epilogue, the landscape was incomplete. "The only way we can experience 'an entire heaven and an entire earth,'" he wrote, quoting Thoreau, "is to bring the wolf back."

The book was published in 1993, and Rick traveled widely to promote it, speaking at venues that ranged from small bookstores to the California Academy of Sciences. He had become a proselytizer for wolves, carrying the gospel to anyone who would listen. When he landed his job in Yellowstone, he immediately began planning his next book: the triumphant saga of the wolf's return.

· · ·

RICK'S TRANSITION TO YEAR-ROUND WORK IN YELLOWSTONE WAS a milestone for him in more ways than one. He rented an old cabin in Silver Gate that had once served as the community's one-room schoolhouse, and for the first time he acquired his own furniture. He was, at long last, settling down, and he found he liked it. As the wolf-watching community grew, he enjoyed seeing the same faces year after year.

Eventually Rick warmed to his new role in the park as well. Ad hoc roadside talks weren't the same as slideshows in a visitor center, but he gradually acquired the necessary skills. Once he found something that worked, he stuck with it. He told the same jokes over and over. When a tour guide brought a wolf-watching client over to see how Rick used his telemetry equipment, he almost always offered some variation on the same basic gag: that the antenna detected brain waves, though none seemed to be emanating from the guide or client, or else the device emitted dangerous radiation and must never be pointed at anyone's head, as it inevitably was at that moment. The joke never failed to garner a laugh or two, assuming the client understood enough English to follow it, the odds of which were increased considerably by Rick's characteristically slow delivery.

He always included plenty of facts and figures about wolves in his talks, but he found that stories about individual wolves were what moved people. Over the years, he learned to tell stories that suited whoever happened to be in his audience on a given day. For a busload of young cancer survivors, he had tales about wolves, like Limpy, who had managed to overcome their disabilities and thrive. For a visitor from the South, Rick might make an allusion to professional wrestling, which he loved almost as much as wolves. It didn't matter to him that the matches were fixed. He loved the larger-than-life personalities, and he saw timeless themes in the endless battle between good and evil that was the hallmark of every match—the same lessons he found in the stories of the wolves he followed.

He liked westerns and Charles Bronson movies for the same reason, along with the new Marvel superhero films, which he drove to Bozeman or Cody to see every time one came out. He was well read and kept abreast of current affairs—he was a particular fan of the wonderful stories featured on *This American Life*—and yet his understanding of what motivated the people around him was shaped by an almost childlike optimism. He cried easily; any story in which an animal or a child got hurt might briefly bring him to tears, or close to them, though he was never ashamed. He was a storyteller who never tired of hearing stories, the more fabulous the better.

Rick's dream, though he seldom described it as such, was to someday tell a story so good that the people who heard it simply wouldn't want to kill wolves anymore. It was an ambition not entirely without precedent. Rick often told visitors about Ernest Thompson Seton, the great nineteenth-century painter and naturalist whose short story about trapping one of the West's last remaining wolves became a national sensation and changed the way many Americans thought about wolves and the natural world in general.

Originally published in *Scribner's Magazine* in 1894 under the title "Lobo, the King of Currumpaw," the story recounted how a friend in the New Mexico Territory hired Seton to kill a wolf that had plagued ranchers in the area for years. Seton, who had some experience as a trapper, tried a variety of poisoned baits and buried traps, but Lobo, as the ranchers called the enormous gray male, was simply too wily.

Finally Seton found the wolf's weak spot. He trapped Lobo's naïve young mate, known to ranch hands as Blanca, and dragged her carcass through a field laden with traps, knowing that Lobo's blind loyalty would drive him to follow her scent heedlessly. When Seton returned to check his handiwork, he found Lobo held fast by traps on three of his legs. Seton had outsmarted him at last.

But when the time came, he couldn't bring himself to shoot Lobo. Something about the nobility of the enormous beast, among the last of his kind, hopelessly ensnared and yet still lunging gamely at his captor—and perhaps the shame of having resorted to such underhanded tactics to catch him—kept Seton from finishing the job. Instead he brought Lobo back to his employer's ranch, where he chained him up with plenty of food and water nearby. The next morning he was dead—the victim, Seton surmised, of a broken heart.

Maudlin and fantastic by modern standards, the ideas in Seton's piece—about a West that was rapidly losing its wildness, about man's duty to be a good steward of God's creation—nevertheless captured the nation's imagination and helped popularize the feeling that the country's natural endowment, and the wonders of the West in particular, were treasures to be savored and protected. The story's success had tangible results, chief among them renewed interest in the national park movement. More to the point, as far as Rick was concerned, Seton planted the seed that eventually flowered into the campaign to protect the nation's remaining wolves.

Rick wanted his Yellowstone book to finish the job that Seton had begun. He was proud of his first wolf book but knew it wasn't the kind of writing that moved people, as the story of Lobo had, along with the dozens of other tales in the "outlaw wolf" genre that blossomed in the years after its publication. He'd made a careful study of how the stories were crafted and the methods the authors had used to inspire sympathy for a species that had been so widely despised for so long. He sometimes imagined turn-of-the-century readers, nestled in their cozy houses back east, following along as the West's last remaining wolves were pursued by men on horse-back, raptly turning the pages as the stories built toward their climatic final scenes. All of them rooting, just this once, for the wolf.

NOW THAT WOLVES WERE BEING HUNTED AGAIN, SETON'S MESSAGE seemed more vital than ever, yet Rick's employment with the Park Service made the politics of the situation delicate. He was careful not to directly criticize the way officials in Montana and Idaho managed wolves; establishing a hunting season was their prerogative.

But hunting near the park was different. Some Yellowstone wolves had become tolerant of humans, especially those who lived in the Lamar Valley, where wolf-watching had become so popular, raising the question of whether it was ethical to shoot them when they left the park. Very few had actually become habituated, the term biologists use for an animal that approaches people, cars, or houses looking for food. In the entire history of the Wolf Project, Doug Smith had been forced to kill only two habituated wolves, both of whom had been illegally fed by visitors and had lost their natural fear of humans. Neither wolf had harmed anyone—in fact, there hadn't been a single recorded instance of a wolf attacking a person since reintroduction. But Smith could not undo what they had learned, and both continued to approach people no matter what deterrents he tried.

Yet even nonhabituated wolves that had grown accustomed to seeing cars and people at a safe distance—as many in the park had—would make easy targets for hunters. Wolf advocates had lobbied for a kind of buffer zone around the park in which hunting would never be allowed, but such efforts hadn't gotten far. The Park Service was still smarting from an attempt in the 1980s to extend its jurisdiction around Yellowstone to improve wildlife management in the park itself. It had met with such a cold reception from members of Congress that park officials had been forced to abandon the issue. Just how vulnerable Yellowstone's wolves would be to hunters was anybody's guess.

When the first Montana hunt began, on September 15, 2009, they found out. Within three weeks, hunters killed four of the ten wolves—including the alpha male and female—in the Cottonwood Creek Pack, a recently formed tribe known to move back and forth freely across the park's northern boundary. Most had been shot on the northern end of the Buffalo Plateau, not far from the rural community of Jardine, which, despite its proximity to Gardiner and its annual summertime flood of wolf-loving tourists, had become something of a locus for anti-wolf sentiment in the Yellowstone area.

Though the pack itself was relatively new, several of the Cottonwood Creek wolves were very familiar to watchers, including a pair of seven-year-old females known as 527 and 716. Both females had once survived a rival pack's lengthy siege of their den by sneaking out for food, a drama that had likely never been witnessed before and that kept Rick and his fellow watchers riveted for days. They were the only animals in the pack wearing research collars, and hunters had shot them both, so there was no longer any way to monitor the pack's movements. The last Rick had heard, 527's stuffed and mounted carcass was now decorating a bar in a resort in Pray, Montana, a tiny hamlet on the road from Gardiner to Livingston. She'd been shot by a hunting guide and professional rodeo rider who lived nearby. With both alphas dead, the pack would most likely fall apart, if it hadn't already.

Rick suspected that 754 and 755 occasionally traveled over the park's northern boundary as well. Now that that the Druids' hold on the Lamar Valley was so tenuous, it was possible that O-Six would eventually move into the valley herself, which would make such excursions less likely. Historically, when the Druids left the park, they had generally gone east, into Wyoming, where there was no wolf-hunting season, at least not yet. Park wolves were still safe there, or as safe as they had ever been, and Rick took some consolation in that.

But it wouldn't last forever, and once hunting was legalized in Wyoming, Rick thought, the park would essentially be surrounded by hostile territory. Rick had gotten a brief glimpse of what that would be like in the spring and summer of 2008, when wolves had temporarily lost protection in Wyoming. The state's wolf-management plan allowed any wolf found outside the narrow mountainous corridor that included Yellowstone and Grand Teton National Park—roughly 85 percent of the state, in other words—to be killed without a permit at any time of year. A federal judge had quickly returned them to the endangered species list, but in that brief window scores of wolves had been shot.

One of them was Limpy. Off researchers' radar for years, he'd been shot the very first day federal protection was removed. He had been with a pair of wolves near an elk feeding ground about eighty miles southeast of Grand Teton National Park. All three wolves were killed, most likely by someone who had been monitoring their movements for some time. His death had been covered by the Salt Lake City papers, where his unexpected appearance had caused such a stir six years before, and picked up by news outlets around the country. Yellowstone's wolf-watching community went into mourning.

Game officials in Wyoming resented the coverage Limpy's death received. Yellowstone's habit of producing "famous" wolves only made their jobs harder, and they weren't shy about calling Doug Smith and letting him know it. Wolf Project biologists didn't encourage the phenomenon; they never gave collared wolves names, like zoo animals, only numbers, and their official reports and published papers were as dry as those produced by wolf biologists anywhere else. But they didn't really discourage it, either, and Smith, for his part, believed that positive accounts about individual wolves, such as Bob Landis's films on the Druids, were good for wolves everywhere. They offered a counterbalance to the steady stream of complaints about livestock depredation or depleted elk herds and frustrated hunters.

But it hadn't been enough to deter U.S. Fish and Wildlife from delisting wolves. Laurie had taken the death of the Cottonwood Creek wolves hard, especially the two females, and she included an obituary of sorts in her daily update. "When Rick writes his book, all of their lives will contribute to knowing and understanding wolves in the wild, and these girls will be standouts," she wrote. For every beloved Yellowstone animal lost to the hunt, Rick knew that dozens of unheralded wolves were being killed across the Northern Rockies. By the end of the season, the combined tally in Idaho and Montana had reached 258. Rick supposed he'd have to get used to it. Every day he'd expected to see something new; now he waited to hear something terrible.

THOUSANDS OF VISITORS WATCHED THE LAMAR PUPS THAT SPRING and summer. When they got home, they posted breathless accounts on Facebook, along with countless photos of the pack and its new pups. The relentless parade of bears through the den area created a chance to photograph two of the West's iconic animals interacting with each other, though the action occasionally got a bit too exciting. One morning as a large group on Bob's Knob watched the Lamar wolves run an elk into the creek, a grizzly began making its way up from the flats in the general direction of the watchers. Rick kept an eye on it, watching the pack and the elk through his scope, and soon realized the bear was making straight for the crowd. He calmly but firmly ushered everyone back to their cars, then followed the bear in his own vehicle until it nosed its way past the parking lot and it was safe for everyone to come back out.

When O-Six finally ventured out of the den to hunt, she came right down to the creek to stalk elk, creating photo opportunities that professional photographers might wait years to get. Stunned visitors saw her kill elk single-handedly right in front of them. Some considered it the experience of a lifetime, while others, perhaps used to seeing somewhat less bloody depictions of predator-prey interactions on television, were appalled by the unedited version. But it left an indelible impression regardless, and O-Six's legend grew.

The crowds on Bob's Knob made 754 and 755 skittish. They wouldn't come down to the creek when the hill above was full of people, and they were still as leery of the park road as they had ever been. But O-Six seemed as oblivious to the watchers as she was to the road. She was perfectly content to spend an hour feeding on a carcass in plain view of a crowd of fifty people, to the delight of visitors with cameras.

Humans away from the road were different, however. Coming down into the Slough Creek drainage from an adjacent valley one morning, O-Six surprised a hiker walking along the hillside. Neither traveler spotted the other until they were close enough to make eye contact. O-Six panicked. She ran west toward the creek, looking over her shoulder as the man stood, equally stunned, watching her flee. She was so flummoxed that her normally sure footing failed her, and she fell into the creek. She eventually made her way up to the den, taking a long and indirect path, calculated to leave danger behind. When she arrived, she nursed her pups. Laurie reported O-Six's encounter in her update that night. "The expression on her face," she wrote, "was one of pure fear."

6

REBELS IN THE SAGE

As O-Six entertained her fans on Bob's Knob, a different sort of crowd was gathering on a crisp, early-summer morning in downtown Missoula, Montana. By nine o'clock, a throng of around a hundred people was milling outside the Russell Smith Federal Courthouse, a two-story shoebox of red brick on an otherwise picturesque street lined with dusty Subarus and full-size pickups. Among them were a father and daughter in matching camouflage hunting jackets. The girl, four years old with a perky blond ponytail, clung to her daddy's neck with one hand and with the other held a fluorescent pink sign that read WILL THERE BE ANY ELK LEFT WHEN I GROW UP? A woman in her fifties with short hair and a lined, angular face wore a camo hoodie over a T-shirt with a silhouette of a wolf framed by a rifle's crosshairs. Her hand-lettered orange sign read: AS YOU READ THIS . . . WOLVES ARE EATING MY FAMILY'S DINNER!

It was June 15, 2010, and inside the courthouse U.S. District Court Judge Donald Molloy was preparing to hear oral arguments in a lawsuit seeking to put wolves back on the endangered species list in Idaho and Montana. It had been only fourteen months since the U.S. Fish and Wildlife Service officially delisted wolves in the two states, and now the agency was back in court again, fending off yet another lawsuit. Reporters from the local television stations worked the crowd, collecting footage for what would be the top story on every broadcast that night. The handful of pro-wolf advocates in attendance weren't especially vocal, perhaps for good reason. "I should yank that wolf tie right off that guy's neck," someone in the crowd muttered, as a group of wolf supporters approached the courthouse.

An attorney named Doug Honnold sidled into the crowd and slowly worked his way toward the courthouse doors. He was fifty-five, with a lean frame, thinning black hair, wire-rim glasses, and a full beard that was turning gray. He wished, not for the first time, that he was not wearing a suit. He knew from long experience that in Montana it was the functional equivalent of lugging around a sandwich board that read I AM AN ATTORNEY, which, in turn, was the same as saying, "I am part of the problem." The Montanans blocking the sidewalk before him did not seem especially inclined to clear a path as he approached.

Even without the suit, some in the crowd might well have recognized him as the enemy. Based in Bozeman, he had been the chief litigator for the Northern Rockies office of Earthjustice, the environmental movement's best-known legal advocacy nonprofit, for almost two decades. "Because the Earth Needs a Good Lawyer" was the group's slogan, and Honnold was certainly that, having won a string of huge and highly controversial lawsuits over the years. He'd stopped a gold mine from opening just outside Yellowstone, and he'd torpedoed a 47,000-acre logging proposal in the

Bitterroot National Forest in Montana, among others. He'd ended the use of off-road recreational vehicles on thousands of acres of grizzly bear habitat in eastern Idaho's Targhee National Forest. And he had filed five suits in defense of wolves in the last six years, none more high-stakes than this one.

The courtroom was not especially large—the gallery included perhaps ten rows of church-pew-style benches—and when every seat was full, the bailiff was forced to close the doors, directing the remainder of the crowd to an overflow room, where a closed-circuit monitor had been set up to display the proceedings. If the spectators were overwhelmingly anti-wolf, Honnold noticed that his side was also outnumbered in the attorney's well. Earthjustice was representing a coalition of environmental groups opposed to the delisting—including the Sierra Club and several smaller nonprofits—with a combined membership in the millions. But Honnold had only two attorneys with him: Tim Preso, a colleague from the Bozeman office, and Deborah Sivas, director of the Environmental Law Clinic at Stanford University, who was accompanied by one of her law students.

Clustered around the defendant's table, meanwhile, were roughly twenty attorneys. Lawyers from the Department of Justice and the Department of the Interior were present, as well as a senior advisor to President Barack Obama's secretary of the interior, Ken Salazar. Joining the federal team were attorneys representing the states of Idaho and Montana. Nobody from the State of Wyoming was present, since Wyoming's wolves had been excluded from Fish and Wildlife's delisting order. Wyoming governor Dave Freudenthal was still battling the federal government over the suitability of the state's wolf-management plan, and as a result wolves in Wyoming were still considered an endangered species and couldn't be hunted. Representatives from various ranchers' associations and hunting groups were present as well.

Honnold spotted Ed Bangs, the Fish and Wildlife biologist who had directed the wolf recovery project since 1988, seated with the defendants. He was an unlikely member of the opposition. As the face of the program for seven years prior to reintroduction, Bangs, who was fifty-nine, had arguably done as much as any other person to bring wolves back to the Northern Rockies. Born and raised in a blue-collar California family, he'd spent thirteen years as a field biologist in Alaska, where he'd come to know wolves well. He had organized hundreds of community meetings to explain the reintroduction program in venues across the West, often in tiny ranching communities where support for wolves was nonexistent.

Plainspoken, self-effacing, and funny, he knew how to talk to his fellow westerners and had won the grudging admiration of quite a few adversaries over the years. He often began his talks by saying he didn't love wolves, and not just because he'd once been bitten by a yearling in a collaring mishap that left him with a bloody puncture wound clear through his wrist. His commitment to reintroduction was about science, not sentiment. Wolves belonged in the Northern Rockies because they played a vital role in the ecosystem, not because they were beautiful or fun to watch.

Now, however, he found himself on the other side of the fight. As far as Fish and Wildlife was concerned, wolf reintroduction had been a success. It was time for the federal government to turn their welfare over to the states, where wildlife management properly belonged.

Honnold and his clients were keeping that from happening, but Bangs didn't take it personally. After the last time Honnold beat Fish and Wildlife in court, Bangs had offered his congratulations. "If I'm ever in trouble," he said, "I want you representing me." For his part, Honnold found Bangs more likable than most bureaucrats (especially the ones he sued) and appreciated his straightforward style. They were both getting close to retirement, and the welfare of wolves had consumed an outsize portion of their careers. For Bangs, delisting would mean wolf recovery in the Northern Rockies was finally complete; for Honnold, one last win for wolves would be the pinnacle of a long and rewarding career.

As the defense team's army of attorneys took their seats, Honnold leaned over and caught Bangs's attention. "Do you think you have enough backup, Ed?" he asked, and Bangs gave a tense laugh.

THE CROWD, SO RAMBUNCTIOUS ON THE SIDEWALK, SEEMED TO lose its verve once inside. A nervous silence fell over the courtroom as everyone awaited Judge Molloy's entrance. Honnold had appeared in Molloy's court many times and knew him well. Appointed by President Clinton in 1995, the sixty-four-year-old judge was extremely hardworking—the first to show up at the courthouse in the morning and the last to leave. He read every brief, and he knew the law; his was not the kind of courtroom where an unprepared attorney was likely to escape notice. Molloy was a lifelong Montanan and looked the part, right down to the bushy mustache. Yet he had a reputation for independence, most notably in a series of controversial rulings rejecting timber sales proposed by the U.S. Forest Service, which environmentalists had argued would destroy essential wildlife habitat.

He had generally been an ally to wolf advocates. It was Molloy who had shut down Fish and Wildlife's short-lived Wyoming delisting in 2008, balking at the state's management plan with its tepid commitment to maintaining sufficient numbers and its enormous "predator zone," in which wolves could be shot at any time for any reason. Fish and Wildlife's unusual response—leaving wolves on the endangered species list in Wyoming, while moving forward with delisting in Idaho and Montana—was what had brought everyone to court today.

But Molloy's support was far from a sure thing. Honnold had filed his suit immediately after Fish and Wildlife published its delisting rule in the spring of 2009. There was no way the suit would be resolved before the coming fall hunting season, so Honnold had asked the judge for an injunction, forestalling any hunting of wolves until the court had a chance to rule on the merits of the case.

Although Molloy had granted a similar injunction in 2008, this time he declined. He conceded that Honnold had a good case, but he disagreed with the attorney's contention that the fall hunt would cause irreparable harm. To the delight of officials in Idaho and Montana, he allowed the first legal hunt in decades to go forward, as each side filed its briefs that winter and prepared for oral arguments the following summer.

That decision led to the destruction of Yellowstone's Cottonwood Creek Pack, along with the death of 254 other wolves across the region by season's end. Painful as it was to Honnold and his clients, the hunt had at least clarified what was at stake. Molloy was either going to reject Fish and Wildlife's delisting rule a second time, sending the agency and the states away to try once more to come up with a plan that passed legal muster, or he was going to give the rule his blessing, which would mean hundreds more wolves would be killed that fall.

THE DOOR TO MOLLOY'S CHAMBERS OPENED, AND THE JUDGE strode purposefully to the bench. A former college football star and navy fighter pilot, Molloy was a big man, with a broad forehead, thinning hair, and a scowling mien. In his brief opening remarks, he acknowledged the charged nature of the issue at hand but dismissed such concerns in his characteristically brusque way.

"We're here this morning to argue the legal issues in the case," he began. "They are not normative questions about the goodness or badness of decision-making." He didn't care whether hunting wolves was good public policy; he was just trying to determine whether it was being done in accordance with the law.

The judge had given each side just an hour and twenty minutes to make its best case, and the plaintiffs were up first. Honnold spoke quickly and confidently, like a college professor addressing a lecture hall full of undergraduates.

"This case is critical to both wolf recovery and the continued viability of the Endangered Species Act," he began. The truth about Fish and Wildlife's latest delisting rule, he told the court, was that it was based on politics, not on science. The agency's recovery plan for wolves in the Northern Rockies covered Wyoming, Idaho, and Montana, along with portions of Utah, Washington, and Oregon. Before wolves could be declared recovered and removed from federal protection, the plan stipulated that state officials in Wyoming, Idaho, and Montana (where the vast majority of wolves were found) would have to come up with management plans of their own that would ensure the continued viability of their respective wolf populations. Idaho and Montana had done that to Fish and Wildlife's satisfaction, but Wyoming had yet to comply, choosing instead to sue the federal government rather than amend the plan Molloy had rejected in 2008.

Lobbied heavily by ranching and hunting interests, Governor Freudenthal wouldn't budge, which meant that wolves could never be declared fully recovered across the whole region. The result had been a long-running stalemate. The partial delisting was the federal government's attempt at circumventing the impasse, allowing game managers in Idaho and Montana to get control over the wolves in their own states, even as wolves in Wyoming remained on the endangered species list.

The problem was that it made no sense from a wildlife management perspective, Honnold argued. If the goal was to ensure the long-term survival of wolves in the Northern Rockies, their numbers had to be stable throughout the region, not just in a portion of it. Fish and Wildlife's logic was legally suspect as well. There was no precedent, he pointed out, for delisting a contiguous population of a species in only a portion of its range. They were all the same wolves, and they moved back and forth across state borders regularly. Maintaining or removing protection according to the wolves' current state of residence was an obvious effort to shoehorn a political solution into a legal framework that wouldn't allow it. In the long history of Fish and Wildlife's implementation of the Endangered Species Act, it had simply never been done.

Honnold glanced briefly at Mike Eitel, the Justice Department attorney in charge of the defense team, who looked on in stony silence. Eitel had written the brief explaining the legal rationale behind Fish and Wildlife's decision. It was creative to say the least, and Honnold looked forward to hearing him defend it in front of Molloy.

But the trouble with the agency's management of wolves went much deeper, Honnold continued, all the way back to 1987, when the original recovery plan was completed. According to the plan, the existence of just one hundred wolves and ten breeding pairs in each of the three key states for three consecutive years constituted a recovered population. (Wolves in Yellowstone National Park were excluded from the count.) This recovery goal was extremely modest—a choice, he argued, that was also driven by politics.

"You can go back and read the 1987 recovery plan," Honnold said. "And there is simply no explanation for three hundred or the thirty breeding pairs that was selected. None whatsoever." How had the magic number of three hundred wolves been arrived at? he asked the court. Why not five hundred, or a thousand, or two thousand? Wolves in the Upper Midwest states of Wisconsin,

Michigan, and Minnesota, he reminded the court, were managed for much higher numbers by Fish and Wildlife. How could it be, he asked the court, that a recovered population in that part of the country meant twelve to fourteen hundred wolves, while delisting in the Northern Rockies, with a much greater expanse of suitable habitat on public land, required only three hundred? The answer, he suggested, was that one hundred wolves per state was the maximum number that officials in Montana, Idaho, and Wyoming had been willing to tolerate when the recovery plan was negotiated. It had nothing to do with science.

Of course, all parties had signed off on the numbers in the plan at the time. KEEP YOUR PROMISE, one of the protesters' signs in front of the courthouse had read that morning, a sentiment that was hard to argue against. In the intervening twenty years, however, many wolf advocates had come to consider the terms of the recovery plan a kind of Faustian bargain. In comparison to the modest recovery goals set by Fish and Wildlife, wolf reintroduction was an unqualified success, immensely bolstering the states' case that the time had come to delist. But now that the outstanding quality of the wolf habitat in the region had been established—now that there were at least seventeen hundred wolves in the region— the numbers in the original agreement were potentially disastrous. The delisting rule required Idaho and Montana to manage for 150 wolves each, as a kind of buffer against reaching the critical hundred-wolf level that would trigger a return to federal protection. Even so, under the terms of the recovery plan, over two-thirds of all the wolves currently in the Northern Rockies could be legally killed with no repercussions.

In any case, Honnold now told the court, it didn't matter what the 1987 recovery plan said. The law required Fish and Wildlife to make delisting decisions based on the best possible science at the time such calls are made. "For unknown reasons, Fish and Wildlife was confident that the area could not sustain more than a few hundred wolves," he said. "This determination has been disproven by wolves on the ground."

Arbitrarily directing each of the three states to manage for the same number of wolves made no sense, either, at least from a scientific perspective. Fifteen years after reintroduction, for example, Idaho now had twice as many wolves as Wyoming, a function more than anything else of the outstanding habitat in the central part of the state, which hosts the largest roadless wilderness area in the Lower 48. Yet Fish and Wildlife was still hewing to the terms of the original recovery plan, a political deal cut with three reluctant states that seemed predicated more on an agreement to "share the pain" than on any sound principle of wildlife management.

It was time to revisit the plan, Honnold concluded, in light of what had been learned since its inception. "None of us wants to go to the doctor who treats us with twenty-year-old medical practices," as he put it.

Yet as flawed as the recovery plan might have been from the advocates' perspective, it also contained a provision that Honnold hoped might be his ace in the hole. Just reaching the three-hundred-wolf threshold wouldn't be enough to delist the wolf, according to the plan. Evidence of "genetic exchange" among the three separate wolf populations in the Northern Rockies—Greater Yellowstone, central Idaho, and northwestern Montana—would have to be established as well. This meant that Fish and Wildlife needed to document wolves dispersing from one core area to another and breeding in their new homes once they arrived.

This interchange was considered critical for the long-term health of wolves in the region. Past research on other isolated populations of large mammals had shown that animals stranded in habitat "islands" might flourish for a short time but then began to suffer from the effects of inbreeding and lack of genetic diversity.

Moreover, the absence of connectivity among populations might place the viability of any one segment at risk from sudden die-offs through disease or other unforeseen causes. It wasn't enough that wolves were flourishing in Yellowstone or other pockets in the Rockies, Honnold had suggested in his brief for the judge. Projects like wolf recovery were about restoring ecosystems on a grand scale, not, as he now told the court, creating "postage stamp replicas of a world long gone."

It fell to Molly Knobler, the young Stanford Law student on Honnold's team, to make the genetic connectivity argument in court. Though she knew the case well, she was visibly nervous as she stood to begin her remarks, more conscious than Honnold of the Montanans behind her in the gallery, quietly glowering in their Wrangler jeans and hunting jackets.

Montana itself could be a little overwhelming for first-time visitors. Landing in Missoula was like stepping back in time, to the days of the Old West. This somewhat surreal sensation was exacerbated by the altitude, which often caused a light-headedness in flatlanders that could last for days. The town was surrounded by the kind of dense forest you seldom saw in the rest of the country, but it wasn't just the thought of what was in the woods that made newcomers feel so unsettled. It was the people, too. You might see a teenager riding horseback down the side of the road, as casual as any kid on a skateboard in southern California, or come upon a Native American butchering an elk in the back of a pickup alongside the highway. Life here was different.

"Can you hear me okay?" Knobler asked the judge, who assured her that he could. Even as the population of wolves in each of the core areas climbed steadily, she explained, biologists had been able to document very little interaction between them. The problem, in part, was the extremely rugged terrain around the borders of Greater Yellowstone. The Beartooth Mountains to the north of the national park, for example, hold some of the most expansive tundra in the Lower 48. Wolves ordinarily disperse in the winter, and the Beartooth, at ten to twelve thousand feet, was all but impassable once the heavy snows began to fall, even for an animal as hardy as a wolf. In twelve years of monitoring, Fish and Wildlife had been able to document only two wolves making the trek into Greater Yellowstone from outside the ecosystem. At one point the service had resorted to trucking in another pair, though as Knobler told the court, describing this as evidence of "connectivity" strained the definition of the word.

As the plaintiffs had pointed out in a brief to Judge Molloy, the existence of densely populated habitat is what forces a dispersing wolf to travel long distances to find a territory of its own. If so few wolves made it from central Idaho or northwestern Montana to Yellowstone when some seventeen hundred wolves inhabited the Northern Rockies, how many would make it post-delisting, when federal protections were removed and the numbers presumably dropped? Fish and Wildlife's own research suggested that a population of around a thousand wolves across the region was necessary to ensure that connectivity was maintained, yet they proposed to allow the states to manage for a fraction of that number.

Even wolves that were inclined to make the journey would find it difficult now that their numbers were being hunted in Montana and Idaho. Under Wyoming's contested state plan, meanwhile, at least some of the wolves dispersing from central Idaho to Yellowstone would likely have to cross the state's free-fire "predator zone" before they made it to the sanctuary of the national park. If connectivity really was essential to recovery, then how could Fish and Wildlife sign off on such an arrangement?

It was a powerful argument, but Honnold noticed that Knobler was having an increasingly difficult time delivering it. Five minutes into her presentation, she paused. "I'm sorry, Your Honor," she said. "Do you mind if I get a drink of water?"

"Are you feeling okay?" Molloy asked, but Knobler didn't reply. She had fainted.

HONNOLD WAS A CALIFORNIA NATIVE, BUT AFTER ALMOST TWO decades in Montana, he was long past culture shock. Still, he understood what pressure could do to a young attorney. He'd felt it, too; nothing compared to the vitriol he'd witnessed in the fight over wolves. Idaho's official wolf-management plan—blessed by Fish and Wildlife prior to its 2009 delisting decision—contained the following declaration on the first page: "Idaho is on the record asking the federal government to remove wolves from the state." Idaho's first-term governor, C. L. "Butch" Otter, a sixty-eight-year-old former agribusiness executive, had campaigned in 2006 on a promise of drastically reducing Idaho's wolf population as soon as federal protection was lifted. Though it never became law, the Wyoming state legislature approved a bill shortly before reintroduction that offered a thousand-dollar bounty to anyone who shot a wolf dispersing from Yellowstone, and directed the state to pay attorney's fees for anyone charged with illegally killing a protected wolf.

The fight had spilled far beyond the Rockies; everybody in the West had an opinion on wolves. Politicians as far away as Texas were taking on the issue. Even the National Rifle Association weighed in, though it had long before ceased to be a hunting rights organization in any real sense. Wolves had become one of those polarizing issues, like abortion or gun control or war in the Middle East, about which the country could not seem to reach a consensus.

But the truth was that wolves were just the latest flashpoint in a fight that had been simmering in the West for decades. The real struggle was over public land—what it should be used for and who should have the right to decide. The federal government owned almost half of all the land in the West, in large part because nineteenth-century homesteaders found much of it too arid or too rugged to settle, unlike the more hospitable Midwest, which settlers had made into the nation's breadbasket.

The government instead adopted a pattern of selling access to the West's rich resources—grazing rights, timber, precious metals, oil and gas—without actually selling the land itself. As a result, the residents of a place like Idaho, where fully two-thirds of the land is federally owned, don't make decisions about how the resources in their own backyards should be used. Instead agencies like the U.S. Forest Service and the Bureau of Land Management call the shots from Washington, and people all over the country—even those who visit a place like Yellowstone or the Grand Canyon only once in their lifetimes—feel that they should have a say in how the West is managed, because it belongs to them just as much as anybody who actually lives there.

As the environmental movement gained steam in the 1970s, rising resentment over conservation measures on federal land boiled over in the so-called Sagebrush Rebellion, when western politicians pressured Congress to turn control over much of the land to the states or even to private owners. Timber companies resented bans on logging in national forests to protect owls and other endangered species. Exhaustive environmental reviews slowed new mining projects for years. For every environmentalist, like Honnold, who resented the fact that cattle were grazed on public lands, there was a rancher in the West who resented paying the fees and believed that the land ought to belong to the people who used it, the sort of common-law notion that underlay the very idea of homesteading that had brought people west to begin with.

When the effort to wrest control of the West from the federal government failed, some of the frustrated anti-government fervor expressed itself in darker ways, like the white nationalist militia groups that cropped up, most notoriously in Montana. Overreaching federal judges, restrictions on gun ownership, job-killing bans on logging and mining—the list of grievances was long, and the return of the wolf was seen by many as just one more burden to bear. When politicians like Butch Otter gathered votes by vowing to wipe out wolves, they were tapping into that strain of conservative, anti-Washington populism.

The anger was real, and from what Honnold had seen it was getting worse. As his list of victories grew, so did his list of enemies. Death threats had been sent to his office in Bozeman. The off-road vehicle suit Honnold had won had inspired someone—presumably a disgruntled ATV enthusiast—to leave an unlit gasoline bomb on the steps of the local ranger station. A note scrawled on the side read, "Bye, bye, fuckers, boom!" The West was caught up in a culture war, and for some people it was more than just a metaphor.

And now, to Honnold's dismay, the federal government was turning management of wolves over to state officials who had promised to kill as many of them as possible. But could Governor Otter and his fellow governors really undo what the feds had accomplished? Ed Bangs didn't think so. He didn't share the plaintiffs' concerns over the number of wolves shot by hunters since federal protection had been removed the previous spring. Bangs believed that wolf numbers would rebound quickly; there were simply too many packs in the woods now, producing too many pups every spring, to eliminate them by hunting alone.

It would take a return to the brutal methods of the nineteenth century—widespread poisoning, gassing of dens, government bounties, and the like—to significantly reduce their numbers. At most, sport hunting might slow the dispersal of wolves to new territories outside their current range—to areas in the West that were currently devoid of wolves, in other words—by reducing the population density that drove lone wolves farther afield.

Privately, Bangs was skeptical that controlling wolves would boost the elk population, which had always been the main rationale for instituting a wolf-hunting season. If hunting wasn't sufficient to significantly lower the wolf population in the Northern Rockies, then it followed that you couldn't really reduce elk predation that way, either. You might be able to temporarily boost elk numbers in certain areas through a brief period of high-intensity hunting, but it wouldn't last. Other wolves would simply move into the unoccupied territory and eat the same number of elk as before. The bottom line, following this reasoning, was that it didn't do any harm—at least at a broad, population-wide level—to shoot wolves, but it didn't do any good, either.

Research in Yellowstone had strongly suggested, meanwhile, that unexploited wolf populations, left to their own devices, would eventually level off on their own, without culling of any kind. When their numbers began to outstrip the available habitat, more wolves would die from conflicts among packs, and breeding females would have smaller litters. Yellowstone's own wolf population, which declined by 43 percent over a six-year period with no human intervention whatsoever, certainly seemed to support the conclusion that wolf populations were essentially self-regulating.

Yet Bangs still thought wolf-hunting was a good idea. He was convinced that allowing the states to manage their own wolves was the only way to deescalate the long-simmering tensions over the issue, which would be good for the species in the long run. People wanted to shoot wolves, and that was reason enough for a wolf hunt.

It might be good for the embattled Endangered Species Act as well, Bangs felt, proving that it could actually work the way it was designed to. His years of talking about wolves with elk-hunters and ranchers had given him some insight into how attitudes change. "What we normally mean by 'education,'" he once told a crowd of wolf advocates, is, "I want someone else to know what I know so they will have my values." In his experience, it didn't work that way. If wolves were hunted like any other animal, then people would begin to think of them as they did any other species in the woods, rather than as objects of resentment.

Honnold wasn't so sure. Plenty of wolves were already being killed on behalf of ranchers, after all—more than most people realized. Beginning with a handful of problem wolves, the pace of the culling had increased as wolves spread and conflicts multiplied. Fish and Wildlife had begun compensating ranchers with confirmed wolf kills, but the money wasn't enough; officials were under pressure to aggressively control depredating packs.

It was not a practice that the federal government was keen to advertise, but taxpayers who knew about the program might have found the logic difficult to swallow: one federal agency was reintroducing predators on public land, a second was leasing adjacent land to ranchers, and a third was dispatching trappers or men in helicopters to kill those same predators when they inevitably crossed paths with livestock. But a deal was a deal, and Fish and Wildlife didn't balk as the numbers killed in the name of livestock protection grew larger and larger. By 2010, more than twelve hundred wolves suspected of preying on livestock had been shot.

Ranchers might have been appeased, but anti-wolf sentiment in general didn't seem to be tapering off. During the previous fall's hunting season, a handful of hunters had posted gory photos of dead wolves on social media, which had only stoked the controversy further. Honnold also believed that Bangs was wrong to underestimate the determination of state officials to drive down wolf numbers as low as possible, especially in Idaho, which had the region's largest population of wolves. Hunters in Idaho had claimed the majority of the wolves shot during the first legal hunting season the previous fall. After the initial four-month season ended in December, Idaho game officials—in keeping with Governor Otter's promise to kill as many wolves as possible—decided to extend the season until March 31.

A seven-month hunting season is unusual for any species, as is a season that extends into a game animal's breeding period; some of the wolves killed in March were likely pregnant, which depressed numbers even further. Montana's packs didn't fare much better: the combination of sport hunting and government culling on behalf of ranchers had destroyed more than a quarter of the state's estimated wolf population in a single year. And it was all perfectly legal, now that Fish and Wildlife had ceded control to the states. There was even talk of adding a trapping season in Idaho in the near future.

Emboldened by the success of efforts in Montana and Idaho, state officials in the Upper Midwest, meanwhile, were pressing for a return to wolf-hunting there as well. At the same time, Fish and Wildlife was moving forward with a plan to remove protection for gray wolves in the remainder of the country, including areas that currently had no wolves at all. The measure was being pushed by ranching and hunting interests in places like Oregon and Washington State, where dispersing wolves had established a growing presence, and in Colorado, as a kind of preemptive measure against their inevitable drift south toward the heart of the Rocky Mountains.

Some of Honnold's clients were opposed to any wolf being killed for any reason, though others were open to the idea of limited hunting. But it had to be done responsibly, and Honnold had seen no indication that the states could be trusted on that front. One thing was clear: fifteen years after reintroduction, the leading cause of death for wolves in the Northern Rockies was back to what it had been for much of the nineteenth century, and wolves had as many enemies as they did advocates.

JUDGE MOLLOY ORDERED THE COURTROOM CLEARED SO THAT PARA-medics could examine Knobler. She soon recovered and declined to be taken to the hospital. The judge directed the bailiff to bring everybody back in, and the proceedings continued after an hour's delay.

Deborah Sivas, the Stanford professor, wrapped up Knobler's presentation, and then Mike Eitel, the Justice Department attorney, opened arguments for the defense. Eitel pointed out that while the original wolf recovery plan might have been twenty years old, as Honnold noted, Fish and Wildlife had vetted its decision to delist much more recently, in 2001 and 2002. As part of that process, the agency had consulted national experts on wolves, the majority of whom agreed that the wolf was recovered in the region and that populations would remain stable under the terms of the delisting rule.

But Judge Molloy seemed less interested in the argument over the merits of the recovery goals set by Fish and Wildlife—or whether those goals had been achieved—than in the legal conundrum posed by leaving one of the three states out of the delisting order. Under questioning from the judge, Eitel conceded that Fish and Wildlife had never before split a population along political lines in a delisting rule, though he argued that the Endangered Species Act might be construed to allow it, under a novel interpretation of certain key provisions.

Molloy listened patiently, but he didn't seem to be buying it. "I still don't understand what the legal argument is that you can subdivide that?" he told Eitel. "I mean, I understand the practical argument. I understand the political argument. It's very, very clear, those two things. The legal argument isn't as clear to me, and so that's what's troubling me."

Molloy continued to prod Eitel with skeptical questions until the attorney found himself deep in the weeds, parsing the meaning of passages from the *Congressional Record* in an effort to establish what legislators had intended in making various amendments to the act over the years.

He seemed relieved to hand the proceedings over to Idaho's assistant attorney general Steven W. Strack, a veteran litigator who had argued cases before the U.S. Supreme Court and defended the State of Idaho in several high-profile suits brought by environmental groups. All the talk about minimum recovery levels, Strack suggested, was beside the point. Idaho's game commission had created its own state management plan that called for maintaining a population of five hundred to seven hundred wolves. The plan wasn't legally binding, and the state could manage for much lower levels if it so chose, but Strack knew the Endangered Species Act chapter and verse, and he knew that courts were bound to defer to the stated intentions of regulatory bodies. If Fish and Wildlife accepted the numbers in Idaho's plan at face value, then the judge must do so as well.

"The plaintiffs' suggested methodology is just to speculate that the commission will not carry out its own plans," he argued coolly, gesturing vaguely toward Honnold. "Well, that's simply unacceptable under the statute, Your Honor. That would be arbitrary and capricious, to ignore the commission's own plans."

Honnold knew Strack was correct. It didn't matter that the governor of Idaho himself had promised to do everything in his power to drive wolf numbers as low as the state legally could. Strictly speaking, none of that should enter into the judge's calculus in making his decision about the legality of the delisting rule.

"So will Idaho maintain greater than fifteen breeding pairs, 150 [wolves]?" Strack summed up. "Well, undoubtedly. We have a management plan that says we will."

As the hearing wound down, Molloy queried the representative for Montana's fish and game department about the legality of partial delisting. The attorney turned philosophical. If Wyoming never came to the table, then what remedy did Idaho and Montana have, he asked the judge, other than to wait indefinitely in a kind of legal purgatory? "It's sort of like that figure in Greek mythology who is condemned to roll the boulder up the hill but never had the strength to get to the crest," he said.

By noon the hearing was over. Molloy gave no hint as to which way he would rule, and everyone would have to wait until late summer to hear his findings. As Honnold gathered his things to leave, Ed Bangs caught his eye. "Maybe I didn't have enough backup after all," he said. Honnold smiled, though he knew that neither of them had any idea what the judge was going to do. He had a familiar feeling as he watched Strack and the other attorneys file out of the courtroom, their faces grim. This might have been his last time to stand up and make the case for wolves, but whether he won or lost, it wasn't likely to be the last time wolves were in court.

IRON MAN

Rick McIntyre didn't attend the court proceedings. Too much was going on at the den, and he couldn't afford to miss it.

Two days after the hearing, he stood behind his scope on Bob's Knob with Laurie at his side, watching 755 mind his offspring. The pups were six weeks old and growing fast, gaining two or three pounds a week. Everything was still new to them, every novel sight or smell a delight. Though it was mid-June, the weather had turned sharply colder, and sudden flurries forced the watchers back to their cars in search of more layers. Snow in summer was something that Laurie was still not quite used to, but the bite in the air had made the pups frisky, and she smiled as she watched one of the pups—at this stage it was hard to tell one from another—screwing up his courage to confront a raven that had landed provocatively nearby. The two-foot-long, jet-black bird was almost as big as the pup and completely unafraid.

There were always a few ravens near the den, hoping to steal a

bit of regurgitated food when the pups were fed. They were ubiquitous in Yellowstone, where they filled the ecological niche occupied
by vultures in most other parts of the country. The birds spent a
lot of time on the ground, down at a pup's-eye level, which meant
they were among the first creatures in Yellowstone's broad menag-
erie that young wolves encountered. The Lamar pups had only
recently discovered the fun of chasing them. The ravens hopped
lightly away but never went far, which made for a game that could
go on for quite some time. It was an early taste of what every adult
wolf knew from long and tiresome experience feeding at kills surrounded by hungry ravens: no matter how far you chased them,
they always returned.

These pups had a lot to learn. After fifteen summers in Yellowstone, Rick had a kind of pup primer in his head, a list to tick
off as their tiny worlds got bigger and bigger. Pronghorns were too
fast to catch, though the pups always tried. Bison were extremely
dangerous and best avoided. Coyotes that normally fled from an
aggressive pack might turn on a lone wolf, especially if the coyotes
had pups in a nearby den. And perhaps the most important lesson
of all, strange wolves were not friends.

One sunny afternoon a Druid finally found the new family.
She was a black female yearling, part of the group that had chased
O-Six across Little America as she was courting 754 and 755. Rick
spotted the solitary traveler at the base of the mountain below the
den site, lying in a meadow and chewing on a bone. He could see
that she was over the worst of her mange, and her frame had filled
out a bit. But she was somewhere she shouldn't have been; O-Six
inevitably picked up her scent and made her way down the mountainside. Rick braced himself for another violent encounter.

O-Six stalked through the brush and long grass until the intruder was in range, then ran to confront her, tail held high. The
Druid female froze. She was face-to-face with the wolf that had

killed White Line, her pack leader, only a few months before. The yearling was no match for O-Six—certainly not with 754 and 755 only a few hundred yards away—but it was too late to run.

O-Six, it turned out, wasn't interested in another fight. As Rick looked on in wonder, she merely sniffed the visitor and allowed her to move on, following her to the east until she was sure that the den wasn't her destination. The lone female wasn't a harbinger of any coming Druid revenge, and O-Six seemed to know it. The truth was that there were no more Druids now, only a few scattered wolves without a pack or a home.

Rick was grateful on behalf of the Druid female, but more than that, he was gratified to see the kind of leader O-Six had become. Good alphas, he felt, modeled wisdom and mercy, as 21 had done. Wolves who rose through the ranks merely because they were the largest or—like the cruel Druid alpha female known as 40—the most ruthless often failed to thrive once they got to the top, and their packs suffered commensurately. O-Six could be fierce, to be sure, but Rick was glad to see that she was no 40.

Rick knew that in the field of wildlife biology, imputing human characteristics to a creature that it doesn't really have—anthropomorphizing, as the habit is known—is considered a cardinal sin and a hallmark of amateurism. Doug Smith sometimes told people that his wolves weren't Rick's wolves, by which he meant that he was interested in science, not in stories. But wolves, Rick felt, were more like humans than they were given credit for, in their tribal ways and territoriality; in their tendency to mate for life; and in the way male wolves provided food and care for their offspring, so unusual in the animal world. He loved to quote the early-twentieth-century English philosopher Carveth Read: "Man, in character, is more like a wolf . . . than he is any other animal."

When human civilization was still built on hunting rather than agriculture, this notion was considered conventional wisdom.

In *Of Wolves and Men,* Barry Lopez recounts the story of an eth-nographer posing a riddle to an elder among the Nunamiut, a tribe in northern Alaska. At the end of his life, the researcher asked, who knows more about life in Alaska—how to escape a blizzard, how to find caribou, how to survive on such a harsh landscape—a wolf or a man? "The same," the elder replied. "They know the same."

IN THE WEEKS THAT FOLLOWED, THE PUPS BEGAN TO WANDER OUT of the bowl, exploring the mountainside in groups of two and three. The adults never let them get too far before rounding them up with a howl or a short pursuit. Bears were still wandering through the den area with alarming frequency, and the adults had to be vigi-lant. By now, O-Six had resumed hunting regularly, as one of the brothers—usually 754—watched the pups. She had lost a little weight from her months in the den, but if anything, her lean frame had made her faster than ever.

One morning a crowd on Bob's Knob watched her chase a cow elk and her calf down from the trees east of the den site and into the creek drainage below. The cow was headed for the safety of one of the stream's deeper pools, but O-Six managed to get between the calf and its mother just as the pair was approaching the water. The cow was forced to double back, and O-Six soon had her by the throat, bringing her down at the water's edge. But the chase wasn't over. As the visitors looked on, the wolf left the cow where she lay and headed back up the bank to track down the calf. In the space of ten minutes, O-Six had killed them both, barely a hundred yards from the crowds above.

It was not a pleasant thing to watch. Rick always recorded every kill he witnessed in great detail; they were of particular in-terest to Doug Smith and his fellow researchers, with whom Rick regularly shared his notes. In her own nightly report, Laurie was more reticent. She didn't elide such moments, but she didn't dwell on them, either. Like Rick, she considered herself an emissary for wolves to the general public, and to her, moments like this—in which the savage side of life in Yellowstone became impossible to ignore—were fraught. More than anything, what wolf advocates fought against was the long-held notion that wolves were nothing more than killing machines. They were so much more, as the wolves of Yellowstone had demonstrated time and again to anyone willing to pay attention. But it was also true that they were among the most effective predators the earth had ever seen.

O-Six, as Laurie frequently pointed out to her readers, was rarely "cuddly." But that wasn't why she and so many other watchers had come to admire her. It was her stunning blend of confidence and competence that inspired them, her indomitable will, her ability to bend a harsh landscape to her own ends, to do what needed to be done to provide for herself and her family every day, without fail. Seeing her in action was like watching a gifted athlete, like the star shortstop who effortlessly turns every double play, no matter how improbable it seems. Fans know they are supposed to appreciate the overachieving striver who improves through constant practice, the type celebrated in a million Horatio Alger stories. But nobody has to be told to love the natural, for whom excellence seems to be a birthright.

THE FAMILY FED ON THE PAIR OF CARCASSES, MIRACULOUSLY unmolested by bears, for three straight days. With hundreds of pounds of fresh meat just a short jaunt from the den, O-Six was in almost constant motion, gorging herself at streamside and then making her way, belly wide and low, back up through the long grass to feed the pups at the den high above. By the third day, all three adults were meat-drunk, O-Six most of all. When the pups tailed after her as she set out at dawn, a would-be hunting expedition turned into a playful romp that ranged all the way down to the creek. Now three months old and weighing around thirty pounds, they had become strong runners, though O-Six was still much faster, a fact she demonstrated again and again as the pack made its way leaping and rolling down the grassy hillside.

The pups' personalities were beginning to emerge. The one the watchers had begun calling Dark Gray Male was the most adventurous. The other male pup had a lighter gray coat and was more tentative, and Laurie had named him Shy Male. There was one in every litter, and Laurie tended to worry about them more than the others. The two female pups were both gray and somewhat difficult to tell apart, though one was slightly bigger and bolder. The smaller stayed close to her mother whenever possible. At the creek, the pups tumbled off the bank and into the stream, delighted by the icy water.

O-Six soon spotted a bull elk grazing by himself in a meadow high above the family, near the den, and began stalking her way uphill as the pups looked on. The bull raised his head, his healthy rack pointing skyward. When he trotted into a stand of nearby trees, O-Six broke into a run. Three of the pups readily joined in, along with 754. Shy Male held back, watched over by 755. The excitement didn't last long; O-Six had merely wanted to test the big bull, and he'd shown no weakness. As first hunts go, it wasn't much of an education for the pups. From O-Six's perspective, however, it was a promise of things to come: it had been a long while since she'd had a line of wolves running behind her on a hunt.

When it turned cold, it would be time to leave the den and hunt the full range of the pack's territory—the extent of which she had yet to fully explore. She would be mobile again, in a way she hadn't been since the previous winter's trials. Even with the Druids gone, there would be dangers, but she wouldn't be facing them alone. As her pack moved by fits and starts back up the mountain-side, she could see all six of them spread out before her: 755, now a willing hunter and equal partner; 754, formidable in size if not in disposition; and the four pups, still gawky and naïve but growing fast. In just a few more months, they would be almost as big as her, their milk teeth replaced by unbreakable daggers, their legs long, their lungs virtually inexhaustible.

This winter things would be different.

RICK RELIGIOUSLY RECORDED EVERY DETAIL OF THE LAMARS' FIRST litter in his journal. It was wonderful viewing, though nothing he hadn't seen before at one time or another in the park. This was his fifteenth summer in Yellowstone, which meant he'd been there for fifteen generations of pups, plus another dozen or so from his summers in Denali. The circumstances weren't always so idyllic: he'd witnessed entire litters lost to disease, pups killed by mountain lions or bears, dens raided by marauding enemy packs. Starvation, usually following an injury or death in the pack's alpha pair, was the worst to witness.

To the more dedicated watchers who returned time and again, Rick was a guru. He seemed to know every last detail about every wolf he spotted: their lineage, their life history, their quirks and habits. Part of his appeal was his presentation. His soothing, mellow voice was easy to listen to, and his flat affect was almost mesmerizing, especially in the bucolic roadside settings of Yellowstone.

His reputation had grown beyond the park as well. The yellow Nissan Xterra he drove had been donated to the Park Service specifically for his use, after a Nissan employee became a regular visitor and wolf-watcher. So had his spotting scope, a top-of-the-line model from Swarovski, the high-end Austrian manufacturer, which sold for thousands of dollars.

Doug McLaughlin had set that up. As word spread about Yellowstone's wolves, he sold more and more scopes until finally he was among the top Swarovski salesmen in the country. One day Doug called his contact at the company and pointed out that Rick McIntyre, the man who had seen more wolves than anyone else on the planet and who spent his days engaging countless eco-tourists— and would-be Swarovski customers—was using a run-of-the-mill Bushnell. It was a question of marketing: if Swarovski was the Nike of spotting scopes, then why wasn't the Michael Jordan of wolf-watching using one? The company arranged for Rick to get a new scope and extended an open-ended offer to send him the latest models when they were released.

Rick was happy to have the scope, but he had never taken the company up on that upgrade. He liked the one he had. As a rule, he wasn't big on change. His daily diet, for example, almost never varied. Frozen blueberry bagels and Diet Pepsi featured prominently. His spaghetti recipe was once featured in a celebrity cookbook, the sales of which benefited wolf research. Rick's dish, which he made with a modest amount of ground bison meat and Ragú sauce, was considerably simpler than Linda McCartney's recipe for aubergine caponata, which appeared on the opposite page. But then again, it had to be: he ate it almost every night. Laurie and Doug did most of Rick's shopping for him, since he rarely made it into a town big enough to have a real grocery store. Laurie had gradually been introducing some vegetables into his diet.

Rick had come to depend on Laurie in more ways than one. Even as he grew more adept at talking to visitors, he remained a little rough around the edges. One day after he abruptly cut someone off midquestion, Laurie approached him. "Rick, you just can't talk to people that way," she said. He was chagrined and grateful to her for pulling him aside. He started seeking Laurie's advice whenever social situations turned sour.

Rick had long compared Doug Smith to 21, his favorite wolf; eventually he began telling people that of all the women he'd met, Laurie was the most like 42, 21's longtime mate. Of course, Laurie already had a mate of her own (and so did Smith, for that matter), but she understood what he meant.

As for Rick, his own relationships never seemed to go anywhere. He had dated a woman, a wolf-watcher who came to the park frequently, a few years after he moved to Silver Gate permanently. One morning she suggested the two of them go to Bozeman to see the new Johnny Cash movie. Rick was amenable, though he was thinking, *Provided we see a wolf before it's time to start driving to Bozeman.* Rick happened to be in the midst of his longest streak of wolf sightings, a stretch that eventually extended to 891 consecutive days. That morning the wolves had proved difficult to find, and as the day wore on without a sighting, he became more and more anxious. He finally decided he was going to have to tell her he couldn't go—when a friend suddenly got a wolf in his scope and hurriedly called Rick over. Disaster was averted for the time being, but the relationship eventually withered. The wolves always came first. They were his family.

The more Rick learned about Yellowstone's wolves, the more responsibility he felt to tell their story. He had come to think of his writing project as not just a single book but a series of books, covering everything from the rise of the Druids to the arrival of O-Six.

But when was the first book going to appear? It had been fifteen years since he'd published anything. He had a mountain of material from his daily observations in the park, enough for an entire shelf of books. His journal contained thirteen years' worth of notes on the Druids alone, and the story was fantastic. And yet he hadn't begun writing any of it.

He worried that he couldn't meet the high standard he had set for himself—to become the next Ernest Thompson Seton—but something else was holding him back, too. Once the first book was finished, he'd have to promote it, which meant he'd have to leave Yellowstone and go back out into the world. He'd have to stop spending time with the wolves and become their emissary, just as Jane Goodall had done when she tore herself away from her beloved chimps to begin her own writing and speaking career, championing their cause everywhere she went. Instead of quiet mornings in the park, there would be airports and traffic and hotels. After fifteen years in the same place, doing the same thing day after day, it was all a little hard to imagine.

So instead he continued to collect material, a little more every day, making the mountain higher. Some of what he recorded made for gripping reading, though for every engrossing account of a wolf like O-Six fighting off a bear or taking down an elk, there were pages and pages describing sedentary wolves engaged in the same mundane behaviors you might observe while watching a dog whiling away empty afternoon hours on a back porch: standing, facing west, sniffing the ground, sitting back down. When Doug Smith and his team began a research project, they were always trying to answer a specific question—the relationship between wolves and ravens, for example—and this gave their note-taking some direction. But Rick wrote down everything.

BACK IN DENALI, WHERE HE'D SPENT ALL HIS FREE TIME TAKING pictures of wolves and other wildlife, he had grown so obsessed with getting the perfect shot that he found himself encroaching on animals, entering their space in ways that bordered on harassment. You learned to rationalize it, he would later tell friends; it was part of being a professional wildlife photographer. Somebody else was inevitably doing something worse than you were, and there were always boundaries you wouldn't cross. Until you did. He began to feel a kind of helplessness in the face of his compulsion, like an alcoholic. The solution, he finally decided, was to stop cold turkey.

By the time he got to Yellowstone, he was done with photography. Now he only took notes.

But the compulsion that had driven him in Denali hadn't really gone away. In some ways, it was even more pronounced than before. A pleasant morning in the park with his friends would turn tense if too many hours went by without a sighting and the prospect of a wolfless day arose. Laurie in particular would grow more anxious as a morning waned, knowing how much it meant to Rick to see a wolf each and every day, and unable to rest until she'd found one. When she finally got a wolf in her scope, she would hurriedly call him over, sometimes interrupting his interaction with nearby visitors midsentence, and Rick would all but run to the scope, lest the momentary sighting be lost before he arrived. Once he had his wolf, he could relax.

Over the years, the daily watching and the meticulous note-taking had become ends in themselves, and Rick savored what he considered to be personal milestones, evidence of his astounding perseverance. Since coming to Yellowstone, he had transcribed close to five million words of field notes into his journal; the King James Bible, the longest book he knew of, had only around eight hundred thousand. Cal Ripken, the celebrated Baltimore Orioles shortstop known as the "Iron Man" because he never took a day off, had played in 2,632 consecutive games. Rick hadn't missed a day in the park since June 12, 2000, the day he returned from his mother's memorial service, which meant that he had surpassed the Iron Man's achievement back in 2008. And Ripken's streak, of course, was interrupted by days off between games, not to mention winters, as Rick sometimes reminded people.

One night during his 891-day streak of consecutive sightings, the park was hit by a blizzard that was bad even by Yellowstone standards. The road from the park's northwest entrance to Silver Gate was the one stretch park officials kept open all year long, so Yellowstone's handful of winter visitors would have at least some access to the park. But with this storm the snow was coming down so heavily that the plows could barely keep up.

The next day brought more snow and high winds. By midday, visibility was near zero, and Yellowstone's superintendent made the unusual decision to close the park. Rick hadn't yet spotted a wolf when he heard the news, and he was in no hurry to leave. He drove his yellow Xterra cautiously through the Lamar Valley, as Doug McLaughlin followed in his Nissan Pathfinder.

There wasn't a soul on the road, not even a ranger. It was just the two of them crawling through the valley, Rick stopping from time to time to check for signals and updating Doug with his hand-held radio. The overcast, snow-filled sky was so dark, it might as well have been night. The wolves were in the valley, it seemed, but not where they could be easily viewed. The conditions continued to worsen, and snow was accumulating at an alarming rate. It was getting difficult to see where the road ended and the ditch began, and the window of opportunity for a safe return to Silver Gate was rapidly closing. If they got stuck, there would be nobody coming to pull them out, at least not until the next morning.

Doug heard his friend's voice come over the radio. "What emergency provisions do you have?" he asked. Rick wanted to see a wolf, and he was willing to push his luck a little further, even if it meant risking a night spent in a blizzard in the back of an uninsulated SUV. Doug always kept a sleeping bag, water, and food in his truck, in case he got stranded, just as Rick did. Just a few more minutes, they both agreed.

On a hunch, Doug left Rick on the side of the road, where he was still trying to pin down a weak signal, and drove about a mile farther on. Minutes later he radioed Rick: he had wolves. Rick hurried to him and looked through Doug's scope, the wind turning the exposed skin on his face a bright red.

There they were.

Distant and difficult to see through the snow, which was now blowing sideways, but there nonetheless. He had his sighting. Both men jumped into their trucks and headed for home, Rick busting through snowdrifts in his Xterra, struggling to stay in the center of what was by then only a suggestion of a road. Somehow they made it back to Silver Gate. For weeks afterward Doug was the hero; he had saved the streak.

Rick didn't have much to report when he sat down to type up his notes that night. It had only been a brief sighting, after all. But he wrote it up anyway, like he always did.

8

RETURN TO THE LAMAR VALLEY

Judge Molloy issued his ruling on Thursday, August 5, 2010. He signed the decision at 2:43 in the afternoon, too late for the news to make Friday morning's papers, buying himself—and every other government official involved—one last day of peace before the storm hit. The news was this: wolves must be returned to the endangered species list throughout the Northern Rockies, effective immediately.

Declaring wolves recovered in Idaho and Montana but still endangered in Wyoming did not pass legal muster, Molloy decided. Nothing in the language of the Endangered Species Act or in its legislative history allowed for such a maneuver, despite Fish and Wildlife's creative effort to reinterpret the code. "Even if the Service's solution is pragmatic, or even practical," the judge wrote, "it is at its heart a political solution that does not comply with the ESA." Doug Honnold had won.

It was just two weeks before Idaho officials were scheduled to announce wolf-hunting quotas for the fall; Montana game regulators had already set a limit of 186 wolves, more than double the number authorized in 2009. Both hunts would have to be canceled. The *New York Times* lauded the ruling in an editorial. "State plans meant to satisfy hunters rather than protect the wolves cannot do that," the editors wrote. "The gray wolf may need federal protection for years to come."

Honnold and his clients were delighted, though in reality it wasn't a total victory. Molloy had declined to rule on any of the other issues raised by the plaintiffs, such as the sufficiency of the recovery standards, or the question of whether genuine connectivity had been achieved. In Molloy's view, the fundamental flaw in the rule's logic—holding that some Northern Rockies wolves were endangered while others weren't—rendered all the other issues moot. Honnold felt he had made a compelling case that Fish and Wildlife's entire approach to recovery needed to be revisited, but Molloy had punted on that question.

Anticipating the backlash, Ken Salazar, the interior secretary, sought to channel blame away from the federal government and toward Wyoming officials, whose recalcitrance had forced the judge to rule as he did. Governor Freudenthal did take some lumps in the days that followed, but inevitably most of the vitriol was aimed at the feds. "I don't know why any state would ever allow another reintroduction of a species because the federal government and radical environmentalists simply cannot live up to their word and allow state management," Idaho governor Butch Otter told reporters.

Civil disobedience—another round of "shoot, shovel, and shut up"—was widely predicted. The response from frustrated officials in Idaho County, who oversaw a stretch of prime wolf habitat in the Lolo National Forest along the Montana border, captured the mood in rural Idaho. "At what point do we consider ourselves backed into a corner?" a county commissioner asked at a meeting shortly after the ruling was announced. "Can we file an action [saying] to the judge, 'You're not a wildlife biologist. Sit down and shut up?'" Officials in Montana and Idaho filed an appeal to the Ninth Circuit, though any possible relief from a higher court would come far too late to salvage this fall's hunting season.

Steven Turnbull learned about Molloy's ruling on the evening news. The situation was so complex, he wasn't sure whom to blame. One thing was clear: Montana and Idaho hunters had been screwed again. *Now they know how we feel in Wyoming* was his first thought. The consensus among the regulars at the Painter Outpost was that it was another example of federal judges overstepping their bounds. Turnbull had a friend who was convinced it was part of a plot to end hunting altogether, not just for wolves but for all big game. It was the first step, he believed, in the federal government's broader scheme to disarm the American public: if hunting were outlawed, then there was no longer any rationale for people to have guns.

You heard all kinds of rumors in Crandall about wolves: that the reintroduction had been illegal from the beginning, that the reintroduced wolves weren't the same species that had once lived in Yellowstone. They were Arctic wolves, it was said, 150-pound monsters, whereas the indigenous wolves had rarely exceeded 80, so small they didn't even prey on elk. It was hard to know what to believe.

Turnbull wasn't crazy about the federal government; he still blamed the EPA for the loss of his gas station. But he didn't hate the feds the way some people in Crandall did. In fact, he admired President Obama for trying to do something about the high cost of health insurance, which Turnbull had only rarely been able to afford. Heart trouble ran in his family—his father had died of a heart attack—and he'd recently had an operation for a clogged artery, the cost of which he was still slowly paying off. He planned to sign up for Obamacare as soon as he could. The law hadn't gone into effect yet, but it was starting to look like he'd be getting insurance before he got a wolf.

ON A CHILLY MORNING THAT OCTOBER, JOHN TESTER, THE DEMO-cratic U.S. senator from Montana, attended the Montana State University Homecoming Day parade in downtown Bozeman. As he often did at such events, he rode a green and yellow John Deere tractor down the street, waving at his constituents from its high seat. Unlike some Montana politicians, he looked very much at home in the seat, a burly man in boots with a flattop haircut and a blue corduroy Future Farmers of America jacket. A third-generation farmer, he had grown up on a piece of land home-steaded by his grandfather in north-central Montana, in the middle of the vast prairie that covers most of the state.

Wheat, not wolves, was what people cared about in Tester's part of Montana; the town nearest his farm—Big Sandy, popula-tion six hundred—was known as the home of Big Bud 747, the world's largest tractor. But wolves were on his mind as he steered the John Deere down Bozeman's picturesque main street, waving to the crowd and nodding to people he knew. Tester had a lot rid-ing on the outcome of the wolf fight, and as he had recently come to understand, so did some very powerful people in Washington.

Tester had been elected to the U.S. Senate in 2006, at the age of fifty. Relatively speaking, he wasn't a powerful person in Wash-ington, a junior member in a body that valued seniority above all else. And yet as the 2010 midterm elections drew near, his for-tunes were becoming a matter of acute concern for Democrats ev-erywhere. Tester's 2006 win had been pivotal: it was one of six races in which Democrats had defeated incumbent Republicans, swinging the Senate back to Democratic control. It wasn't much of a majority—fifty-one Democrats to forty-seven Republicans, with two independents—but it was all they needed. It meant a Democrat, Harry Reid, was the new majority leader, giving him control of the flow of legislation and the power to make key appointments in the Senate's all-important committee system.

Coupled with a new Democratic majority in the House and in 2008 the election of President Obama, Tester's win meant the Democrats had complete control in Washington—at least for the moment. The rise of the Tea Party movement had radically changed the political calculus in the country, and pollsters were predicting a bloodbath for Democrats in the 2010 midterms, which were less than a month away. Republicans would almost certainly regain control of the House, bringing Obama's legislative agenda to a halt.

Reid, Obama, and the big Democratic donors were already thinking ahead to the 2012 elections, when the Republicans' goal would be to take back the Senate as well. Tester would be up for re-election then, and his seat would undoubtedly be one of the GOP's primary targets. He had won it by the thinnest of margins—less than 1 percent—and Montana had a tendency to swing back and forth between Democrats and Republicans in statewide elections.

If the anti-Obama fervor that was sweeping the nation's rural areas lasted into the 2012 campaign season, Tester would be vulnerable. He was friendly with the president; the two had been junior senators together. Tester had supported Obama's massive stimulus bill—the original animus for many Tea Party adherents—as well as Obamacare, though neither had been especially popular in Montana. On other issues, such as gay marriage, he'd taken a more independent line, in keeping with the attitudes of his relatively conservative constituents.

At the time of Molloy's ruling, a new opponent for Tester had yet to come forward, but Republican congressman Denny Rehberg was widely considered to be preparing a run. A wealthy rancher and real estate developer, Rehberg had been in politics for most of his adult life. He'd made an unsuccessful run at the Senate in 1996 and was already laying the groundwork for taking on Tester. He had the backing of the state's powerful mining industry, which he had long championed in Washington.

Lately Rehberg had been touring the state, holding town hall meetings. Like rural elected officials across the country, he was getting an earful about the bailout of the banks and runaway federal spending—but he was also hearing a lot about wolves. After Molloy's recent ruling, he had written an opinion piece for the Bozeman paper, promising to hold hearings on the issue. "It's like a bad horror movie where the monster keeps coming back no matter how many times you think it's been killed," he wrote. The piece also took a more direct dig at Tester, who he suggested was out of touch with his constituents: "Montanans overwhelmingly opposed federal bailouts, the nearly trillion-dollar spending bill that has yet to stimulate the economy, and of course Obamacare. It's because I was listening before I voted that I'm the only member of Montana's delegation who voted against them all."

Shortly thereafter Rehberg signed on to cosponsor an anti-wolf bill that had been floating around Congress for months, a resolution that would specifically exempt the gray wolf from the Endangered Species Act. It was meant as a kind of legislative solution to the legal impasse over the management of wolves, an end run around the courts. The resolution was a long shot; Congress had never before put its thumb on the scale in a fight over a specific animal, deferring instead to the bureaucracy at Fish and Wildlife and the act's interpretation by the federal judiciary.

The bill was going nowhere—the Democratic majority in the Senate would never let it through. But that didn't matter; Rehberg, who kept a stuffed wolf in his Capitol office, was getting credit for trying to fix a problem that a lot of Montanans cared about, and that edge might make all the difference in a close race against a Democrat tainted by his association with Obama. Tester couldn't do much about his voting record on the stimulus and Obamacare, but he needed to find a way to take the wolf issue off the table.

AS THE HOMECOMING PARADE WAS WINDING DOWN, TESTER spotted Mike Phillips, the former Yellowstone Wolf Project coordinator, shaking hands and working the crowd. Phillips was running for reelection, too. He had represented Bozeman in the Montana House of Representatives since 2007, though he was also still working for Ted Turner as the director of the Turner Endangered Species Fund. Bozeman, a bastion of progressive politics and environmentalism, was one of the few places in Montana where Phillips's résumé was completely noncontroversial. He was somewhat less popular in the halls of the capitol in Helena, where he was disdainfully referred to in some circles as "Ted Turner's personal wolf biologist" and where his legislative agenda was met largely with stony indifference. Yet Phillips was ambitious and he understood politics. Standing together on Main Street under an impossibly blue sky, the two men went over Tester's options for how to deal with Rehberg and the wolf issue.

The irony was that Tester shouldn't have been vulnerable at all on wolves. He'd proposed a federally funded program to compensate ranchers who lost stock, and he'd come out strongly in favor of state management of wolves and a regular hunting season. And the idea that Tester—whose farm rarely earned more than twenty thousand dollars a year and who famously butchered his own meat and carried it on the plane to Washington—was out of touch with rural Montanans was risible.

Yet he wasn't one to grandstand. After Molloy's ruling, he sent a letter to Secretary Salazar, urging him to convene stakeholders from all three states to restart the process of negotiating a solution to the impasse. But after talking to Harry Reid about the high stakes of the 2012 elections, he realized he didn't have that kind of time.

Reid was more than eager to help. He'd promised to steer plenty of campaign cash Tester's way, and observers were predicting his next race would be the most expensive in Montana's history. But money might not be enough, especially if Rehberg outmaneuvered him on the wolf issue. If Democrats were going to keep a toehold on power in Congress—if Obamacare was going to live past its infancy—wolves needed to start dying in Montana, in large numbers, and soon.

If he could find a way to reverse Molloy's ruling, Tester asked Phillips, should he do it?

Phillips was a pragmatist. He didn't think wolves should be hunted near Yellowstone—he felt it wasn't fair chase—but he wasn't against wolf-hunting in general. He agreed with Ed Bangs and the wildlife professionals in the states: wolves were back to stay, and no amount of hunting was going to change that. Still, he didn't like the idea of Congress intervening in a decision about how the ESA should be applied. It was a bad precedent, he told Tester.

But it wasn't bad science, in his opinion. "Biologically, you're fine," he said. Yes, it was a political solution to what was essentially a legal conundrum, but life was politics. There was no getting around it.

"We need you reelected," he told Tester. "So go ahead."

IN THE FALL OF 2010, O-SIX FOUND HERSELF RANGING FARTHER and farther east to find elk, and Rick began to pick up signals from her packmates' collars in the Lamar Valley on a regular basis, and even to points beyond. On one foray, O-Six made a kill in an area known as Round Prairie, four miles up Soda Butte Creek, the tributary of the Lamar that ran southwest from Silver Gate and down into the park. Getting the meat to the pups meant trekking back down Soda Butte, through the entire Lamar Valley, and back to the den above Slough Creek—roughly ten miles. To the amazement of the watchers, O-Six made the round-trip twice in one day, traveling forty miles altogether. It was a herculean effort, but it wasn't sustainable. It was time to move the pack to where the food was. It was time, in other words, for O-Six to go back to the Lamar Valley, the place her mother had been born, the place the Druids had once ruled.

The problem was that despite the Druids' demise, the valley wasn't completely free of wolves. A small pack known as the Silvers—a mated pair and two adult daughters—had moved in the previous winter, taking advantage of the Druids' decline. They were soon joined by O-Six's onetime companion 147, the black male she and her sister had been running with when she first encountered 754 and 755. His brief dalliance with O-Six's sister hadn't lasted, and she'd eventually gone back to her natal pack. The Silver females had welcomed 147's company, while the resident alpha male had done his best to run him off. But the Silver alpha was past his prime, and when the inevitable showdown came, 147 defeated him. The old male wasn't seriously injured, however, and 147 allowed him to stay, in a kind of emeritus role.

This behavior was not unprecedented, but it was unusual, and Rick watched with interest as the two males adjusted to their new arrangement. In time, 147 began to treat the old wolf like a big brother, clutching him around the neck with his paws and licking his face. For their part, the old male's daughters, one of whom was just a yearling, chased and tumbled with 147 as if they had known him since birth. In the spring, the alpha female gave birth to a litter of 147's pups, the first born in the valley to a pack other than the Druids in over a decade.

The presence of the Silvers in the valley might have been what was pushing the Lamars so far east, up into the Soda Butte drainage. The packs were roughly the same size, though the Silvers had more adults, and dislodging them would have been a somewhat risky proposition for O-Six.

On October 20, Rick discovered just how far east the Lamars were roaming. That morning in the frosty predawn darkness, he climbed into his Xterra and started the motor. As the SUV idled in front of his cabin, he turned on the rooftop antenna as he always did. To his surprise he immediately got a powerful signal from 754 and 755. It was too strong to be coming from the park; the Lamar males were in Silver Gate.

He took a quick look out his window, but it was still black outside. He picked up his radio and called Laurie and Doug, the two people in town he knew would be awake already. Like Rick, Laurie was already in her driveway, warming up her Subaru. In the calm, professional voice he always employed on the radio, he told her to stay put: the Lamar males were nearby. It was unclear if O-Six or the pups were with them; it might have been just the two males out hunting. Laurie was ecstatic, but there was nothing to do but stay near the radio and wait for the sun to come up.

Then she heard a howl. She got out of the car and listened. It was high-pitched, almost certainly that of a pup, and very nearby. She stood in the driveway, waiting for an answer. When it came, it was like nothing she had ever heard. The pack's calls to one another echoed against the sheer walls that towered over the town, and she stood dumbfounded, just a few yards from her front door, immersed in the sound of their voices.

When the darkness at last began to give way, she saw three figures moving through the trees east of the house. It was O-Six and the two males. They were close enough that had they been her dogs, she could have called them to her. Over the next hour they moved in and out of her view, sometimes in the woods to the north of the house, sometimes across the street in the meadow to the south. The pups were somewhere out of sight; periodically they howled in distress, and the adults answered. Rick joined Laurie in her driveway, and they watched together, too excited to get out their scopes and not really needing them in any case.

Rick looked up and down the road as the sun rose and the handful of buildings scattered along Highway 212 came into view. Every morning he left for the park in total darkness and returned in the afternoon or evening; this was the first time he could remember in his fifteen years here that he had actually seen the morning sun on the narrow valley. His absence from the park didn't go unnoticed, and as word got around that the Lamars were in Silver Gate, watchers began to join them in ones and twos. By the time a small crowd gathered, the three adults were walking boldly along the side of the road. O-Six crossed the highway at will with 755 in tow, and 754 darted furtively across when he had to. Scarcely any cars were on the road at that hour.

Rick's joy at seeing the pack right outside his front door was tempered by the significance of this excursion: The Lamars considered the area east of the park to be part of their territory. Nothing good could come from that. There may not have been a wolf-hunting season that fall, thanks to Judge Molloy's ruling, but there were cattle east of the park—especially along the Clark's Fork and its tributaries, like Crandall Creek—and cattle and wolves didn't mix. In recent years, Wyoming officials had taken an increasingly aggressive stance toward livestock depredations in the area. After ten cows were lost in 2008, government hunters destroyed an entire pack based near Crandall Creek and all but a handful of members of a pack that denned in Sunlight.

. . .

THAT FALL THE SILVERS SUFFERED A SERIOUS LOSS THAT SUDDENLY made the Lamar Valley look much more attractive to O-Six and her family. On November 1, as Rick scanned for the Silver pack, he detected a mortality code coming from 147. A few days later Wolf Project biologists hiked in and found him lying under some pines. He had puncture wounds, most likely from a fight with other wolves, though it wasn't clear which pack had been in the area. The perpetrator might have been a lone wolf roaming through the valley, which was not uncommon. It was a sad occasion for the watchers. 147's kindness toward the old Silver alpha had made him a favorite.

Still, his death was a good omen for the Lamars. Without an alpha male, the Silvers' claim on the valley would be tenuous. With no collared wolves remaining among the Silvers, the watchers had no way to track the pack. Rick guessed they would likely scatter. It showed how fragile pack life was, even in a wolf paradise like Yellowstone. A pack was thriving one moment, and then it was simply gone the next.

Shortly after 147's death, the Lamars began frequenting a site on the eastern end of the valley that the Silvers had been using for months. There was no sign of the Silver alpha female, the old male, or the pups, and O-Six had apparently moved her brood in without a fight. It was a piece of land Rick knew well: the Druids' old summer rendezvous. O-Six had presumably never visited the spot, but somehow she found it and made it her own, just as generations of Lamar Valley wolves had done before.

The Lamars' move to the rendezvous made them easy for the watchers to locate in the mornings, though viewing was not quite what it was back at the den on Slough Creek. The best spot for watching the pack was a full two miles from the site, and there were trees and foothills that tended to obscure the action. But it was possible to keep tabs on their comings and goings and, with a little luck, to catch a few glimpses of domestic life.

Now six months old and weighing perhaps fifty pounds, the pups were beginning to rank themselves. Dark Gray Male was the most assertive, snapping and snarling at his littermates from time to time, though they didn't always appear to notice. Shy Male tended to fall behind when the family was on the move and would often bed by himself, some distance from the pack. He was leery of the road and sometimes refused to cross, hiding in the trees and howling instead. Rounding him up when it was time to move on required no small effort by the adults. The task more often than not fell to his uncle, 754, who seemed to take a special interest in the pup.

The pups were now feeding at kills, though they sought food from the adults at the rendezvous site as well. Regurgitation is less a choice than a reflex, and to keep their own stomachs full, O-Six and the two males were obliged to pin the pups when they came running, tails wagging, to solicit a meal. The adults held them down for a few seconds, their enormous jaws clamped lightly on the pups' throats, until the youngsters got the message and stopped trying to lick at their mouths. After a few weeks of pinning, a simple curled lip was usually enough to keep the hungry pups at bay.

When it came to joining in the hunt, however, the young wolves needed little encouragement. The valley was full of elk that fall. One rainy morning shortly after they'd moved, the entire pack bedded atop an embankment above a curve in an old course where the Lamar River no longer ran. An enormous herd was passing about a mile to the north, not far from the park road. This end of the valley was the part that most resembled the Serengeti, to which it was so often compared: flat and grassy, with wide-open vistas that allowed predator and prey alike plenty of warning about what was coming their way. Adults and pups were lounging on the dried-up riverbank, like lions in the hot Serengeti sun, passively watching the distant ungulates. The fickle nature of Yellowstone's own sun made no difference to the wolves, and neither did the chill wind, which at that moment was blowing a steady rain into their faces. They did not miss the sun, nor did they mind the rain.

The elk drifted south, moving in the pack's direction. When the lead animals spotted the family hunkered down in the wet sage, the herd turned abruptly east, and the wolves found themselves staring at the flank of a passing parade of cows and calves, with a few young bulls in the mix, snorting and huffing in alarm as they got within range and prancing to show their fitness. O-Six and the two adult males scarcely moved, but the pups popped up and down like prairie dogs, alternately excited and intimidated by the hooved mass of buff-colored hide thumping and surging before them. Dark Gray danced back and forth, ready for action, though when a solitary elk broke from the herd in his general direction, he immediately turned and ran for the protection of his parents.

When the last elk had passed, the pups waited for a cue from O-Six. Would they give chase? They would not. Whatever their mother was looking for in the passing herd, she hadn't seen it. One by one the adults roused themselves and left the bank. 754 paused briefly to submit to his brother, who rewarded him with a high wagging tail, then lingered behind to make sure each of the pups, including Shy Male, kept up with the family as they drifted across the valley.

It was unusual for so many elk to be in the valley this early in the winter. They typically stayed at higher elevations until a bit later in the season, not coming down until the deep snow on the mountaintops forced them to seek lower ground. But this year they were already coming to the valley in droves. As the elk arrived, hundreds of trumpeter swans were leaving, though it was somewhat early for their migration as well. The elk and the birds appeared to know something that the wolves and the watchers did not.

What that was became clear on November 20, when a massive snowstorm hit the Northern Range. Even for Yellowstone, the snowfall was staggering. The roads in and out of the park were all but impassable, and the power and phones were out for days in Silver Gate. Trees overloaded with snow and buffeted by the wind collapsed, falling across the roads. Snowplow crews managed to clear enough snow and debris to open the park for a couple of days, but then another round of flurries, coupled with a relentless wind, created dangerously high drifts, and the superintendent closed the park again. (Rick still managed to get his daily visits in, of course.) When it reopened, the plowed roads were jammed with bison desperate for some relief from trudging through snow up to their bellies. No wolves were sighted for four straight days.

The storm was unusual only in its intensity. During the winter, Yellowstone was one of the coldest inhabited places on earth. Trees at higher elevations in the park had been known to simply explode, succumbing to the rapid expansion of their frozen sap. The park was also one of the snowiest places in the nation. Snow could fall any day of the year, even in the middle of summer. Average snowfall north and south of the park was roughly twenty feet per year, but Yellowstone itself usually got more than twice that amount. The November snowstorm was the beginning of what would become one of the harshest winters in years. O-Six's first winter in the valley would be one to remember.

A FEW WEEKS AFTER THE STORM, A SOLITARY WOLF STOOD HOWLing high atop Specimen Ridge. He was perched on a thick cornice of snow, looking down into the valley from a vantage point roughly a mile west of the rendezvous site. Far below, the Lamars heard the call and turned their attention to the mountain. With the Silvers gone, the pack had roamed the valley unchallenged for over a month. From time to time they picked up the scent of a lone wolf wandering through, but there had been no real threat.

This was something different. The wolf on the ridge was 586, the beta male of the Agates, O-Six's natal pack. In late fall, the Agates had begun frequenting the eastern end of Little America, which had seen less use since the Lamars moved from the den above Slough Creek into the Lamar Valley. The Agates, who spent most of their time farther to the south along the Yellowstone River, were still led by O-Six's mother, known as 472, though she had now reached the advanced age of nine. One of O-Six's sisters was still with the pack as well. Her father had died in 2007, but two dispersing wolves—a pair of Mollies from the park's interior—had recently joined the Agates, and one had become 472's new mate. The other was 586, a barrel-chested 130-pound gray, bigger even than 754.

The Lamars still considered the eastern end of Little America—at least as far as the natal den above Slough Creek—to be part of their territory, and the packs had been ranging closer to one another in recent weeks. On December 1, they'd gotten close enough to exchange howls, raising the possibility that a confrontation was coming. With nine wolves, the Agates had greater numbers, boasting five adults to the Lamars' three. O-Six chose retreat that day, leading her clan higher and higher onto Specimen, until the Agates were far out of range. Whether O-Six and her mother recognized one another's howls was unclear; in any case, mother and daughter never got close enough on that occasion to test the resilience of their familial bond.

As it happened, they never would. On December 6, O-Six's mother was found dead on the western edge of Little America, not far from Junction Butte. She'd been killed by other wolves, most likely the neighboring Blacktail Pack, which made occasional forays down into the outskirts of Agate territory. Her tenure as an alpha had been among the longest since reintroduction, and she had left a considerable legacy in Yellowstone's Northern Range, most notably in female leadership: at least five of her daughters had become alphas in other packs.

Now, three days after her death, 586 was alone in Lamar territory. The Agates had entered the valley the day before, chasing elk, and he'd become separated from the pack. He was old—one of the oldest wolves in the park—yet he was still very hale, with a thick gray coat and a deep, basso howl. He was also heavy. As he leaned over Specimen's sheer drop, the fresh snow under his feet suddenly began to give way. He leaped back just as the cornice crumbled, sending a river of snow cascading toward the edge. Suddenly an entire section of the ridgeline gave way, and thousands of pounds of snow and ice plummeted down the mountainside with a thunderous roar, slamming into the trees below and sending a spray of fine white powder high into the air.

If the Lamars had been unsure of his location before, they certainly knew where he was now. They also knew from his unaccompanied howl that he was alone. The pack replied in a confident chorus, and then for good measure jumped atop one another in a licking, rollicking heap. Undeterred by the avalanche or the challenge of the wolves below, 586 continued to look for a likely place to descend Specimen. As he made his way down, the Lamars approached from the south, moving through the trees in the rippling foothills. When the intruder finally reached the flat plain of the valley and broke into the open, the Lamars spotted him and began advancing at a run, the two adult males in the lead, with O-Six just behind. The old Agate didn't flee; instead he approached with ears flat and tail wagging low, as though he were greeting his own pack, as he might well have believed; at his advanced age, his eyesight and hearing were likely not what they once were.

By the time he realized his mistake, 754 and 755 were within striking distance. The old male turned and sprinted for the river, breaking trail through the deep snow. The Lamars followed, loping easily through his wake, and were on him in seconds, with 755 leading the attack. Outnumbered and desperate as he was, the solitary Agate was not an easy victim. He was a more experienced fighter than either of the Lamar males, and his wide leather collar and thick winter coat offered some protection from their slashing teeth. The pups joined in as best they could, snapping at the intruder's rear legs and hindquarters to no real effect.

The Agate broke for the river again at his first opportunity, only to be overtaken once more by his younger and faster pursuers. Had the pups been a bit older, he might have succumbed to his attackers' greater numbers. Instead, twisting and turning between the males and O-Six, he managed to protect his flanks long enough to make a third dash for freedom, and this time the Lamars gave chase for only a short spell before letting him go.

The conflict was unlike anything the pups had ever experienced. They excitedly retraced the course of the running battle, sniffing the ground and lingering in the spots where the fighting had been most intense, the rent snow leaving a chaotic record of the fracas. The emboldened pack spent the rest of the afternoon tracking down every last place the Agates had visited in the preceding days, but the intruders were long gone, and the confrontation turned out to be the last between the two neighboring families. The old male recovered from his wounds, but the Agates, bereft of their longtime matriarch, retreated to their core territory. It was O-Six's first successful defense of the valley.

ON JANUARY 3, DOUG SMITH SPOTTED THE LAMARS IN THE SLOUGH Creek flats from the passenger seat of a helicopter. It was collaring time again. He'd agreed not to dart O-Six out of deference to the wolf-watching community, who felt she was too special—too wild—to wear the mark of any human endeavor. Bob Landis was particularly insistent, though for more practical reasons. Some of his best footage from the previous year had featured O-Six; in his mind any film he might make of her story would be ruined if she suddenly appeared in a research collar halfway through.

Yet Smith wanted at least one more collared wolf in this particular pack. Currently, project members could track both of the adult males, but how much longer 754 would stick around was an open question. Unless something happened to his brother, he would have to leave the pack to find a mate, which would mean 755 would be the lone remaining collared wolf. Smith knew how fast a pack's fortunes could reverse; he didn't want a repeat of what had occurred with the Silvers, when 147's abrupt death had left researchers wondering what had become of the pack he left behind.

He doubted he could dart O-Six even if he wanted to. As the pilot banked over the creek, she headed straight for the nearest trees as she always did. The pups weren't as savvy, and Smith managed to bring down the smaller of the two females after a few passes. He found her in good health, if a little on the thin side at seventy-one pounds. Her collar number was 776.

The pack was now on the move almost constantly. O-Six had managed to keep her entire brood alive almost to adulthood, which was a rare trick. This was a dangerous time for the pups, however. Now that the pack was roaming across its entire territory, the chances of being left behind were greater than ever. The pups were nearly full grown but still naïve and would be hard-pressed to feed themselves if they became separated from the pack.

On January 31, the watchers spotted the Lamars on Druid Peak, nosing around the old Druid den site. It was halfway up the mountain, completely obscured from the road. Rick knew from long experience where the wolves would be visible as they came and went from the den area, however. A narrow trail along a rock outcrop, known as the Ledge Trail, was the preferred route to the den forest. It was exposed enough that watchers could spot comings and goings. Sure enough, though none of these wolves had ever visited the Druid den before, they used the very same trail.

Laurie noticed that Shy Male was not among the wolves visiting the den. A watcher on the radio reported that he was far to the west, under a copse of trees above Lamar Canyon, howling for the pack. He was only a few miles away, which meant he could likely track them down in the night, if the weather held. Wolves have glands between their toes that leave their unique scents behind as they walk, but heavy snow could make it difficult to scent-trail. For the time being, Shy Male was by himself, not far from the border of the Lamars' territory. If strange wolves found the pup before his parents did, he might become the young family's first casualty.

At first light the next morning, Laurie spotted a single pair of tracks in the valley but no wolves. The pack was gone. Rick had signals indicating they were far to the east, likely up the Soda Butte drainage. The temperature meanwhile had plummeted to forty below. It was so cold that steam from the valley's warm springs was freezing in the air, forming tiny crystals of ice that hung on the breeze and caught the morning sun. The phenomenon, called fairy dust by park veterans, was usually cause for delight. But now the brutal cold felt like a bad omen for O-Six's lost pup.

Shy Male eventually was spotted howling forlornly as he made his way east. There was no reply; the pack was simply too far away. He was at least headed in the right direction. In the afternoon, however, the pup lost the pack's trail. To Laurie's dismay, he turned and headed west. There was no way to know how long it had been since he'd had something to eat. The pack was still far to the east the next day, which dawned just as cold. Shy Male, meanwhile, had continued in the wrong direction. By midmorning, he had made it all the way to the old den above Slough Creek, where he wandered about in circles, looking for his family in the place where he had been born.

The next morning the Lamars were back in the valley, and the watchers counted them anxiously. There were seven. After three days on his own, Shy Male had found the pack at last. Or more likely, Rick thought, the pack had found him.

THE PUPS NOW LOOKED LIKE LITHE VERSIONS OF THEIR PARENTS. Both female pups resembled their mother, and as their frames filled out, it became more difficult to tell the three Lamar females apart as they moved across the valley. Soon they would be considered yearlings, yet they hadn't become any less playful. That winter the pups spent countless hours stalking mice. The rodents had marginal nutritional value for animals as large as wolves, but mousing wasn't about being hungry—it was about having fun. Hidden beneath two feet of snow in tunnels of their own making, the mice couldn't be seen from the surface, but the wolves could hear them moving. With their uncannily sensitive ears cocked forward, heads tilted to one side, the pups listened for the telltale scrabble beneath the snow, then reared up, foxlike, for a two-footed pounce. Most often they missed. When one of the pups managed to catch one at last, he paraded around with the hapless mouse dangling from his mouth, daring his littermates to try to take it, or tossed it high into the air and pounced on it again.

One evening Laurie watched 776 and her sister, whom she and Rick had begun calling Middle Gray, lounge on the snow in the trees near Soda Butte Creek. The rest of the pack was nearby; they had a carcass in the woods. As she studied the two sisters, Laurie noticed something black on the snow between 776's paws: she'd caught a raven. She had no interest in eating it—her belly was already full of elk—yet it was clearly a cherished prize.

The young wolf stood up, gathered the limp bird in her jaws, and began looking for somewhere to hide it. She set the raven down briefly on a frozen stream, only to have it slip off the ice and into the shallow water, necessitating a brief bobbing exercise to retrieve the now-sopping wet bird. She trotted along until she found a suitable nook under some brambles, where she carefully tucked her package, pushing some snow across the entrance.

No sooner had she made her cache than her brother, Dark Gray, began nosing among the feathers scattered around her former resting place. He promptly began scent-trailing the bird, only to be distracted by a hole along the bank of the creek, from which he pulled an enormous chunk of ice. Something about its size and texture appealed to him, and he settled down with the chunk between his paws and began gnawing away at it as though it were a bone, as content with his find as his sister had been with hers.

The pack's adults, meanwhile, were more interested in one another. It was mating season again, and the love triangle that connected the three of them was much in evidence. O-Six did little to discourage 754's affections, but 755 policed their interactions diligently, and when O-Six was ready, the alpha male didn't miss his opportunity. Rick had gotten into the habit of timing such couplings, known as ties, over the years with his wristwatch; a particularly long one was marked on the calendar, the better to predict when the pups might be born.

AS THE BRUTAL WINTER WORE ON, BISON LEFT THE PARK BY THE hundreds, searching for lower ground. It wasn't the cold they were fleeing: their fur had an underlayer so efficient that scarcely any body heat reached the ends of the longer guard hairs above. The relentless snow was what drove them out. For every bite of grass they ate, a mound of heavy snow had to be shoved aside. It was a task for which the bison's broad forehead and muscular neck and shoulders were well suited, but even so, there were limits to how much snow the beasts could move before the effort outweighed the meager reward, and this year the snowpack was much deeper than usual.

Most of them left the park near Gardiner, which meant they wouldn't survive to see the spring. Some of Yellowstone's bison carry brucellosis, a disease that under rare circumstances can be transmitted from wildlife to domestic cattle. Thanks to a long-standing agreement with ranchers north of the park, Montana authorities slaughtered most of the bison that left the park in the winter to prevent any possibility of contagion; this year the migration was bigger than usual, and five hundred were killed.

Those that remained in the valley were slowing down, conserving what energy they had left. More and more they resembled white statues, almost indistinguishable from the granite boulders that dotted the valley's endless fields of snow. The elk were suffering, too.

The wolves, on the other hand, could not have been healthier. Their fur kept them so warm that they seldom sought shelter from the cold. Even when it was time to rest, they simply curled up in the snow wherever they were and closed their eyes. And every winter-killed animal was a free meal, so the Lamars were eating well.

One morning 776 spotted a bison on its haunches near Soda Butte Creek, surrounded by ravens. She approached with caution—bison were dangerous, even when they were half-starved—but the animal didn't move. It was dead, frozen in place as it dozed upright in the deep snow. The ravens had done their best, but there was little they could eat until the carcass was properly opened. 776 made a few experimental tugs at the bison's hide, but the carcass was so stiff that she couldn't get good purchase. In the end, she decided it wasn't worth the effort; there was no shortage of food, after all. She left the bison sitting there, still upright, its massive head staring straight ahead at nothing, a strange sentinel in the frozen silence.

IN MID-MARCH IT WAS CLEAR THAT O-SIX WAS PREGNANT AGAIN. Rick watched her soliciting food from the males, a sign that she was slowing down and would be denning soon. Unlike last year, this spring she would be well provisioned in the den. The pups had become accomplished hunters, and Rick had watched them join 754 and 755 to take down elk without O-Six's help. But where would the new litter be born? O-Six had been spending more time in the old Druid den site on Druid Peak, though Rick had also spotted her checking out the Slough den as well.

By the end of the month, she'd made her choice. The new pups would be born on Druid Peak, in the same den where O-Six's mother had been born, or very near it. The den site was not especially high on the mountainside, nor very far from the road that ran along its base, yet it was impossible to see from the ground, nestled as it was in a heavily wooded recess. This time there would be no grand unveiling of the pups as there had been at the Slough Creek den, no scenes of O-Six moving her newborns around by the scruff of the neck or chasing them down when they wandered too far. The trees around the site were just too thick.

But Rick didn't mind. O-Six had chosen a den that had been used by the park's most successful pack for more than a decade, and that seemed propitious. He'd documented at least a dozen litters born there, had watched 21 and 42 come and go from the den forest every spring, year after year. Localized on Druid Peak, the Lamars were now officially Lamar Valley wolves, and he welcomed the idea of spending the spring and summer here, watching them move through the landscape he knew so well.

He had spent so many years in the valley, scanning the sides of Druid Peak to the north, Specimen Ridge to the south, and the river corridor in between that he might as well have lived there himself. When he closed his eyes, he could see every hill, every contour of the river, every dip and rise in the valley's floor in his mind—the way lifelong residents of a neighborhood knew every tree, every building, every street—and could tell a story associated with each. Now the valley would be the stage for a new story.

O-Six had come home.

9

BETRAYAL

In early April 2011, an alarming memo came down from the superintendent's office: if the Obama administration and the new Republican majority in the House of Representatives couldn't reach an agreement on a spending bill by April 15, Yellowstone National Park—along with the rest of the federal government—would shut down. The park road through the Northern Range would remain open, but only for purposes of travel between Silver Gate and Gardiner; there would be no stopping within the park for any reason, including wolf-watching.

Talk of a government shutdown had been brewing for months. As predicted, the fall elections had resulted in a GOP takeover in the House, and the new Republican speaker, Ohio's John Boehner, immediately demanded massive budget cuts as a condition for any new spending agreement, along with the repeal of Obamacare. The Republican caucus now included a sizable Tea Party contingent, and the new members let it be known that they were prepared to stop at nothing—furloughing thousands of federal employees, even defaulting on interest payments on U.S. government debt, one of the pillars of the global economy—to achieve their goals. A lengthy game of brinksmanship between President Obama and Speaker Boehner had ensued, dominating the headlines for months.

At the last possible moment, Obama acquiesced to the cuts, signing a federal budget bill funding the government for the remainder of the fiscal year. (A separate bill unraveling Obamacare never made it to his desk, having been shot down by the Democratic majority that still held the Senate.) Disaster had been averted, but a new era of hyperpartisanship in Washington had begun.

The 459-page funding bill made no mention of wolves or the Endangered Species Act, but tucked deep inside was a paragraph, barely a hundred words long, that radically changed the terms of the debate. It read:

> Before the end of the 60-day period beginning on the date of enactment of this division, the Secretary of the Interior shall reissue the final rule published on April 2, 2009 (74 Fed. Reg. 15123 et seq.) without regard to any other provision of statute or regulation that applies to issuance of such rule. Such reissuance (including this section) shall not be subject to judicial review and shall not abrogate or otherwise have any effect on the Order and Judgment issued by the United States District Court for the District of Wyoming in Case Numbers 09-CV-118J and 09-CV-138J on November 18, 2010.

In plain English, the provision reversed Judge Molloy's ruling—reinstating Fish and Wildlife's decision to delist the wolf in Idaho and Montana—and stipulated that neither Molloy nor any other judge would have the power to overturn Congress's intervention. In Wyoming, meanwhile, the wolf would remain under federal protection, pending the outcome of the state's lawsuit against Fish and Wildlife. The directive, known as a budget rider, had been inserted with the approval of the lead budget negotiators for each side—Harry Reid for the Democrats and John Boehner for the Republicans—just two days before the House and Senate voted on the bill. It was authored by Montana senator John Tester.

Tester's rider was unprecedented. It marked the first time in the thirty-eight-year history of the Endangered Species Act that Congress had intervened in the rule-making process to force a desired outcome. With a single paragraph, lawmakers had upended years of jurisprudence based on countless hearings and hundreds of pages of expert testimony.

If the move was brazen, it was also cunning. Had the rider's language been in a stand-alone bill put to an up-or-down vote on the Senate floor, its passage would have been extremely unlikely. Pinning it to the coattails of the must-pass budget bill, however, gave Democratic members the cover they needed; they weren't voting *against* wolves, they were voting *for* a budget that their leaders had negotiated, a compromise that represented the best possible deal they could get in the face of a Tea Party–dominated Republican caucus that was intent on cutting federal spending to the bone and was willing to hold the federal government hostage to get it done. The rider was Reid's favor to Tester, the boost he needed to climb past Rehberg in the polls.

As is often the case with changes slipped in at the eleventh hour, there had been no debate on the merits of the rider, nor even any formal announcement of its adoption. Environmental lobbyists caught wind of the move shortly before the scheduled vote, however, and spread the word to liberal bloggers, who were outraged. But it was too late. The deal was done, and no hundred-word paragraph—no matter how controversial—was going to be allowed to derail a budget agreement months in the making, sealed

just hours before a looming government shutdown was set to begin. Tester's rider was just one of a laundry list of policy changes
tacked onto the bill—like those governing the fate of prisoners
at Guantánamo Bay or low-income women seeking abortions in
Washington, D.C.—during the backroom negotiation between
Reid and Boehner. Wolves had become another commodity in
Capitol Hill's never-ending swap meet.

Judge Molloy was equally powerless to undo the maneuver,
as he conceded in a short ruling that seethed with unconcealed
anger. Congress's action represented "a tearing away, an undermin-
ing, and a disrespect for the fundamental idea of the rule of law,"
he wrote. And yet his hands were tied. The rider "sacrifices the
spirit of the ESA to appease a vocal political faction," he wrote,
"but the wisdom of that choice is not now before this Court." The
only question was whether the rider was constitutional, and Molloy had to concede that it was. The rule was reinstated, and wolves
were no longer protected in Montana and Idaho. The great victory
that wolf advocates had won in Molloy's court the previous summer had lasted less than a year.

State officials in Idaho and Montana were exultant. Four days
after Tester's rider became law, Governor Otter signed a bill declaring gray wolves a "disaster emergency" in Idaho and authoriz-
ing state officials to take immediate action to reduce their numbers.
It played well with anti-wolf forces, though state officials quietly
conceded that they were content with waiting for the regular fall
season to renew hunting in the state. Montana would do the same.

"Things will be better tomorrow": that was the credo wolves
lived by, Rick had long ago decided. Regardless of the hardship and
misadventure that every pack inevitably faced, they were essentially
optimists. He tried to see life that way, too, but it wasn't easy. In
the weeks that followed, he found himself fielding questions from
visitors about wolf-hunting around the park, and he answered as

best he could, with the studied neutrality he'd learned to adopt as an employee of the National Park Service. The federal government officially supported delisting of wolves, after all, and good relations with game managers in states adjacent to the park were essential. During Montana's 2009 hunt, Doug Smith had made some mild comments to reporters about the setback to his research caused by the death of collared wolves, prompting a personal rebuke from the park superintendent. The two weren't always on the best of terms, despite the project's success and popularity with visitors. "Why does the Wolf Project stick out like a sore thumb?" Smith's boss had once asked.

This time Smith's reaction was pragmatic. Another hunting season along the park's northern and western borders was only five months away, and he was determined to limit the damage. He met with Montana wildlife officials to discuss limiting the take in hunting zones adjoining the park, especially around Jardine, where so many park wolves had been lost in 2009.

Still, it was inevitable that some Yellowstone wolves would be killed. Rick thought of the jaunt through Silver Gate that the Lamars had taken back in October. National Forest land lined both sides of the road through town and up to Cooke City and beyond, and the woods were full of hunters during elk season. If O-Six were to lead her charges on the same excursion this fall, one of Rick's neighbors could step outside his home and shoot her in his front yard. Silver Gate was definitely a wolf-friendly town, but you never knew; Laurie sometimes heard old-timers muttering about all the watchers—"wolf groupies," they called them—in the local motels.

TESTER'S RIDER WAS ALL ANYBODY IN CRANDALL TALKED ABOUT for days afterward—Congress had finally done something sensible about wolves. Of course, it didn't change the local situation in the slightest, since Wyoming still had no wolf-hunting season. Turnbull supposed he could head up into Montana and get a permit to shoot one, but he wouldn't even know where to begin to look. The country he knew was in Crandall, as were the wolves that needed shooting.

Turnbull hadn't seen too many signs of them in recent months, though he'd been out in the woods as much as he could, collecting shed elk antlers as he did every year, and keeping an eye out for the best-looking black bear he could find, the one he'd be taking that season. Crandall hadn't really had a resident wolf pack since government hunters eliminated the local wolves almost entirely in the summer of 2008. They had done the same thing to a pack denning in nearby Sunlight in 2010 after a rancher there lost some cattle, and now only a pair of wolves were left in that basin. The word was that they weren't denning, so there'd be no pups that spring.

Still, Turnbull knew there were wolves around. Louie Cary usually kept pretty good tabs on what was happening on the other side of the mountains in the Lamar Valley, and he kept everyone in Crandall up to date on which Yellowstone wolves he'd seen coming and going. It seemed a new pack was denning in Lamar, and they were coming east from time to time, as park wolves tended to do. In fact, Turnbull had a friend at a bar in Cooke City, where he went for beer and barbecue almost every Sunday, who had spotted a pack that spring walking right down the road from Silver Gate. He thought he'd heard a howl or two himself recently, coming maybe from Hunter Peak, behind Louie's place.

Calf survival in Yellowstone's northern herd had been dismal again that spring, which meant another lean fall was coming for elk-hunters all around the park. Turnbull wasn't sure who represented Wyoming in the U.S. Senate, but he was starting to wonder what exactly it was they did for a living. If John Tester could do what he did for Montana, then why couldn't Wyoming's senators do the same thing?

WHEN DOUG SMITH AND ROGER STRADLEY, THE PARK'S LONGTIME pilot, flew over Yellowstone's mountains and valleys, Smith didn't always look for wolves. Sometimes he counted beavers. Once a year he and a handful of other researchers flew over almost the entire park to make note of beaver food caches—piles of wood big enough to be spotted from the air—each of which signified the presence of a beaver colony. Not long after wolf reintroduction, Smith noticed that he was finding more and more colonies; from just 49 in 1996, the number had ballooned to 118 by 2009. The increase was partly due to a reintroduction of beavers that had taken place just north of the park in the mid-1990s, but that didn't explain why the animals had found Yellowstone's streams so hospitable after decades of absence. The answer seemed to be a resurgence of willow, the riparian shrub that is the beaver's preferred food.

And why was the willow coming back? Smith was still trying to figure that out, but he knew the answer almost certainly had something to do with wolves. As their numbers grew after reintroduction, elk numbers had of course declined, but—just as important—their behavior had changed as well. No longer free to congregate at their leisure along stream banks, elk were spending less time browsing on willow, which left plenty for the beavers.

More wolves, it seemed, meant more beavers, but that wasn't all: the return of Yellowstone's top predator was having repercussions up and down the park's food chain. The Lamar Valley that O-Six claimed as her own was not the same landscape that her Druid ancestors had been introduced to fifteen years before. It was healthier in ways that even some of the wolf's most ardent advocates hadn't anticipated. Biologists called this type of chain reaction a trophic cascade, and by the spring of 2011—ironically, just as the political situation was turning sour for wolves—it was the hottest research subject in the park, not only for Smith's own colleagues at the Wolf Project but also for visiting biologists from around the country. At a time when species were disappearing from the earth at a rate faster than that of any period since the extinction of the dinosaurs, here was a rare success story: Greater Yellowstone, the largest intact temperate ecosystem left in the world, was returning to its former glory. Smith happily greeted every visitor and kept tabs on every study, proud to be at the center of so much intellectual ferment.

One of the most dramatic changes concerned coyotes. Yellowstone had long hosted one of the densest coyote populations in North America, but that quickly changed with the reintroduction of wolves. After decades as Yellowstone's top canines, the park's coyotes seemed to have lost their collective memory of how to coexist with their much larger relatives. They routinely approached wolves feeding on carcasses, as was their habit when they spotted an easy meal. Time and again wolf-watchers observed coyotes realizing their fatal mistake far too late, as the faster and more powerful wolves easily ran them down and killed them. Wolves colonizing new areas of the park routinely dug up and destroyed coyote dens, killing any pups they found, to eliminate competition for prey and to make their own dens safer. In short order, Yellowstone's newly dominant canines reduced the Northern Range's coyote population by half.

What happened next was revelatory. The park's rodent population, long depressed by years of unchecked predation by everpresent coyotes, rebounded immediately. This meant a sudden increase in the food supply for raptors like owls and hawks. Healthier birds began having larger broods, and Yellowstone's bird-watching community began seeing an avian renaissance, something they never realized they were missing. Weasels and foxes also benefited from the rebounding rodent population, and their numbers began to grow, too. Even pronghorn numbers were up. Though no predator in North America can run down a healthy adult pronghorn, coyotes routinely fed on helpless newborn calves, which had long depressed the park's herds. Wolves, however, seldom take pronghorn calves, so their displacing of coyotes meant more antelope survived to adulthood.

Another surprise for Smith and his colleagues was the sheer number of animals that fed on wolf kills. Not only ravens and magpies but also coyotes, foxes, and eagles routinely visited almost every carcass, despite wolves' efforts to keep them away. Smith began calling the phenomenon "food for the masses," and the Wolf Project biologists Dan and Erin Stahler, a husband-and-wife team, began turning out paper after paper on the phenomenon.

Wolf kills were also a major new source of nutrition for the park's bears and, it turned out, a very timely one. Wolf reintroduction coincided with a steady decline in the production of whitebark pine nuts in the park, a key source of protein for bears. They routinely raided nut caches created by the park's squirrels in the fall, the season when bears were preparing for hibernation and needed to feed as much as possible. Climate change was considered the most likely cause for the decline, and researchers expected to see less healthy bears and fewer cubs as a result. Yet the bears seemed to still be thriving, possibly, researchers theorized, because elk carcasses brought down by wolves were offsetting the loss of the nuts.

New research on declining elk numbers brought unexpected results as well. Each year state game managers tabulated the number of elk taken by hunters—the harvest, as it was known. The northern Yellowstone herd had declined dramatically, limiting the harvest in a few areas immediately adjacent to the park, but state-wide elk harvests hadn't dipped at all in Wyoming, Montana, or Idaho. In fact, they were trending up: in 2010, for example, Wyoming hunters took 25,420 elk, a new record for the state and a 30 percent jump from 1995, the year wolves were first reintroduced.

Even more promising, from Smith's perspective, was a new study by the young biologist Arthur Middleton, who set out to measure elk calf survival rates in the region east of the park. Wolf critics, especially the Wyoming Farm Bureau, were acutely interested in Middleton's study, correctly anticipating that he would report the numbers to be at almost historic lows. But they were somewhat less enthusiastic about the findings from the second phase of Middleton's project—his assessment of what was causing the decline. After months of observing elk interact with predators, he concluded that grizzlies, not wolves, had taken the majority of the calves, and that most elk in the region rarely encountered a wolf at all. He also concluded that stress caused by drought, not wolves, was the main driver of low pregnancy rates among cows, which further depressed herd numbers.

The science was on Smith's side, but it didn't seem to matter to ranchers and hunters, or to state legislators. The debate wasn't about science anymore, if indeed it ever had been.

BY MID-APRIL, O-SIX HAD DISAPPEARED ALTOGETHER, AND RICK knew that a new litter had been born. The watchers set up camp across the road from the base of Druid Peak in a large parking lot known informally as Hitching Post, since guided horse trips into the Lamar Valley often left from the spot. News that the den was once again in use traveled fast, and Hitching Post, along with a pair of adjacent pullouts, filled up quickly every morning, as a hundred or so people set up shop to wait for the Lamar wolves to make an appearance.

With the yearlings now joining in the hunt, the den was well provisioned and well protected. Though hidden from view, it was not far from the road, and wolves bringing food home crossed the blacktop so frequently that rangers were obliged to put up signs prohibiting stopping along a stretch near the base of the mountain, to prevent endless traffic jams caused by wolf sightings. There was a particular spot where the Druids had always crossed, a narrow gully now immortalized as 21's Crossing, and the Lamars instinctively used it as well, drawn to the cover it provided right up until the unavoidable dash across the blacktop.

On June 21, the watchers finally got their first view of the new pups, in a meadow a short hop east of the den forest. This time there were five, three blacks and two grays, all healthy and eager to explore. In the weeks that followed, Hitching Post was more packed then ever: watchers were deterred only slightly by the washout of the park road a few days after the first sighting, as Soda Butte Creek jumped its banks just upstream from the parking lot. As the days warmed up, the park's unusually heavy snowpack led to enormous runoff, and every stream in the park had become a gushing torrent of ice-cold snowmelt.

The Lamars were now twelve members strong, and the constant coming and going from the den forest meant there was almost always something for the watchers to see. Although it took a good while, and countless observations of urinations and comparing of notes, the watchers eventually determined that both gray pups and two of the three blacks were females. Along with the two female yearlings, the family had become female-heavy, which meant that sooner or later 755 would be dealing with suitors from other packs.

• • •

IT WAS BEGINNING TO LOOK LIKE HE MIGHT BE DOING SO WITHOUT his brother. 754 was spending more and more time alone, which wasn't uncommon in summer, when the pack was at its least cohesive. The new litter of pups kept the alphas relatively immobile, leaving subordinate wolves largely to their own devices. Hunting was happening singly or in parties of twos and threes for the most part. Yet the den was still the axis of each pack member's orbit, and 754 was returning to check in less and less often. In his absence, Shy Male had stepped into the favored caregiver role for the new litter of pups. He shared his uncle's gentle nature, along with the boundless reserves of patience the job required.

754 also seemed reluctant to come in to feed on kills when other pack members were present. He was leery of O-Six in particular, who had begun forcing the brothers to wait to eat, snarling and snapping at them until she had filled her belly with meat for the pups. When she was in this state, 754 didn't even bother groveling, though that was always his first instinct. Instead he would sometimes appeal to his brother, as though 755 might somehow hold the key to getting the pair a spot at the table. But 755 had learned to simply wait until she was gone. When he got too close on one such occasion, she'd seized his lip between her teeth and given a vicious shake, and he didn't need a repeat lesson. If it meant the brothers seldom got the choicest bits—the heart and other organs, for example—that was just the way it had to be.

One morning 754 tagged along with a hunting party consisting of O-Six, 755, and Dark Gray Male as they tested a herd of perhaps two hundred elk above Slough Creek, not far from the old den site. With four yearlings and five pups, the pack now had a lot of mouths to feed, and kills were becoming fewer and farther between as midsummer in the valley pushed the elk up into higher elevations, where it was cooler and the forage was better. The prey that remained were approaching their physical peak, well fed on the valley's abundance.

754 watched from a distance as the threesome approached the herd from below and the elk closed ranks. O-Six drove into the milling mass, trying to split them apart. But there were too many, and instead of marshaling her quarry, she succeeded only in creating chaos. She found herself fleeing east across the mountainside with a bold cow in pursuit, only to be caught beneath the hooves of a large group of elk bolting heedlessly in the opposite direction. She was rolled like a dog between the wheels of a pickup but leaped up unscathed. The elk regrouped, and the hunters came away with nothing.

As his packmates considered their options, 754 maintained his distance. Not long ago he would have been running alongside his brother and O-Six. Now that the yearlings were becoming accomplished hunters, his presence wasn't so important. He was still the pack's beta male, which meant that O-Six, long the object of his desire, would become his mate if something were to happen to 755. But it had now been eighteen months since she chose 755 instead of him, and though he still showered her with all the affection she would tolerate, it was clear that he would have to leave home if he was going to find a mate of his own.

Rick had grown so accustomed to seeing the three adults together, it was hard to imagine what the pack would be like without 754. It had only been a few seasons, but it seemed like much longer. The brothers just seemed of a piece with each other, 754's goofy antics complementing his brother's workmanlike demeanor.

If 754 did leave the pack, nobody would miss him more than Doug McLaughlin. 754 had become his favorite wolf. Every watcher had one, just as a teacher always has a favorite student or a parent (secretly) a child. To Doug, there was something tragic about

754: his gentleness in spite of his great size, his boundless loyalty to his dominant brother, somehow untainted by his hopeless pursuit of his brother's mate. His continued presence in the pack had always been at the whim of his brother, and every gesture 754 made seemed to be an apology, every decision colored by the endless drive to seek approval.

If 754 left the valley, the watchers could still track his collar's signal, but he might relocate somewhere remote where sightings were virtually impossible. Or he might not survive the effort at all.

THAT SUMMER WYOMING'S HUNTERS FINALLY GOT THE NEWS THEY had been waiting years to hear. On July 7, Interior Secretary Salazar met with Matt Mead, Wyoming's newly elected governor, at the state capitol in Cheyenne. With Salazar was Dan Ashe, whom President Obama had just appointed his new Fish and Wildlife director. They hadn't made the long journey from Washington by choice. Wyoming senator John Barrasso had demanded the meeting as a condition of Ashe's confirmation by the Senate, where by long-standing tradition even a single member can hold up a presidential appointment indefinitely at his or her own discretion. Barrasso, a Republican from Casper, wanted a deal made to get wolves delisted in Wyoming once and for all, and he wanted it done now. Seven days after Ashe was confirmed, he was on a plane to Cheyenne.

The next day Governor Mead announced that the two sides had reached a tentative agreement. Wyoming's recalcitrance seemed to have paid off in the end; despite lengthy negotiations over the preceding year, state officials had made scarcely any concessions. Under the proposed management plan, almost the entire state—everything south and east of the Yellowstone–to–Grand Teton National Park corridor—was still a "predator zone," in which wolves could be killed at any time for any reason. Back in 2009, this had been a deal-killer for Fish and Wildlife, yet now the department reversed itself and signed off on the arrangement, under the somewhat circular logic that an almost total lack of wolves in the eastern four-fifths of the state meant that it wasn't critical wolf habitat. (The same could have been said for Yellowstone National Park prior to 1995.) In fact, by the agency's own count, there were forty-six wolves currently living in what would become the predator zone, including three breeding pairs. Under the terms of the agreement, it was assumed that all these wolves would be killed in relatively short order, once the delisting order was approved.

Likewise, the state's plan still lacked any firm commitment to maintain a buffer above the absolute minimum of one hundred wolves outside Yellowstone. But that didn't seem to matter anymore, either. If it was becoming abundantly clear to wolf advocates just how few friends they had left in Washington, officials at Fish and Wildlife were just as capable of reading the tea leaves. The fight over wolves was moving from the courts to the political arena, and it was a war the wolves were losing.

No firm deal had yet been made, so there was no timetable for Wyoming's first wolf hunt. It wouldn't happen that fall, which was fast approaching. Still, Crandall's remaining outfitters began exploring the idea of adding a wolf hunt to their menu of services. It was starting to seem like the feds really meant it this time.

On August 19, Doug spotted 754 bedded with his brother in the heather not far from Soda Butte Creek. Eventually he stood and, after rousing 755 with a submissive lick, began heading east. Through his scope, Doug could immediately tell something was wrong with the way 754 was moving: his front left leg was broken.

He had apparently injured it the night before, most likely during a hunt. The leg wouldn't hold any weight at all, which meant that 754 could barely manage more than a trot. A broken leg was the most common injury for wolves and, next to a wounded jaw, the most worrisome. For a lone wolf, it was often a death sentence.

A few days later a watcher spotted 754 far up the Soda Butte Creek drainage, limping alone through Round Prairie, with four coyotes tailing him relentlessly. So formidable on four legs, a wolf with only three is a humble creature. The huge black wolf was three times the size of any of his pursuers, but in his reduced state he could only tuck his tail and plod along, ears flat and head low, until he reached the woods. Had those coyotes in Round Prairie been strange wolves instead, 754 would easily have been killed.

Over the next six weeks, as his leg slowly healed, 754 returned to the fold, never straying far from his brother and O-Six and feeding off of the pack's kills as he always had. Even with nothing to contribute, he was as welcome as he had ever been, though elk were now becoming truly scarce. Between kills, the wolves were reduced to gnawing on the dusty, suntanned hides and scattered bones of winter-killed bison that had died months before.

In one respect, the timing of the injury was fortunate: had the break occurred in winter, when the pack was fully mobile and wandering the length and breadth of its territory, 754 would have been hard-pressed to keep up. He hopped along as best he could at his brother's side, plopping down for a rest at every opportunity. Even so he found himself left behind from time to time, especially when the pack crossed the road. The blacktop was more intimidating than ever, now that he couldn't dart across. He was so flustered one evening that Rick had to stop traffic for him so that he could join the rest of the pack heading up Druid Peak to the den.

In the end, it was not 754 who left the pack that summer but Dark Gray. He'd begun turning up in the watchers' scopes less fre-

quently since early August. By the first week in September, he was
gone. It wasn't surprising that he was the first to strike out on his
own; even as a pup, he had stood out for his boldness. Still, the
watchers missed him, especially Laurie. She could still remember
him tumbling down off the narrow landing in front of the den above
Slough Creek and being dragged back up in his mother's jaws.

Wolf generations were so short: just when you got to know
one litter of pups, some of them would inevitably disappear, and
another group was on the way. Without a collar on Dark Gray, the
watchers would likely never know what the future held for him or
where in Greater Yellowstone he would end up. He might become
an alpha and sire generations of pups of his own, or he might be
killed the moment he left the Lamar Valley. Rick liked his chances.
If nothing else, he was an outstanding hunter, having learned from
the best.

On August 30, 2011, the wolf-hunting season opened in
Idaho. Montana's would follow two weeks later. Montana set a
statewide quota of 220 wolves, but Idaho set no upper limit, the
goal still being to drive wolf numbers as low as legally permitted.
What might have been a gloomy day in the park became full of
excitement as O-Six finally moved the pups out of the den forest
and onto the valley floor, to a spot she had chosen near the base
of Mount Norris, about two miles east of the old Druid summer
rendezvous.

Always a traumatic event for pups born on Druid Peak, the
move down off of the mountain began smoothly enough. After
months of high water, Soda Butte Creek had finally returned to
normal flow, and the pups crossed without incident. Set up on a
hill at the base of Druid Peak, the watchers could see the family
moving through an early-morning fog in the valley south toward

the river corridor. The pups were awed by the new surroundings, by turns cowering and running excitedly ahead. The yearlings helped O-Six herd them south toward the rendezvous, chasing the pups down when they occasionally made a break for the mountain and home.

Just as the family reached the river, two visitors on horseback riding a trail through the valley spotted them and began to approach. At the sight of the horses, 755 panicked and fled east, with 754 limping along behind as best he could. O-Six made for the trees on the far side of the valley, with two of the pups in tow. The remaining three were still in the river corridor, but the curious riders decided to follow O-Six, and she couldn't turn around until she reached the trees. Over the next hour, the watchers looked on apprehensively as O-Six methodically searched for the three missing pups, howling periodically and pausing to listen for their replies. By the end of the evening, she had found only two. Laurie feared the worst, but two days later all five were sighted in the rendezvous.

Just after dawn on September 20, Laurie spotted a pair of female Agates not far from Junction Butte in Little America, moving north across a frost-covered plain toward the ford in the Lamar River. She'd been following the progress of the two wolves, one of whom was O-Six's younger sister, for months as they tried to form a new pack. Hearing a howl, Laurie scanned the landscape until she spotted a slender gray bedded in the sage, calling after the two females. To her delight, it looked very much like Dark Gray, the missing Lamar yearling. If she was right, it meant he hadn't gone far after all, and he seemed to have found a home, or at least a decent prospect.

BY LATE SEPTEMBER, THE LAMARS WERE BEGINNING TO GO ON longer jaunts from the rendezvous with the pups in tow. They were big enough now that it was sometimes difficult to tell them from the yearlings, and when all eleven members set out together, they were a force to behold. One evening Rick watched as the pack boldly drove off a grizzly that had tried to take over a kill the wolves had made near the river the night before.

776 was emerging as the beta female, frequently taking the lead position as the pack moved across the valley floor, and joining her mother in the vanguard of hunting forays. Like her mother, she showed no fear of the road. She was clearly an alpha in the making and wasn't shy about dominating her sister Middle Gray when she felt it was necessary. Now that 754 was back in the fold, Shy Male had resumed his habit of shadowing him, never missing an opportunity to submit to his uncle.

The pups, meanwhile, were flourishing. One of them, the light gray female, had become a favorite of the watchers. Her very light coat—almost white in the summer—made her easy to recognize, but it was her beautiful facial markings that truly set her apart. Her face was almost two-toned, white on the cheeks and gray through the nose and eyes, which were unusually expressive.

Aside from their traumatic move to the rendezvous, the new litter seemed almost charmed. They had little trouble from bears; Laurie even watched the pups play with a young grizzly, perhaps two years old, who had just left his mother and was still adapting to life on his own. For a half hour, the pups chased him playfully as he spun and bluff-charged this way and that, never making an aggressive move and seemingly enjoying every moment. Days later the pups experienced their first real snow, gleefully sliding down embankments and rolling on top of one another.

So often in summer, packs tended to drift apart in Rick's experience, with yearlings that seemed to come and go, neither fully committed to the pack nor completely independent of it. Or there would be succession struggles, as subordinate adults bucked against the alphas' leadership. But the Lamars were unusually co-hesive, O-Six's powerful presence the pole around which the rest of the pack orbited.

DESPITE RICK'S PLEASANT MORNINGS IN THE PARK WITH THE Lamars, it was impossible not to think about the hunt when he returned to Silver Gate in the evenings. The woods were full of elk-hunters, and he frequently heard gunshots as he sat in his cabin, typing up his notes or eating his bison spaghetti. Every time a wolf was spotted in the back of a truck in Gardiner, Rick would hear the report. The first legal trapping season in decades would soon begin in Idaho.

October 5 brought more bad news. Fish and Wildlife had of-ficially endorsed the Wyoming delisting plan announced back in the summer. As expected, the state's management plan for wolves was essentially the same document that Fish and Wildlife had rejected three years before. The plan was sent out to experts for a lengthy peer-review process, with the tentative goal of turning management over to the state in time for a hunting season in the fall of 2012, which was roughly fourteen months away. If it came to pass, Yellowstone would essentially be surrounded by wolf-hunting zones, and no wolf foraying out of the park in any direction would be safe.

For the watchers, a kind of siege mentality set in. Laurie had always been sensitive about the dirty looks she sometimes received from locals passing through the park when she was on the side of the road with her scope. Now it seemed to her that it was happen-ing more often. "Get a good look," a man in a passing pickup told her, "they won't be there much longer." The scowls always seemed to come from drivers with Wyoming plates. She imagined them heading down into Crandall, where so many Yellowstone wolves had been lost over the years, and waiting for their chance to shoot another—legally this time.

Shortly after Fish and Wildlife's announcement, the Wolf Project recorded the season's first confirmed losses to the hunt. Both of the former Agates that Laurie had spotted traveling with the Lamar yearling Dark Gray had been shot north of the park. There was no way of knowing whether Dark Gray had been with them at the time, and his whereabouts were unknown. Project staff spotted a female yearling, the last known living member of the ill-fated pack, traveling far and wide in the months after the death of her companions. She was alone.

Thanks to Doug Smith's efforts, the quota for the hunting zone just north of the park had been reduced from twelve in 2009 to just three, and the two Yellowstone wolves were the second and third taken, closing the area for the season. That should have meant no more Northern Range wolves were in danger, at least until fall came around again. Nevertheless the park lost one more, when a hunter illegally shot a wolf known as 692 near Jardine on November 5, 2011. She was a five-year-old female, well known to the watchers as one of the founding alphas of the Blacktail Pack, though she had been wandering more or less on her own for some time. She had been born an Agate, in the same litter as O-Six. The hunter, a local, told authorities he was unaware the limit had been reached in the area, though it had been closed for a full month. He was fined $135.

10

RAMPAGE OF THE MOLLIES

On a clear morning that fall, Erin Stahler flew over the Pelican Valley in Roger Stradley's Piper Cub, looking for the Mollies Pack. Known for its brutal weather and dense grizzly population, the Pelican wasn't ideal wolf habitat, but then the Mollies had not come there by choice. The high, snowy valley in the park's interior was where the pack's original alpha female, driven from the Lamar Valley by the Druids fifteen years before, had finally stopped running.

The Pelican had few elk in winter, but the original Mollies taught themselves to prey on bison, and their descendants remained the only pack in the park that did so regularly. They seldom got to enjoy their meals as they would have wished, however. The Mollies lost most of their carcasses after an hour or two to the Pelican Valley's ubiquitous grizzlies, which could smell a fresh kill from miles away.

Still, the pack endured. Theirs was a story of perseverance, and Stahler, like Doug Smith and the rest of the team, had come to admire those original pioneering wolves and their descendants. Now that the Druids were no more, the Mollies had officially become the last of the original handful of packs brought down from Canada.

In Stradley's capable hands, the tiny plane swept the windy, craggy terrain as methodically as a crop duster working a wheat field, while Stahler scanned through the pack's frequencies on her receiver. Eventually she spotted the alpha female, 486, in the southwestern part of the valley, traveling alone. In the Pelican's upper reaches, Stahler found what seemed to be the rest of the pack. She counted nine adults sleeping in the snow, along with seven pups. The Mollie alpha male, 495, was not among them.

After another pass, Stahler found out why: her receiver picked up 495's collar transmitting in mortality mode. Discoveries like this were why project biologists flew the park so often. Outside the Lamar Valley, it was impossible to know what was going on with most of the packs without a plane, and this was a major development—though just how big Stahler didn't yet realize.

A few days later a crew hiked in to investigate and found 495's carcass in the snow. He had suffered traumatic injuries, most likely from a bison kick. Even past his prime at nine years of age, 495 was an amazing specimen. At the time of his collaring in 2005, he weighed 143 pounds, making him one of the largest Yellowstone wolves on record. With his dark coat and massive head, he resembled a juvenile black bear lumbering across the snow. Many of his male offspring had grown up to be almost as formidable as their father.

He had been the pack's alpha male for a little over two years, and his reign had been a productive one. With five adults, seven yearlings, and seven pups, the pack was flourishing. Now, however, the longtime Mollie alpha female 486 would have to find a new mate, most likely from outside the pack, since most of the subordinate males were related to her. Ordinarily a dispersing male from another pack would fill that position, but a large pack could intimidate would-be suitors, and the Pelican was so remote that lone wolves seldom wandered through. In the end, 486 decided to leave the pack to seek a mate on her own.

The problem was that it was almost time for the Mollies' annual journey out of the valley, the time when the pack needed leadership the most. Elk tended to leave the Pelican early in winter when the snows got too deep. Bison were a viable, if much more difficult, alternative, but the pack had also formed the habit of coming north to the Lamar Valley, revisiting the same rich hunting grounds the Druids had wrested from them so long ago. Over the years, the watchers had learned to expect some conflict, like the ambush that claimed the life of 42 in 2004. Yet the Mollies rarely stayed long. They were after elk, not territory. Within a few weeks, they usually returned home to the Pelican, not to be seen again until the following year.

But this winter things were different. When the Mollies left home, they were nineteen wolves strong, less a pack than an army—but one that was in considerable disarray. A subordinate female had stepped into 486's place, but there was no new candidate to take over for the dead alpha male. The result was mayhem on a scale not seen since the Wolf Project began.

On December 2, the Mollies killed the alpha male of the Mary Mountain Pack in the Hayden Valley, an area along the Yellowstone River west of the Pelican. From there, the pack moved north, engaging O-Six's natal pack, the Agates, in a series of skirmishes. On December 22, Doug Smith detected a mortality code from Agate 775, the alpha male. Nobody had witnessed the conflicts, but Smith wasn't surprised that two alphas were among the casualties. They tended to do the heavy fighting when packs collided. The trail of destruction made it clear enough where the Mollies were headed, and it was only a matter of time before they arrived.

ON JANUARY 6, RICK AND LAURIE WERE IN A PULLOUT NEAR THE midpoint in the Lamar Valley when they spotted the Lamars bedded on a bald knob near the top of Specimen Ridge. Suddenly the wolves were up and moving in unison to the east. Rick scanned in the opposite direction and saw the reason: the Mollies were coming over Specimen a mile to the west, all nineteen of them.

O-Six drove her family along the side of the ridge, determined to put several miles between herself and the invading pack. The Mollies began scent-trailing, following their noses down to a meadow where the Lamars had bedded the day before. They milled about like army ants, inhaling every trace of the resident pack's presence, parsing what intelligence they could gather about O-Six and her considerable brood. They were undeterred by what they learned, pushing farther east along the Lamars' trail, giving up only when it became clear that the pack was by now miles away.

A week later Rick saw firsthand what happened when a pack didn't flee, or at least not fast enough. Just east of Lamar Canyon, a group of nine Mollies chasing elk through the trees came upon a quartet of Blacktail wolves that had ventured out of their own territory, most likely pursuing elk as well. Curious about the oncoming wolves, the Blacktails hesitated, and the Mollies overtook them not far from the road. Three of the four Blacktails ran wildly for home after the skirmish, but the next morning the body of a four-year-old male was found on the frozen Lamar River, not far from the bank. He'd recently injured a leg, no doubt making him the slowest among his comrades and the first to be run down.

In the update she sent out that night, January 4, 2012, Laurie gave him her customary obituary, a task she'd found herself doing with disturbing regularity since the Mollies first left the Pelican some five weeks earlier. She tried to be diplomatic about it; the Mollies were just doing what came naturally to wolves, she pointed out. But the truth was she dreaded their inevitable clash with the Lamars as much as everybody else in Yellowstone's wolf-watching community.

ON FEBRUARY 4, O-SIX WAS FINALLY COLLARED. DOUG SMITH hadn't meant to dart her. When he came across the pack flying over Jasper Bench, he'd thought he was targeting 776, the two-year-old gray female who had lost her collar and needed a new one. The mother and daughter were difficult to tell apart, especially from the helicopter, with the snow swirling below the blades. When he landed and examined the gray lying in the snow, however, he was surprised to find a bit of blood in her vulva—a sign the wolf was in proestrus, a hallmark of the breeding female. Was he about to collar O-Six? It could have been 776—she was just old enough to breed. The truth was he couldn't be sure which wolf he'd brought down; he hadn't spent hours watching the pack through a scope as Rick had.

He returned to the chopper and radioed Rick, who was watching from the road. "I think I've got the old lady instead," he said, using his term for an alpha female.

But despite the distance and the chaos caused by the chopper's appearance above the pack, Rick was certain he'd seen O-Six head into the woods before Smith had taken the shot. Laurie, who was standing beside him, felt the same. It had to be 776.

Smith trudged back through the snow and looked at the gray again. She was in remarkable shape: no broken or worn teeth, her muscle tone excellent. She weighed ninety-seven pounds. Convinced he had the daughter, not the mom, he fitted her with the improved collar the project had begun using—a state-of-the-art four-thousand-dollar device that could be tracked not only by radiotelemetry in the field but also by GPS from a desk in the Wolf Project's offices. Then he loaded her into the chopper and ferried her across the valley to a secluded spot on the northern side, far from the Mollies' last known location, where she could safely recover from the effects of the tranquilizer.

By the following evening the mistake was plain. At the first good sighting of the pack, Rick could clearly see that Smith had collared O-Six, not 776. He was chagrined, and Laurie was beside herself. She was their favorite wolf, the one they had watched more than any other for the last two years. How could they have been so wrong?

Smith had told himself the gray in his sights couldn't be O-Six, he later confided in Rick, because O-Six would have immediately run for the trees, and he wouldn't have been able to get her. Rick supposed that subconsciously he had felt the same way, that O-Six would never allow herself to be caught. She was too clever. Her official number was now 832, though she would always be O-Six to the watchers.

That same week Smith also collared the light gray female pup, the one the watchers had singled out for her unusual beauty. She was now known as 820.

BOTH WOLVES RECOVERED WELL AND RETURNED IMMEDIATELY TO the pack. A few days after the collaring operation, Laurie was standing behind her scope in the parking lot at the Slough Creek turnoff, scanning the hillside south of the park road. It was mid-morning, about twenty degrees, and an inch of new snow lay on the ground from the night before. She could hear the Lamars howling. The pack was somewhere in the trees on a shoulder jutting north from Specimen Ridge. The watchers called the area Divide Ridge, because it stood between Little America to the west and the Lamar Valley to the east. It was a spot rich in wolf history; one of the acclimation pens had been built near the base of the ridge, in a drainage known as Crystal Creek. It was surprisingly close to the road, roughly four hundred yards from where Laurie now stood.

Eventually she spotted the Lamars. All eleven of them had moved into an open area not far from where the pen once stood. They seemed to be howling at something above them on Specimen Ridge. Rick, just down the road in the next pullout, had radioed earlier that the Mollies were in the area chasing a coyote, though Laurie hadn't yet seen them from her vantage point.

Another watcher stood next to Laurie, a wildlife photographer named Peter Murray who had recently moved to the area and was now spending all his free time following the wolves. He scanned the skyline at the top of Specimen, looking for whatever it was that had set the Lamars off.

"Holy shit!" he blurted.

Laurie pulled away from her eyepiece and followed Murray's alarmed gaze. Ten wolves were coming down Specimen, stretched out in a long line parallel to the horizon, like a cordon of sheriff's deputies searching the woods for a lost child. The Mollies had found O-Six at last.

They paused perhaps a quarter mile above the Lamars, who had now fallen silent, and waited. Laurie wanted to yell, "Run!" Instead she radioed Rick, lowering her voice to a whisper because the Lamars were so close. Rick had already spotted the two packs squaring off. There was nothing Laurie could do but sign off and hold her breath as O-Six and the rest of the pack paced back and forth excitedly.

By now the Mollies had been roaming the Northern Range for over forty days. In that time, they had killed four wolves—that the watchers knew of. The Blacktail they had slain had been caught on the very ridge where the Lamars were now trapped. If the Lamars ran now, they might still escape unharmed. On the other hand, only ten of the nineteen Mollies were present, and among the missing was the wolf that seemed to have become the new alpha female. O-Six, meanwhile, had 755 by her side—along with hulking 754 (his leg now mostly healed); her two adult daughters, 776 and Middle Gray; and their brother, Shy Male. Together with her five pups, now almost full-grown yearlings, she had eleven wolves of her own. If O-Six was ever going to stand and fight, this was the time to do it.

Her answer came in the form of a bellicose howl, which the rest of her pack lustily joined. There would be no retreat. When the Mollies heard the challenge, they jumped to their feet and raced down the hill with tails raised, still spread out in a long line like a cavalry charge. The Lamars moved steadily uphill to meet them, spreading out until the rival packs faced each other in two almost perfectly matched lines, each advancing on the other.

Just before the lines met, however, the Lamars panicked and broke ranks, fleeing in every direction. The charging Mollies were upon them almost immediately. A black Lamar pup was caught and dragged down, and soon eight snarling wolves were around him in a circle so tight that Laurie couldn't see him at all. She had watched wolves kill coyotes in just this way: all you saw from a distance were the raised tails and straining haunches of the attackers, but you could imagine all too easily what was happening at the bottom of the pile. It was usually over in a few seconds. The pup was almost twice the size of a coyote, but he was still in serious trouble.

After perhaps a minute the attackers left the pup lying in the snow and headed off en masse to pursue other Lamars careening through the trees. Laurie could hear bark-howling coming from all over the ridge as the splintered Lamars ran for their lives.

Wolves were everywhere, and it was impossible to follow them all. She couldn't find O-Six, though she did spot 755 fleeing west at full sprint, trying, it appeared to her, to draw the Mollie wolves away from the pups. Unnoticed in the chaos, the downed black pup roused himself and limped off down the slope, heading for the road.

Rick tossed his scope into his SUV and rushed from one lot to the next, steering with his left hand and operating his radio with his right, trying to get the best view of the conflict and dreading what he might find when he did. But there were too many trees, and too many folds in the ridge swallowing the wolves as they scattered. Eventually watchers on the opposite side of the divide reported that fleeing Lamars had made it into the valley, unpursued by the invaders.

By nightfall they had managed to count ten Lamar wolves; only the black pup was missing. All ten seemed to be moving well, with no major injuries. It could have been much worse. That night the pack retreated far to the east, out of the valley and up the Soda Butte Creek drainage. To the watchers' relief, the black pup, bloodied but not seriously injured, eventually joined them in their temporary exile.

THE MOLLIES, MEANWHILE, SET ABOUT MAKING THEMSELVES AT home. Rick knew they hunted bison back in the Pelican Valley, but the area was so remote that he had only ever seen them in action in a remarkable video taken many years before. Fearless and unpredictable, bison were the undisputed lords of Yellowstone, roaming the park with impunity, jamming up the snowplowed roads in winter where the walking was easiest, and ignoring even the giant RVs that passed within feet of them. Mature bulls stood six foot tall at the shoulder and could reach two thousand pounds, and even cows might grow to half that weight. Their docile appearance was deceptive; getting butted by a bison moving at full speed was like being hit by a car traveling at thirty-five miles per hour. Bison seldom ran when confronted by predators, preferring to stand and face the danger head-on, their massive horned skulls held low like shields. In the Lamar Valley, this display of bravado and power was enough to deter wolf attacks most of the time, at least on healthy adult bison.

The same dynamic did not hold in the Pelican. The video Rick watched showed fourteen Mollies attacking a bison at least ten times their size. In the heat of the battle, they leaped onto the flee-ing bull's back, holding on to his flesh with their teeth until the bison flung them through the air, swinging his massive head in an effort to hook them on the way down. Bison are herd animals, but the Mollies had learned that their solidarity held out only as long as the footing was good. Again and again they drove their quarry into deep snow and set upon him, until eventually, after nine hours, the bull succumbed and the wolves had their prize.

Now Rick was watching the descendants of those wolves doing the same thing right in front of him in the Lamar Valley. On Feb-ruary 12, two groups of Mollies took on a herd of bison in a snowy meadow below Jasper Bench. One faction, twelve wolves strong, chased a string of adult bison out of the trees and onto the valley floor. The panicked bison—unaccustomed to such bold and reck-less attacks—ran for their lives, struggling to break trail in the deep snow. A second squad of Mollies, consisting mostly of year-lings, went up the hillside and made contact with a calf, only to be driven back by its nearby mother. When the yearlings high on the hillside saw that their comrades on the valley floor had managed to take one of the bison down, they came sliding down the absurdly steep hill with reckless abandon, pivoting this way and that, tum-bling head over heels, reaching the bottom by sliding on their rears.

In short order all nineteen Mollies were around the downed behemoth, and together they made it disappear. Not since the heyday of the Druids, when thirty-seven wolves stalked this same landscape, had the Lamar Valley seen a force like this.

WHEN THE LAMARS RETURNED TO THE VALLEY, SHY MALE DIDN'T come with them. He was nearly two years old, so it was a natural time for him to be moving on. Still, Laurie was surprised. She had thought, or maybe just hoped, that he might spend one last summer with the pack, helping his younger siblings corral another litter of pups. She still held out hope that his brother Dark Gray, the first of O-Six's offspring to disperse, would make his way home someday. But after five months without a confirmed sighting, it hardly seemed likely. Now there were only two wolves left from O-Six's first brood, the females 776 and Middle Gray.

O-Six would be denning on Druid Peak again soon. She had already begun frequenting the den forest, no doubt cleaning out the burrow she'd used last season or digging a new one. With the Mollies in the valley, it was the worst possible time to have pups. The pack had avoided the invaders so far by being mobile, relying on O-Six's unfailing instinct of when to fly from trouble. Now they would be tied to one spot; the roaming Mollies were bound to find them sooner or later. It was hard to shake the feeling that history was repeating itself—the same wolves that had killed O-Six's grandmother, the valley's longtime matriarch, were now coming for the new queen.

But what choice did she have? Unless O-Six was willing to leave the valley and cede her territory to the invaders, the pups would have to be born there. In any case, leaving her territory to give birth somewhere else would have been no less dangerous.

Over the next three weeks, as O-Six settled into the den, the

Mollies killed at least two more wolves, including one of O-Six's littermates in the Agate Creek Pack. Every day the watchers hoped to see them heading back over Specimen toward home, but the pack showed no signs of leaving.

WHEN THEY FINALLY CAME TO THE DEN, THEY CAME IN FORCE. Rick, Laurie, and Bob Landis were at Hitching Post one evening, quietly chatting and checking their scopes from time to time, hoping to spot a Lamar wolf coming or going from the den before it got too dark. Suddenly Rick noticed movement, but it wasn't the wolves he was hoping to see. Sixteen Mollies were coming around the shoulder of Druid Peak, heading east toward the den. The Mollies were using the Ledge Trail, just as the Lamars did and the Druids had before them, though Rick couldn't remember a time when he had seen so many wolves on the narrow rocky trail at once. An uncollared gray was in the lead, and Rick could clearly see that she was scent-trailing, following whichever Lamar wolf had passed that way most recently. There was only one logical place that scent trail would lead.

It was April 25, 2012, five days after O-Six's estimated due date. She hadn't been seen for several days, and Rick couldn't get her signal, which meant she was probably inside the den, in all likelihood nursing newborn pups. He quickly scanned for the remaining collared Lamars on his receiver. He got signals from 754, 755, and the yearling 820; they were on the mountain, though how far from the den was difficult to tell. The Mollies were advancing slowly but with purpose, moving inexorably closer to the point where the trail to the den forest dropped down and into the trees.

"No, no, no," Laurie said as the seemingly endless string of wolves threaded unchallenged through the trees toward the den. They had known this day was coming. So far the Lamars were the only pack in the Northern Range yet to suffer casualties during the Mollies' five-month rampage, a testament to O-Six's abilities as an alpha. But this time she couldn't run, not if she wanted her pups to survive. She couldn't hope to prevail in a fight, either. She was Butch Cassidy holed up in the cantina with the Sundance Kid, and the Bolivian army was moving into position.

After the last Mollie disappeared into the den forest, Rick and Laurie hefted their scopes and headed up onto a hill behind the lot to get a better view. Landis scrambled to do the same, lugging his heavy camera and tripod. This wasn't the end any of them had anticipated, but if it was going to be O-Six's last stand, they wanted to be there with her until the last moment.

The trio found the den forest again from their new perch, but nothing was moving in or out of the trees. Five minutes passed in near-total silence.

Suddenly O-Six came exploding out of the woods with a gang of wolves in pursuit. She was alone, separated from her pack, racing downhill through a small meadow. Rick instinctively began mapping her escape route, but to his horror he saw immediately that she had none. Fleeing heedlessly, she had allowed herself to be driven to the edge of an outcrop bordered by a sheer precipice. Behind her were the charging Mollies, closing in on their target; in front of her was a fifty-foot drop. O-Six was going to turn and face her attackers head-on, or else she was going to go over the cliff and die at the bottom.

She didn't stop at the cliff's edge. To Rick's amazement, she flew straight over. A controlled leap brought her to a precarious ledge not far below the advancing Mollies. Pivoting, she managed to drop down even lower to a second spot as her pursuers stopped short, unwilling to try their luck. O-Six was in a steep, narrow gully moving straight down the face of the bluff, one Rick had never noticed before. It was the kind of route only a bighorn

sheep or a mountain goat might tread with confidence, but O-Six
had taken her chances, and the decision had saved her life.

From the Mollies' perspective, she had simply disappeared.
Suddenly they wheeled and began loping east. Rick swung his
scope and spotted Middle Gray sprinting away from the den forest
and drawing what appeared to be the majority of the invading pack
off with her.

O-Six shimmied to the bottom of the bluff and ran all the
way to the base of the mountain and crossed the road not far from
Hitching Post. When she realized she had left her antagonists far
behind, she began cautiously making her way back up toward the
Ledge Trail. The Mollies, meanwhile, broke off their pursuit of
Middle Gray and headed back toward the den forest. Rick could
hear Middle Gray's yipping alarm call as she watched the invaders approaching the den. O-Six crept cautiously up the mountain,
where she found 820 cowering on an outcrop just below the Ledge
Trail.

Some of the Mollies seemed to have become separated from
the main group, and now it was chaos on the mountainside, as
Rick's radio crackled with reports from watchers to the east and
west. Mollies had been spotted in twos and threes moving off in
every direction, and it was unclear how many, if any, had actually
made it to the den. O-Six remained on her perch, her head cocked
to one side, listening intently for signs of the enemy's location. 776
and Middle Gray were howling from opposite sides of the den forest, but there was no answer, either from the Mollies or from 754
or 755. Finally O-Six hazarded a foray down the ledge trail toward
the den, as 820 held back. Meeting no resistance, she sidled back
down into the den forest and out of sight.

When the Mollies finally reconvened an hour later, it was a
half-mile to the west, on a foothill below Druid Peak. They rallied
and howled, long and loud. Then all sixteen moved off in a group

to the south, crossed the road and the river, and headed toward the far side of the valley. None of the Mollies were bloodied or visibly limping, and the watchers hadn't observed any of them make contact with a Lamar wolf—though it was anybody's guess what had happened in the thick trees around the den site. The entire encounter had lasted about two hours.

There was still no sign of the Lamar males, and Rick suspected they had missed everything, despite the howling and yipping from their daughters. O-Six's signal had disappeared, suggesting she was back in the den, which was a good sign. But the pups' fate remained unknown.

The watchers had to wait three days for a definitive answer. In the days after the battle, Rick got strong signals from each Lamar collar, so there was no question that those wolves, at least, were alive and in the vicinity of the den, which suggested that the pups were still there, too. Finally O-Six was spotted slipping down out of the den forest, off the mountain, and across the road. She was moving with purpose, most likely to a carcass the rest of the pack had taken somewhere in the valley. If she returned promptly, that would be a sure sign she was still tending the pups.

To Rick's relief, she came straight back about two hours later, her belly bulging. She had saved the youngest generation of Lamars. O-Six might have led the invaders away from the immediate vicinity of the den with her desperate dash through their ranks, but Middle Gray was the one who had kept them from returning, drawing the Mollies away at the crucial moment. Rick had long assumed that 776 was the most likely of O-Six's daughters to emerge as an alpha. Now that Middle Gray had been tested and shown her mettle, it seemed there might be two future pack leaders in the Lamars' midst.

Sightings were difficult over the next few weeks, limited mainly to small hunting parties of two or three wolves coming or going from the den. It would remain that way until the pups were big enough to move down out of the den forest. Thus it wasn't until mid-May that Rick realized the black male yearling hadn't been seen for some time, not since the raid on the den. He'd somehow cheated death in February, when the Mollies caught him during the clash on Crystal Creek, but this time it seemed he hadn't been so lucky. The watchers had no way to know for sure, but the most likely explanation for his absence was that he was dead, another victim of the Mollies. He was the first pack member O-Six had lost.

BY MIDSUMMER, THE MOLLIES HAD SPLIT APART, AS PACKS THAT reached their ungainly size often did. To the watchers' relief, a half-dozen of them, including the alpha female and a new mate she had picked up, returned to the Pelican Valley. It might well have been the case, Rick speculated later, that finding an alpha male to replace the deceased 495 had been the pack's objective in staying abroad for so long. All that chaos and conflict, caused by one kick from a bison's hoof. The Mollies that remained north gradually went their separate ways, some drifting off alone, others joining neighboring packs. More troubling to O-Six's clan, a few had connected with a new group that had come together in the Lamar Valley. The Wolf Project hadn't given them a pack name yet, but they seemed to be settling in for a long stay.

With only five members, however, this faction was a force that could be reckoned with. On August 3, the Lamars came upon the interlopers at a bison carcass on a bench along the south side of the valley. Eight of the nine adult Lamars were there, and they came barreling in with tails raised, catching the smaller pack off guard. When the surprised wolves scattered, the Lamars pursued a wolf known as 822, a three-year-old black Mollie who had been present for both last winter's confrontation near Crystal Creek and the attack on the den forest in late April. Slight and fast, she led the Lamars on a mile-long chase, fleeing at full sprint down the bench, across the river, and all the way to the road, with her pursuers, led by 755 and the fleet-footed 820, close behind.

On a hillside just north of the road, 755 caught her, burying his teeth in the base of her back and dragging her down so that the rest could pile on. Pinned and helpless, the Mollie female made no attempt to fight them off. After about sixty seconds of violent thrashing, most of the Lamars withdrew. But O-Six remained, grabbing her opponent by the throat and whipsawing back and forth savagely until she was satisfied that the bloodied and broken wolf would not get up again.

After the showdown in the valley, the Lamars had no further trouble from the Mollies, though the months-long struggle did ultimately cost them a bit of territory. A pair of Mollie females joined with some males from the neighboring Blacktail Pack and settled into an area on the far west side of Little America. It was never a core part of the Lamars' territory, but the pack had sometimes ranged that far west, especially in the winter. Now they fell into an uneasy truce with the new group, which came to be known as the Junction Butte Pack.

By the time the dust settled, the Mollies' rampage had profoundly reordered affairs in the Northern Range. They had killed at least nine wolves in four different packs. O-Six's natal pack, the Agates, had disappeared altogether, virtually all its senior adults lost to the Mollies.

One thing remained the same, however: O-Six still controlled the Lamar Valley. She had won.

11

"The Worst Possible Thing
I Could Tell You"

The late-summer weeks that followed were warm and hazy. Smoke from a fire burning northwest of Gardiner drifted into the valley, dimming the watchers' scopes. It was the last month of the 2012 tourist season, and the park was packed with visitors, as full as Rick had ever seen it. Getting from one pullout to another had become a frustrating exercise in patience and perseverance. Hitching Post in particular was a zoo.

Everybody wanted to see O-Six. She had never been the star of a documentary like 21 and 42 (though Bob Landis hoped to change that), never made the papers from coast to coast, like Limpy, whose thousand-mile journey briefly turned him into a celebrity, but everyone seemed to know who she was anyway. She had become one of the sights to see when you went to Yellowstone, like Old Faithful or the Upper Falls.

The pups from her third litter, now four months old and becoming quite active, put on a lively show as they romped around the meadows near the den on Druid Peak. They were lucky to be alive, though they didn't realize it. Neither did the scores of visitors who stopped by to watch the charmed pups for an hour or two, unless they were lucky enough to catch Rick recounting the story of the attack on the den.

South of the lot, meanwhile, random groupings of the scattered Mollies were making regular appearances in the river bottom. When they were in view, some visitors couldn't resist the temptation to venture out, cameras or binoculars dangling from their necks, trying to get just a little closer. Rick policed them as well as he could, but he couldn't be everywhere at once. The wolves ignored the interlopers up to a point, beyond which they inevitably retreated, as often as not to some haven invisible to the frustrated crowd back at the roadside. It was hard to fault the guilty parties for their excitement; most would never get a chance to see a wolf again as long as they lived. Still, Laurie in particular looked forward to the end of summer vacation and that first dusting of snow, when the park would become theirs again.

Middle Gray and 776, both now two years old, spent more time than most tending to the new pups, which included two grays and two blacks. Of the two sisters, Middle Gray was the more maternal, constantly shepherding the youngsters back toward the den forest, whereas 776 was cut more from her mother's cloth, inclined to join the hunt whenever she could. The pups were also drawn to 754, just as the first two litters had been, and he allowed them to jump on him with as much forbearance as ever, though the last vestiges of his own youthful exuberance were almost gone. He often sat by himself, slightly apart from the pack, gazing down from his high perch, like some stone griffin, at the tiny comings and goings on the park road far below.

There were plenty of elk in the valley, and the pack was eating well. The scattered Mollies occasionally visited a Lamar kill when the coast was clear, sneaking what meals they could. No such visit went undetected, and the adult Lamars spent an inordinate amount of time examining the scent trails of every wolf that had come and gone in their absence. But the intruders gave the Lamars a wide berth, and their presence was no more than a nuisance. The Lamars' biggest worry was getting across the busy road to feed the growing pups. But soon O-Six would move them down to their summer rendezvous, and even that minor annoyance would disappear.

STILL, REAL DANGER WAS LOOMING, AND IT WOULDN'T GO AWAY. On August 31, 2012, just as hunters in Montana and Idaho were gearing up for the start of the second season since wolf-hunting was legalized by Senator Tester's budget rider, the U.S. Fish and Wildlife Service officially removed wolves in Wyoming from the endangered species list. After a contentious peer-review process, the five experts Fish and Wildlife had selected to review Wyoming's plan returned a split decision—three agreeing with the agency that the plan passed muster, and two finding that it didn't offer sufficient protection. That was good enough for Fish and Wildlife, which issued its rule just in time for Wyoming's long-delayed first legal hunting season to go forward.

For wolf advocates, the timing could not have been worse. Earthjustice was forced by law to give the government sixty days' notice before filing suit, which meant the hunting season would be well under way before any judge reviewed the legality of the delisting rule. When they did file, it would not be Doug Honnold's name on the suit. After more than fifteen years of litigating on behalf of wolves, he had finally returned to his native California, leaving his colleague Tim Preso in charge of the Northern Rockies office. Rather than take his chances in Wyoming, Preso decided instead to sue Fish and Wildlife in federal court in Washington, D.C., where the agency was headquartered.

Yellowstone wolves now had no safe way to leave the park. To the north was Montana, where hunting guides with clients, especially around Jardine, were all but guaranteed to see Yellowstone wolves in the woods. To the west was Idaho, where hunters and trappers would be allowed to take up to five wolves per person in a season that would last six months. To the east, in woods that were still full of hunters despite the declining elk herds, Wyoming's sportsmen would all be vying to see who could get the first legal wolf. Game officials set a quota of eight wolves in the hunting zone that included Crandall. Wolves leaving the park to the south, meanwhile, would most likely find their way into Wyoming's predator zone.

On September 10, the first day of the Wyoming season, a hunting guide named Mike Hirsch shot a wolf from a local pack on the Two Dot Ranch, an enormous spread between Cody and Crandall. It was the first wolf legally taken by a trophy hunter in Wyoming in decades. Wyoming law prohibited state officials from revealing the name of a hunter who shot a wolf, or the exact location in which the wolf was taken, in order to protect the privacy of everyone involved. But Hirsch happily gave an interview to the paper in his hometown of Powell, twenty-five miles northeast of Cody. He was proud to be the first, and he wanted everyone to know it.

When the news reached Crandall, Turnbull called Hirsch, an old friend, to get the story himself. He was surprised that Hirsch had allowed his name to appear in the paper. "Aren't you worried someone is going to come after you?" he asked. Turnbull had never met any of the park's wolf aficionados, but he worried that some of them were angry enough about Wyoming's new hunting season to do something crazy.

Turnbull already had his wolf tag and had been out every morning that week, driving the Chief Joseph Highway looking for wolf tracks in the fresh snow. He figured it was his best chance of finding a pack, though so far he'd seen nothing.

NEWS OF THE HUNT COLORED EVERYTHING THE WATCHERS SAW IN the park that fall. A few days after Hirsch got his wolf, O-Six moved the pups to the summer rendezvous at the base of Mount Norris, the same spot she had used the year before. Behind Norris was a drainage known as Cache Creek, which eventually led to the headwaters of Crandall Creek at the park boundary and, turning due east, down into Crandall proper. The Lamar adults sometimes ventured out that way in search of elk, but they usually didn't get too far before turning back toward home.

Still, Rick was worried. Over the years, the Druids had sometimes ranged out of the park that way, but Crandall had been thick with wolves in those days, and the Druids had seldom lingered long for fear of a conflict. Now that government hunters had thinned the local packs, however, a Yellowstone wolf might travel for miles without meeting another wolf or smelling another pack's mark. O-Six might even decide to claim Crandall as her own.

BY THE FIRST DAY OF FALL, SEPTEMBER 22, THE CROWDS HAD DI-minished and the watching was easier. The Lamar pups were now big enough to accompany the adults on longer jaunts, and the family, fully mobile at last, seemed unusually carefree and playful. As Laurie and Rick watched, O-Six led the entire pack on a long ramble across the southern side of the valley and up onto a prominent bench. One of the black female yearlings was leaping over tawny 820 and her other littermates. Later Laurie spotted them playing with something slightly shiny, tossing it high into the air and jostling one another to catch it when it landed. On closer inspection, she saw that it was a plastic water bottle, probably left behind by a hiker on the Specimen Ridge trail.

Watching the pups play with a piece of litter was disconcerting, but it was also a sign of how far park officials had come in their drive to make Yellowstone a true wilderness. Bears once routinely fed on garbage heaps in Yellowstone, as visitors gathered around to watch at the behest of park rangers; now a single piece of trash was an exotic toy for an animal that had come back after a decades-long absence.

The delighted pups took turns crunching the bottle and bounding after one another. The enthusiasm was infectious, and soon 755 and O-Six were cavorting like yearlings themselves, racing across the bench until O-Six was running full out, her figure gliding over the thin snow as if she were on skates. Even at six and a half years of age, she could still outdistance her younger mate. "I have never seen an alpha female and alpha male enjoying each other so much," Laurie wrote in her note that night. Later she and Rick watched as 754 and one of the black pups chased each other around a log. They were still getting to know this litter, but this one, a male, was spunky and adventuresome—one to keep an eye on.

ON NOVEMBER 6, ELECTION DAY, THE ATTENTION OF THE NATION was focused on Montana once again. As expected, control of the Senate hinged on John Tester's contest against Denny Rehberg, along with a handful of other competitive races. Mitt Romney was polling at least ten points ahead of President Obama in the state, but Tester, amazingly, had managed to stay almost dead even with his Republican challenger. When the last returns were tabulated, deep in the night, he had edged Rehberg by fewer than twenty thousand votes and the Democrats had preserved their majority.

Rick spent the day tracking the Junction Butte wolves as they made a foray through O-Six's territory. After a lengthy détente, the pack was becoming bolder, venturing more and more frequently from its base in Little America through Lamar Canyon and into the west end of the valley in pursuit of elk. Now Rick watched as the ten of them wandered deeper into the valley, howling at one another when they became briefly separated, then coming together en masse to feed on an old bison carcass north of the road. Later they all crossed the road and climbed up to a good resting spot on Jasper Bench on the south side of the valley.

The Junctions seemed unaware that all thirteen Lamar wolves were already on the bench, perhaps a mile away, watching them. O-Six had spotted the pack as soon as the howling began, but she made no move to confront them. She didn't seem to consider them a threat, despite their frequent incursions into the valley, perhaps because she herself had begun making more forays east of the park, expanding her territory in the opposite direction.

Later that afternoon, as Rick had the bedded Lamar wolves in his scope, he heard gunshots from across the valley. The Lamars heard it, too. It was park rangers taking target practice on a hill behind Buffalo Ranch. O-Six stood and gazed across the valley as the sound of each shot reverberated off Specimen Ridge. Rick wondered if she had any notion what that sound signified. It wasn't likely; she'd spent the vast majority of her six and a half years inside the park's boundaries. Her pack had never been in the woods with hunters, never endured the consequences of preying on livestock.

As the shots continued, she began heading east, away from the troubling sound, and away from the Junction Butte wolves. The rest of her charges rose and followed. That night they continued

east, all the way through the valley, up over Norris, and down into
Crandall.

SIX DAYS LATER DOUG MCLAUGHLIN ARRIVED HOME TO FIND MUL-
tiple phone messages from Rick and Laurie waiting for him. He'd
been on a polar-bear-watching expedition in Canada and hadn't
heard anything about the Lamar wolves for a week. Something
told him the news wasn't good. He called Laurie first.

"What I have to tell you is the worst possible thing I could tell
you," she said. "Your favorite wolf was shot." 754 was dead.

He'd been killed by a hunter in Crandall on November 11, the
day before Doug got home. The shooter wasn't a local, nor was he
an elk-hunter. He'd come to Crandall specifically to hunt wolves
and had tracked the Lamars across Hunter Peak on horseback for
days before he spotted his opportunity. He'd brought 754 down
the mountain on the back of his horse, stopping at the Painter
Outpost to show anyone who was interested. It was the kind of
story Turnbull loved, though he hadn't been around when the wolf
was brought in and had to hear about it secondhand the next day.
The hunter had driven to Cody to check the carcass in at the Wyoming Game and Fish office there. A supervisor had called the Wolf
Project to arrange for the return of the collar, and the serial number had confirmed 754's identity. The fate of the rest of the pack
was unknown.

Doug picked out his favorite photos of 754—he had hundreds—and sent them to Laurie, who posted an online memorial
for her readers. In the days that followed, the watchers received
word that three more Yellowstone wolves, including the only collared wolf in the Junction Butte Pack, had been shot north of the
park, not far from Jardine.

Still the Lamars did not return to Yellowstone, and GPS data from O-Six's collar indicated the pack was still in Crandall, not far from where 754 had been shot. Rick speculated they might be looking for their lost packmate, though it was impossible to say without knowing the exact circumstances of his death. Had the rest of the pack been present when he was shot? Did they know he was dead, or did he seem to just disappear into the endless wilderness east of the park, as Shy Male had done the previous winter?

On November 15, after nine days in Crandall, the Lamars returned to the valley. Rick spotted them on the west side of Druid Peak, counting anxiously until he found the twelve who remained: O-Six and 755, the eldest daughters 776 and Middle Gray, 820 and her three yearling sisters, and the four pups. He got on the radio and spread the word: the Lamars were back, and they were safe.

O-Six howled long and low, unaccompanied by the pack. She might have been letting the Junction Butte wolves know that the valley was still hers, despite the Lamars' long absence. Or, Rick thought, she might have been trying to bring 754 home, summoning him with her call as she had in Little America three years before, when he and his brother were just yearlings, and everything laid out below her still belonged to the Druids.

On November 28, the *New York Times* reporter Nate Schweber called Doug Smith to ask about the death of 754 and other collared wolves; he was writing a piece for the paper's environmental blog. Smith was measured in his comments to Schweber, pointing out that losing the only collared wolf in the Junction Butte Pack had made his job harder. Nathan Varley, the biologist-turned-guide who published Laurie's nightly updates, struck a more strident tone. For years, anti-wolf forces had hammered away at the harm that wolf reintroduction—and the concomitant decline in elk numbers—had caused to the hunting economy. But what about the money lost when hunters killed wolves like 754? Guides had been bringing paying clients to see the Lamar wolves for years. As many as half a million people might have seen 754 in his lifetime, Varley told Schweber. Who was going to compensate guides like him for the loss, as he put it, of "a million dollar wolf"?

Varley had grown up in Yellowstone, the son of the park's chief of scientific research, and his opinion carried weight. Still, some of his fellow advocates, mourning the death of a beloved wolf, were taken aback by his effort to put a dollar figure on 754's life. But not Doug McLaughlin. For years, he'd been trying to convince activists that the only way to get a seat at the table with state game regulators was to speak their language. Elk were a valuable resource, but so were wolves.

A few watchers, including McLaughlin, began to suspect that the preponderance of collared wolves among those taken in the hunt thus far was more than just a coincidence. The collars identified wolves roaming outside the park as Yellowstone wolves, which, at least in theory, allowed hunters who were angry about reintroduction to single them out. Killing a collared wolf, the watchers speculated, was a way of sending a political message to the federal government; it was a kind of terrorism. Doug even suspected that hunters were illegally using radio receivers to locate and track collared wolves, as the park's biologists did. The list of frequencies used by the Wolf Project was a closely guarded secret, but a hunter with a relatively inexpensive handheld scanner could eventually find which ones were in use.

Rick was skeptical of these claims. The collars weren't easy to see at a distance, especially during hunting season, when the wolves' winter coats were thickest. And he knew from long experience how difficult it could be to find a collared wolf in a mountainous, wooded landscape, even with a receiver tuned to the correct frequency and an intimate knowledge of the target's preferred trails and resting places. Still, there was no denying that it was shaping up to be the worst hunting season that Yellowstone's wolves had ever endured.

A LARGE BLACK MALE WOLF HAD BEEN SHADOWING THE LAMARS since their return to the valley, drawn by the presence of so many breeding-age females in the pack. Rick had never seen him before, and his provenance was a mystery, though he was clearly a young wolf, perhaps only a yearling. The females seemed interested, especially 776 and Middle Gray, but 755 was leery of the newcomer. With 754 gone and the only other males in the pack just pups, it fell to him to chase the black off by himself.

But the young wolf was persistent. On a snowy morning in early December, he approached the Lamars in the river bottom once again. Creeping forward, tail tucked, his posture was as deferential as could be. He clearly had no intention of ousting 755, and it occurred to Rick that he might make a good addition to a pack that had just lost its beta male. He marveled at how socially adept the park's wolves were. There was no telling how long or how far the young male had roamed, yet he had shown up in the right place at just the right time, scarcely three weeks after 754 was shot. How could he have known there might be a place for him here?

But 755 drove him off, and that night the Lamars headed up over Norris once again. The next day O-Six's collar confirmed Rick's worst fear.

The pack was back in Crandall.

12

A Good Day in the Park

Through the rifle's scope, the wolves looked like statues in the snow—one black and one gray, standing perfectly still, their ears cocked forward, their eyes on him. Turnbull had cut their tracks on the Chief Joseph Highway at dawn, about a mile and a half from his cabin, and pulled over to investigate. A few minutes of studying the ground told him what he needed to know. There were at least a half-dozen of them, and they had passed through not long before he did, heading south toward a ridge known as Cathedral Cliffs. He'd left the two-lane highway on a private drive that belonged to a friend, then angled as best he could toward the ridge on gravel roads before he was forced to park and head out on foot, sounding his predator call as he went.

He'd been lucky. If the wolves had made the timber at the base of the mountain, he'd likely never have spotted them. Instead they'd still been in the willows not far from the road, and they'd come to investigate his call, just as he'd figured they would. He saw only two, but there was no point in waiting for the rest; he might never get a better opportunity than the one he had right now. He decided he wanted the gray. He exhaled and squeezed the trigger.

At the rifle's crack, the black wheeled and flew into the brush.

The gray staggered and dropped.

It was a long walk through the snow to where she lay, but Turnbull barely felt the weight of the rifle and his snow boots as he got under way. This was a trophy very few people in his part of the world had ever taken.

When he came within fifty yards of his prize, he caught a glimpse of movement in the brush behind her. The black wolf had returned. His eyes on the hunter, he stepped cautiously out of the willows and sat down not far from where the gray lay. They formed a rough triangle in the snow, the three of them. The black was so close that Turnbull could see that he wasn't entirely black after all. His fur was tipped with white along his withers, giving him a grizzled look. The wolf didn't come any closer, but he didn't retreat, either. He seemed to be waiting to see what the hunter would do next.

Turnbull paused, uncertain. He had never seen an animal behave this way. The rifle's deafening retort, the death of his comrade, the advancing hunter—the wolf should have been half a mile away by now. Then the black lifted his snout into the air and howled. It was a sound Turnbull had heard many times over the years but never like this, alone in the snow with the wolf a stone's throw away. He stood still and listened, transfixed. The wolf howled again, longer and louder this time.

From the willows behind the black, more wolves began to emerge.

There had been no way of knowing for certain the size of the pack Turnbull was stalking. Now there seemed to be no end to them. They arrayed themselves in a loose semicircle around the black, all silently focused on the body of the gray, the snow beneath her torso now a bright red. Turnbull counted eleven in all. He instinctively dropped to one knee and raised the rifle. Wolves didn't attack people; he knew that. But what did it matter what you knew or didn't know when you were alone with eleven enormous predators? He'd seen what they could do to a five-hundred-pound elk. He glanced back at his truck. It was only 150 yards away, but it might as well have been a mile. If they came at him, he wouldn't last sixty seconds.

The black howled a third time, and suddenly they all joined in. Turnbull lowered the rifle and slowly rose to his feet. He stood there, agape, disarmed by the otherworldly sound, by the sheer overwhelming sadness of the cry. She was their leader, he thought. She wasn't just the black's mate; she was the one they couldn't do without, and that's why they wouldn't leave.

But he could, and he did. He left his trophy in the snow and began trudging toward the truck, following his deep tracks through the snow. He glanced back from time to time to make sure he wasn't being followed. The wolves were still huddled together around the downed gray, howling. He could still hear them when he reached his truck. He racked his rifle behind the seat and began a three-point turn, fumbling and clumsy from the cold and the adrenaline rush that still hadn't left him. He pulled out onto the Chief Joseph Highway, suddenly wishing somebody had been with him to see what he had just witnessed, what he was sure nobody in the State of Wyoming had ever seen.

An hour later he returned to the spot, armed this time with his .44 Magnum. His trophy was still lying where he had left her, but there was no sign of the pack. He began moving cautiously toward her, swiveling his head from side to side, certain that every disturbance he heard was an approaching wolf. When he reached the gray, he saw that he had put the bullet right through her chest, exactly where he wanted it. He also noticed that she was wearing a wide leather collar with a battery pack on it. She was a Yellowstone wolf.

Her thick winter coat had kept him from seeing the collar before, but he wasn't surprised to spot it now. A collared wolf had been shot in Crandall just a few weeks before. He reached down to get an idea of her heft. Her coat was unbelievably thick, her paws enormous. Somehow her fur was still perfectly dry underneath; she'd been lying in one place for an hour, yet her body hadn't melted the snow at all. She was heavy, at least a hundred pounds. He was not a small man, but he tried to imagine what her six-foot-long body would feel like draped across his shoulders. He looked back at his tracks in the snow, marking the long walk back to the truck. There was no way.

He slid his hand beneath the sturdy collar and began dragging.

The law said hunters had to check wolves in with Wyoming Game and Fish within twenty-four hours. He drove into Cody later that morning, Thursday, December 6, 2012, with the wolf in the bed of his truck. Inside the agency's familiar office, he found Mark Bruscino, the large carnivore section supervisor. Bruscino was in his mid-sixties, balding, with the standard-issue Wyoming cowboy mustache. Turnbull had met him at least thirty years before, when he was still a young man hunting in the woods around Cody, and Bruscino was the local game warden. Now he spent his time managing grizzlies, mountain lions, and for the first time in his long career, wolves.

He wasn't happy to see the collar on the animal in the bed of the pickup. For the second time that month, he'd be calling the wolf office in Yellowstone to tell Doug Smith that another one of his wolves had been shot in Crandall. Bruscino pulled the collar off the gray and took a look at the serial number printed on the inside surface. It meant nothing to him, but Smith would know which pack she came from. He called and left a message on his voicemail, reading off the serial number so that Smith would have it when he returned to the office.

Back in his cabin a few hours later, Turnbull was surprised to get a call from Bruscino. He'd heard back from the wolf office in Yellowstone. "You just pissed off a whole bunch of people," he said.

THE NEXT MORNING RICK MCINTYRE SAT IN HIS SUV IN A PULL-out beneath Druid Peak in the predawn darkness, trying to get a signal on the Lamar wolves. Doug McLaughlin sat shivering in his own truck with the engine idling nearby, waiting to hear what he found. Laurie was out of town, and nobody else was around; they had the valley to themselves. As he scanned through the frequencies, Rick heard a text alert from his cell phone. This often happened when he entered the valley first thing in the morning. Silver Gate had no cell tower, so messages sent the night before tended to stack up while he was at home, and then all come through at once as soon as he got far enough into the park to get service. The first message was from Dan Stahler in the wolf office.

Through the window of his truck, Doug saw his friend's posture sag and his head swing slowly from side to side. Rick put his phone back in its cradle and stared at the steering wheel for a moment. When he rolled down his window, his face was ashen.

"O-Six is dead," he said.

The two friends sat together in the dark and cried.

Rick thought about the last time he had seen her, heading up over Norris. It had been snowing steadily and visibility wasn't ideal, but he'd still been able to track the Lamars through the trees the entire way up the mountain. All twelve of them had been strung out in a line across the mountainside, moving back and forth across the slope as they ascended, like hikers on a switchback trail.

Middle Gray had been in the lead, with O-Six content to follow in her wake, keeping everyone moving in the same direction, holding the family together as she always had. Laurie and Doug had been there, too, watching alongside him.

Laurie would later remember how purposeful they seemed, like a troop of soldiers; there was no play, no straying to investigate strange scents, no pausing to rest. Just up, up, along the ridgelines that ran parallel to the floor of the valley, toward the skyline. Near the top they crossed paths with a nervous group of bighorns, which drew together at the sight of the pack and then bolted when the time seemed right. The wolves held their course. They stopped momentarily at the top, twelve figures beautifully silhouetted against the skyline. And then they were gone. Rick had lingered awhile behind his scope, hopeful that the pack might come back down, but O-Six didn't return.

And now she never would.

Laurie. Rick would have to call her and tell her. He would have to tell everybody. He thought of all the people he would see in the park in just a few hours' time, all the watchers who were in town that week. He knew what he had to do, but he couldn't.

"I—I want you to go ahead and tell the other people when you see them today," he told Doug. "I'm not sure I'll be able to say another word."

THE FIRST WATCHERS DOUG ENCOUNTERED THAT MORNING WERE in a pullout west of Little America, where the park road climbed steeply to an overlook with a dramatic view of a valley known as Hellroaring, hundreds of feet below. As soon as he pulled in, Sian Jones, the retired English detective, strode over to greet him. When she saw the look on Doug's face, she pulled up short.

"Something terrible has happened, hasn't it?" she asked.

Doug found himself at a loss for words, but she guessed it anyway. It was what they'd all been fearing since the Lamars returned to Crandall a few days before.

"Is it O-Six?" she asked.

He nodded. She crumpled where she stood, sagging until she was seated on the ice, and began bawling.

Word spread through the park. At the wolf office, Doug Smith's phone rang constantly, as one colleague after another called to see if it was true. Smith wasn't in Yellowstone when the news came in. He had been invited to give a lecture at the University of Nevada in Reno, and he was waiting backstage in a packed auditorium when Dan Stahler called to give him the news. He barely had time to digest it before stepping out onto the stage.

Driving home from the airport that night, Smith called Rick. Over the years, he had developed a soft spot for his eccentric colleague, and he hadn't forgotten how crushed Rick had been that day on top of Specimen when the two rode up together to recover 21's remains. As a wildlife biologist, Smith was used to death. He'd examined countless elk stripped to bones and bits of bloody hide; he'd done necropsies on wolf pups that had died of starvation; he'd watched wolves kill other wolves through a spotting scope. But the truth was that he did get attached to individual wolves; how could you not, after you'd followed the same packs for generations? Unlike most of the watchers, he actually handled the wolves, during the annual collaring operations, and somehow that made him feel even more protective of them, particularly the special ones. But he couldn't protect them. Nobody could.

He'd called to console Rick, but he found himself breaking down instead. Rick tried to comfort him, in his own way. He began to list all the wolves that had been spotted that morning and the behavior that had been observed. The intensive winter study period was under way, and Rick had helped the crews find a pair of packs. "It was a good day in the park, Doug," he told him softly.

Smith had thought he was finished crying, but he wasn't, and he got off the phone as quickly as he could.

AS SOON AS ED BANGS HEARD THE NEWS, HE KNEW THERE WAS going to be trouble. He had tried to warn state game officials about allowing hunting too close to the park for fear something like this would happen. He'd seen it time and again during his years in Denali—hunters could shoot a hundred wolves on the other side of Alaska without engendering a peep of protest. But shoot one park wolf that people had come to know and love, and suddenly everyone in the state was talking about the evils of wolf-hunting. He had retired back in the summer of 2011—two months after Senator Tester's rider became law—but he still talked to Doug Smith about once a week. Bangs didn't offer much in the way of condolence when he reached his old friend on the phone Saturday morning. Most wolves died from misadventure of one kind or another; as far as he was concerned, there was no difference between a bullet from a gun, a bite from another wolf, or a kick from an elk. Smith didn't take it personally; he knew it was something Bangs had needed to believe in order to do his job.

Bangs was more worried about what was going to come next. "The media is going to have a field day with this," he told Smith. "Don't do anything to feed the frenzy."

That evening Nate Schweber, the *New York Times* reporter who had written about the death of collared wolves back in November, filed another story. This one, which ran not on the website's Green blog but in the much more widely read National section, was titled "'Famous' Wolf Is Killed Outside Yellowstone." By the time it ap-

peared in the next morning's paper, it had already been read online
by reporters around the world, many of whom filed their own stories the same day, including for such far-flung outlets as the *Daily
Mail* and the *Guardian*, both major London newspapers. The Associated Press picked up the story, and suddenly O-Six's death was
being discussed all over the country. ABC News ran a segment on
the death of "the most famous wolf in the world," as did National
Public Radio, bringing the story to millions of people who hadn't
even known there *were* wolves in the Rockies, much less that they
were being hunted. Doug Smith found himself doing interview
after interview from his desk in the wolf office.

With each new report, vitriol in the comments section was
showered on Wyoming officials and the Fish and Wildlife Service
in equal measure. "Why are there trophy zones right next to the
park?" one reader of the popular magazine *Science* wanted to know.
"Let's send Wyoming, Montana and Idaho the bill for the 117 million dollars US Taxpayers spent to restore the wolves to their original territories!"

A FEW DAYS INTO THE FUROR, SMITH GOT A CALL FROM MARK
Bruscino. Until O-Six was shot, Bruscino had had only a vague
notion of who she was or why she was so celebrated. Now he was
getting calls from people demanding to know why he had allowed
a hunter to shoot her. As diplomatically as he could, Bruscino told
the callers that his office managed wolves at the population level;
they didn't take into consideration the fates of individual animals.
He didn't add what he told colleagues in private, which was that as
far as he was concerned, O-Six was just another wolf; she contrib-
uted nothing more to the Yellowstone population than any other
alpha female did.

Nor did he really believe she was that well known, beyond the small group of dedicated watchers in the park. Bruscino seemed to think Smith was to blame for the backlash against her death, that'd he'd been stirring the pot by calling reporters. "You need to tamp this down," he told Smith.

"I can't," Smith replied, "because it's not me that's causing it."

It was true. Smith hadn't called the *Times*, and he hadn't been the one who referred to O-Six as "the most famous wolf in the world," the line from Schweber's piece that would be repeated time and time again in follow-up coverage of O-Six's death. Schweber had been quoting a Los Angeles photographer, one of dozens of professionals who had photographed her over the years. It was hard to quibble with that description, however; thousands of people had watched her in the park since she first denned at Slough Creek in 2010. And yet it was also true that the *Times* report on her death, and the avalanche of coverage that followed, had brought her story to a much wider audience than she had ever enjoyed in life. Calling her the world's most famous wolf in the pages of one of the world's most widely read newspapers had become a kind of self-fulfilling prophecy.

Nobody was more surprised than Rick by the attention her death received. It hadn't happened when 21 died, but then 21 had died of natural causes. The irony of O-Six's death was irresistible to reporters: Who could have foreseen that one of the very first wolves killed in Wyoming's first legal hunt would be Yellowstone's best-known animal? Stories on her death inevitably mentioned the hundreds of other wolves that had been taken in the hunt across the three states that fall. Such statistics had been reported before for previous hunting seasons in Idaho and Montana, but now it was as if people were finally hearing the hard truth about wolf-hunting for the first time, since they could put a name and a face on the phenomenon. Memorial pages sprang up on blogs, where fans were encouraged to leave their favorite O-Six photos and memories. A celebrated sculptor in Gardiner captured her in bronze. *National Geographic's* NatGeo Wild channel began working with Bob Landis on a documentary about her life.

Doug Smith, like Bruscino, was fielding his share of angry calls. Some longtime wolf advocates seemed to feel that collaring O-Six had led to her death, and more than one called for Smith's resignation. Much of the funding for the Wolf Project came from private donors, money raised by Smith himself. He had long told donors that the project offered a chance to invest in research on an unexploited wolf population, a rare opportunity in North America, or anywhere else in the world for that matter. But the death of O-Six, along with so many other collared wolves that fall, called the entire premise into question. Why should donors continue to sponsor collars if hunters were just going to shoot the wolves wearing them?

Everybody wanted to know what would become of the pack, but Smith had no answer for them. Four days had passed since O-Six's death, and the Lamars still hadn't returned from Crandall. It was possible they would not return at all. When an alpha died, especially a female, packs tended to splinter. 755 would certainly need to find a new mate, at least, and there were no females in the pack who were unrelated to him. With breeding season approaching, he was probably already looking, and the search might lead him anywhere. The best Smith could tell people was that with O-Six's death, the quota had been filled in the Crandall area. As long as the pack didn't drift too far east, they should be safe, at least for now.

THE MONTANA FISH AND WILDLIFE COMMISSION MET THE MONday after O-Six was shot. The meeting had been scheduled for months, but her death dominated the agenda. Commissioners announced that they would entertain a proposal to close down several hunting zones north of the park, including the subunit near Jardine where three collared wolves had been taken already, in response to the high number of collared wolves killed in the hunt that fall. With the trapping season set to begin in just a few days, the prospect of the park losing several more wolves was a real one. Doug McLaughlin and several other watchers made the trip to Billings to attend the meeting and speak in favor of the closings. In the end, the commission voted 4–1 to close down the zones.

That night the Lamars came back to the park at last, and the next morning all eleven were sighted rallying near the base of Druid Peak. Rick observed 776 scent-marking like an alpha. She was the clear candidate to succeed her mother, but just how that would happen was anybody's guess. The watchers enjoyed a few days with the pack all together in their old haunts, but it didn't last. On December 15, they were spotted heading over Norris once more, and for the next two weeks Rick was reduced to receiving periodic reports from a friend with telemetry equipment east of the park. The pack stayed in Crandall for a few days, but then, leaderless and adrift, they set out farther east. By December 22, they were forty miles out, which put them in an open hunting zone where the quota hadn't yet been met.

Fortunately they didn't stay long. By New Year's Eve, 755, 776, and 820 were back in the park, but the remaining pack members were nowhere to be found. The trio howled and howled from Druid Peak, but there was no reply, except from the Junction Butte Pack far to the west. If the Junction wolves decided it was time to take the valley, 755 could do little to stop them, with only himself and two daughters to defend it.

On January 2, the Montana Outfitters and Guides Association, joined by a local Montana state representative and a trio of hunting groups, sued the game commission, arguing that the vote to close the wolf hunt near Jardine had been taken illegally, since it wasn't posted on the original agenda and the public was not given the proper notice. A local judge granted a temporary injunction, and the areas were immediately reopened to hunters and trappers. The state legislature, meanwhile, began debating a bill that would prevent the commission from instituting any such midseason closures in the future or creating any kind of a buffer zone around Yellowstone where hunting wolves was prohibited. The message was clear: as far as the State of Montana was concerned, there was no such thing as a special wolf.

Doug McLaughlin decided he'd had enough. He announced that he was raising money for a new campaign, to be known as the War of 754, in memory of his favorite wolf. Publicly, he told donors that the money would go to raise awareness about the killing of collared wolves, which was true as far as it went. But he felt more drastic measures were in order, and these plans he discussed only with a few close friends. He went to the wolf office and requested logs of locations recorded for wolves wearing GPS collars. The logs were public information, and Doug wasn't obliged to tell anyone why he wanted them. From the location data, he identified the most common paths that Northern Range packs used when they left the park.

Over the course of the next few months, he hiked out to the locations marked on his map, his backpack loaded down with tools for a guerrilla campaign against hunters: high-pitched noise emitters and radio signal jammers, along with car batteries to power them. At the park's boundary line, he planted his noise emitters, each equipped with a motion sensor, facing back toward the park's interior, to discourage approaching wolves from leaving by their accustomed routes. The signal jammers he pointed in the opposite direction, to prevent anyone nearby from monitoring signals from radio-collared wolves coming down out of the park. He wasn't sure if the devices were legal, but he didn't care. He was certain the other side was breaking the rules, and he had no interest in losing an unfair fight.

ON JANUARY 13, TWO LAMAR PUPS, NOW ALMOST FULLY GROWN, were captured and collared in the Crandall area, where the pack, including 755 and his adult daughters, seemed to have localized. Now that wolves had been returned to state control in Wyoming, Mark Bruscino had begun his own collaring program, to keep tabs on their numbers and movements. One of the pups he caught was the spirited black male who had caught Rick's eye. He was now known as 859.

It was an ominous development. In addition to general research, state wildlife officials used collars for a purpose that never came up in Yellowstone: tracking wolves believed to have been involved in cattle depredations. The collars made them much easier to find and kill. Beyond that, the symbolism of the act wasn't lost on the watchers: the Lamars, or at least some of them, were Wyoming's wolves now.

On January 20, 755 came back to the park alone. He was spotted on a knoll above Slough Creek, cautiously investigating a kill the Junction wolves had made in the area a few days before. Rick and Doug stood behind their scopes on Bob's Knob with a couple of other watchers, as 755 moved slowly across the mountainside, his nose to the ground, warily watching for the pack he knew couldn't be far off. He made his way up to the old den site, the center of so many good memories for both him and the watchers. Rick was grateful that he was back in the park, but it wasn't easy to watch him come back to this spot as he was now, a lone wolf, bereft of 754, his constant companion, and O-Six, his leader and mate. As they looked on in silence, Rick heard one of the watchers nearby break down and begin sobbing.

Over the next few days, Rick followed 755 around the Lamar Valley as he scavenged off kills, running from the younger and faster males in the Junction Butte Pack when he got too close for their liking. The Junctions had available females that 755 seemed interested in, but he could never seem to get close enough to draw one out.

On January 25, his fortunes reversed. He was spotted near the den on Druid Peak with a gray female, a Mollie known as 759. She had lost her collar some time ago, but her unusually short tail made her easy to identify, and the watchers were familiar with her from the previous spring and summer when the Mollies rampaged through the Northern Range.

Now all the acrimony between the two packs seemed to have been forgotten. The pair stayed near each other for the remainder of the week and were spotted in a tie. 755 had found a new mate. The project began calling the pair 755's group, just as they had when he and his brother first connected with O-Six three years earlier. Doug Smith managed to dart 759 and fit her with a new collar. She was spending more time near the den on Druid Peak, suggesting that she was pregnant and looking for a good place to settle in.

It was the first bit of good news about Yellowstone's wolves in some time. When a reporter from a paper in Missoula called wanting to do a follow-up story on O-Six's death, Rick told him that despite everything that had happened to the pack that winter, 755 had landed on his feet, and the prospects were good for another litter of pups to be born in the Lamar Valley. The pair were not as inseparable as O-Six and 755 had been, but at least he was no longer alone.

The fate of the rest of the pack was difficult to discern. Then, in late February, Middle Gray was spotted in the Soda Butte drainage, not far from 755 and 759. For some reason, 755 seemed hesitant to greet her, and the source of his apprehension became clear when a second wolf came out of the trees behind her. He was so blond he was almost white, and he was big. It was 856, the alpha male from a pack known as the Hoodoo Pack, which held the territory north of Crandall. Middle Gray seemed eager to reconnect, but 755 was leery of his daughter's new suitor. 755 was still in his prime, but 856 was a formidable wolf, and it was far from clear which of the two would become the alpha, if the Lamars were somehow to reunite as a single pack. Finally the two couples came together, Middle Gray sniffing the strange new female accompanying her father, and 755 tentatively investigating 856. There was no hostility during the brief encounter, which ended with each couple moving off in a separate direction.

To the watchers' delight, 820 began turning up in the valley, too. She was sighted near the Druid Peak den area in early March. Though still technically a yearling, she was now almost two years old, and her beautiful tawny coat had grown just a bit darker. Her father wasn't around, but she smelled him and seemed determined to summon him home. As the watchers looked on, she howled for several minutes, methodically turning in every direction until she had filled the valley with her calls. She seemed to be on her own. If Middle Gray wouldn't return to the fold, then perhaps 820 would.

WHEN THE LAMARS DID RETURN IN NUMBERS TO THE VALLEY, ON March 12, it was not the homecoming the watchers were hoping for. Doug, Laurie, and Rick heard howling from the den area and spotted 755 running for his life, heading east across the mountainside. Then, to their amazement, the entire Lamar clan emerged from the woods. With them was not only Middle Gray's new companion but a second Hoodoo male as well—a suitor, it seemed, for 776. It was clear that some kind of confrontation had taken place in the thick woods around the den, but exactly what had happened, the watchers could only guess.

The collared black pup, 859, trotted down the mountainside and out toward the river, scent-trailing 755 and his new mate, 759, who had also been spotted fleeing from the den forest after the morning's chaotic encounter. Confused about the confrontation and clueless about its significance, the pup knew only that his father was nearby, and he wanted to find him. When the pair finally came together in the sage, it was a happy reunion, one that Rick was pleased to see.

But then Rick got a good look at 759 and realized how disastrous the encounter at the den had been. She had clearly been brutalized, her entire back end covered with blood. She was hobbling along after 755 gamely, but she didn't look good. When they paused and bedded in the sage for a short while, 755 licked her wounds. It had to have been Middle Gray and 776 who did the damage, Rick thought, and probably some of the yearling females, too. As far as he knew, Middle Gray was the only Lamar who had actually encountered her father's new mate before; to the rest of the pack, she was a stranger. They had found her near the den they considered their own, and they had done what their instincts told them to do. With the two new males present, 755 had likely been powerless to intervene, or perhaps he had come too late.

The next morning 759 was curled up in the trees on the south side of the valley, near death. The watchers didn't yet realize it, but 755 did. Leaving his mate behind, he'd begun searching the valley for the rest of his pack. He found 776 near the park road not far from the Buffalo Ranch, but the reunion didn't last long. The two Hoodoo males came loping down the side of the hill above the road, with the rest of the Lamar wolves behind them.

The young males were moving stiffly, suggesting that 755 hadn't fled the fight at the den the day before without inflicting some damage himself. But now 755 retreated, and when the chase ended, 776 accompanied the Hoodoos and the rest of the pack back up onto the hill. She couldn't have her father and her new mate, too, and it seemed she had made her choice. They all bedded in the sage: Middle Gray and 776, the only two left from O-Six's first litter, 820 and the other yearlings, and the pups.

755 hadn't run far, and now he slowly made his way back toward the pack. He stood in the snow on the south side of the road and howled at his family high up on the hillside above him. When he got no response, he came closer, across the road to the base of the hill. The two males could plainly see him, but they didn't stir. Neither did the rest of the pack, lying on the snow nearby. They were his offspring, all he had left from his time in the Lamar Valley, but they were no longer his.

It wasn't his valley anymore, either, and he seemed to realize it all at once. He began moving west at a slow pace, stopping to look back up the hill one last time. When he set off again, he moved with a purposeful trot. He left the valley through Lamar Canyon and passed through the flats of Slough Creek, heading over Bob's Knob as he made his way. He continued west, following the creek to its confluence with the Yellowstone River, and still farther, all the way through Little America, without stopping, until he had left his home far behind.

13

Enough Is Enough

In the days that followed, Rick tracked 755's movements as he continued to roam alone, heading ever westward into territory he had likely never before seen. Twenty-four hours after leaving the valley, he was far out on the desolate and treeless Blacktail Plateau. The next day his signal was detected near the Wolf Project offices in Mammoth, on the opposite side of the Northern Range, some thirty miles from the Lamar Valley. That spring Rick watched as 755 roamed from one pack's territory to another, trying unsuccessfully to find a mate. It occurred to Rick that perhaps he never would.

By the time the hunting and trapping seasons around the park concluded, twelve Yellowstone wolves had been lost, including six collared animals. Of the park's ten packs, seven had lost at least one member to the hunt. But a final insult was still to come. On April 24, a rancher and outfitter in Jardine named Bill Hoppe found thirteen dead sheep on pasture he leased a few miles from the park boundary. Montana wildlife officials determined the culprits were a pair of wolves. Rather than send government trappers, they issued Hoppe a special permit that allowed him to shoot the pair himself, should they return to his property. In an effort to streamline the removal of problem wolves, the state had recently begun using such permits more often, though critics of the practice warned that ranchers didn't have the resources to determine whether a wolf spotted on their property was really a livestock killer or merely in the wrong place at the wrong time.

Two weeks later Hoppe shot a collared female from Yellowstone's Canyon Pack known as 831. He hadn't observed 831 attacking livestock; he had merely spotted her on his pasture. When Doug Smith heard the news, he looked up 831's tracking data and found that she had been near Mammoth, ten miles away, both the day before and the day after the sheep were killed. He couldn't be sure, but he strongly suspected that the State of Montana had allowed Hoppe, long an outspoken critic of wolf reintroduction, to kill the wrong wolf. Word got around, meanwhile, that Hoppe hadn't promptly removed all the sheep carcasses from the property, as was customary in Greater Yellowstone to prevent other predators from coming to the scene. 831 might have been attracted to Hoppe's pasture not by the presence of livestock but by the smell of carrion.

Smith had reached his limit. He told a reporter from the Bozeman paper what he thought had happened, and the paper ran a story that did not look good for Hoppe or Montana game officials. Its suggestion that the wrong wolf had been shot outraged game commissioners, but Smith didn't care—he was tired of playing politics. Montana officials came to Hoppe's defense, noting that he had legally shot 831 and disputing Smith's claim that she probably hadn't attacked the sheep. Not long after the story came out, however, Hoppe surrendered his right to shoot the second wolf and moved his remaining stock to another pasture.

THE IDENTITY OF THE HUNTER WHO SHOT O-SIX REMAINED SOMEthing of a mystery. Unlike his friend Mike Hirsch, Turnbull had kept his name out of the papers. Rumors were flying in the park, however, about who he was and where he might be found. Rick had learned his name—several people in Silver Gate knew Turnbull—but kept the information to himself. He'd heard quite a few watchers say they'd like to chew him out, but that wasn't Rick's style, and he'd discouraged them from seeking a confrontation.

One afternoon, however, he found himself at the Painter Outpost in Crandall. Overhearing two men talking, Rick realized that one of them had to be Turnbull. He was only a few steps away, but Rick was uncertain about what to do. He felt he should say something, but he wasn't sure what. *Hey, I don't want to be any trouble,* he imagined telling the hunter. *I knew her. If you want to talk about her, I'd be happy to do that.* He thought it would be good to know something about Turnbull, to know what had motivated him to shoot a wolf. And maybe Turnbull would tell him what O-Six's final moments were like. He was the only one who could.

In the end, however, Rick said nothing. He just walked out to his car and drove back to the park.

THE ENORMOUS BACKLASH FOLLOWING O-SIX'S DEATH SEEMED TO change the dynamic in the national debate over wolves. Six months after her death, Fish and Wildlife published its proposal to delist wolves throughout most of the Lower 48. The agency received more than one million comments, the most ever submitted in response to any such proposal for any species in the history of the Endangered Species Act. The vast majority opposed the move, including the young followers of an enterprising ninth grader from Olympia, Washington, named Story Warren, who had created a popular Instagram account called Kids4Wolves in the wake of O-Six's death. On February 7, 2014, a panel of experts assigned to review the delisting rule released their long-anticipated report. To the surprise of many, they unanimously rejected the proposal, finding that it wasn't based on the best available science.

It was the first in what would become a string of victories for wolf advocates that year. On September 23, Judge Amy Jackson reversed Fish and Wildlife's delisting rule for wolves in Wyoming, immediately returning them to the endangered species list. Jackson found that the state's refusal to agree to manage for 150 wolves, as Idaho and Montana had done, instead of the bare minimum meant that the species wouldn't be adequately protected under state management. She directed Fish and Wildlife to return to the bargaining table with the State of Wyoming. The state's fall hunt was canceled, to the jubilation of advocates everywhere, especially those who were following the fate of O-Six's offspring east of Yellowstone. Wolves in Crandall would be safe, or at least as safe as they ever were.

Less than three months later advocates had cause to celebrate once again. U.S. District Court Judge Beryl A. Howell, another Washington, D.C., justice, ruled that wolves in the Upper Midwest must be returned to the list as well. Since hunting was first authorized in 2011, Michigan had yet to hold a full wolf-hunting season, and in fact voters there had already rejected wolf-hunting in a statewide referendum held shortly before Judge Howell's ruling came down. In Wisconsin and Minnesota, however, hunters and trappers had killed more than fifteen hundred wolves over the previous three years. That was too many, according to Howell, who chastised Fish and Wildlife in her decision. "The D.C. Circuit has noted that, at times, a court 'must lean forward from the bench to let an agency know, in no uncertain terms, that enough is enough,'" the judge wrote. "This case is one of those times."

By the time the Yellowstone Wolf Project marked its twentieth anniversary, on January 12, 2015, the tide seemed to have turned. The nation's papers and news sites were filled with stories about the benefits of wolves in the ecosystem; the term "trophic cascade" suddenly seemed to be everywhere. *National Geographic* and a host of other publications, meanwhile, prominently reported on a study by a Washington State University ecologist that called into question the benefits of culling wolves to protect livestock. It seemed that more culling led to more livestock predation, unless the culling was large enough to seriously reduce the wolf population. The reasons were unclear, though some biologists speculated that smaller packs and the existence of more lone wolves from splintered packs—both functions of exposure to hunting and culling—led to more attacks on easier prey like livestock.

In the fall, members of Congress tried once again to attach a wolf-related rider to a must-pass budget bill, as Senator Tester had done in 2011. This version would have reversed both Judge Jackson and Judge Howell's rulings, legalizing wolf hunting in Wyoming, Wisconsin, Minnesota, and Michigan. Like Tester's rider, the language in the measure would have prevented a judge from reversing the move. But this time, things were different. Perhaps mindful of the overwhelmingly negative public response to Fish and Wildlife's proposal to delist wolves nationwide, twenty-five senators, led by Barbara Boxer, the California Democrat, signed a letter to President Obama urging him to veto any budget bill that undermined protection for endangered species.

Obama let it be known he wanted a clean budget bill with no mention of wolves or any other endangered species, and congressional leaders declined to adopt the rider. After years of defeats, wolves were finally winning again.

In Idaho and Montana, however, things had changed very little, at least from the wolf's perspective. Livestock depredations were down, in part because wolves had learned to avoid ranches after two decades of heavy culling, but also because ranchers had become more savvy about how to protect their stock. The Forest Service had retired some of the national forest grazing leases with the most conflicts, like the Diamond G south of Crandall, under an arrangement with a pro-wolf nonprofit that compensated ranchers for the value of the leases and the cost of relocating stock.

But hunters and trappers in both states were still killing a lot of wolves, especially in Idaho. In the five years since legal hunting began, trophy hunters had taken over 2,500 wolves in the Northern Rockies, 1,500 of them in Idaho alone. Wolf populations are notoriously difficult to estimate, but official counts showed that the total in Montana at the end of 2014 was 554, down about 100 from pre-hunting levels. In Idaho, game officials had managed to reduce the population from a high of 893, in 2009, to 770.

Montana's elk populations, however, were trending up, somewhat lessening the pressure on state game officials to drive down wolf numbers with large quotas and long seasons. The same thing was occurring in Wyoming. Despite the court-imposed ban on wolf-hunting, game officials reported another outstanding elk harvest in 2015, though hunters near Yellowstone were still enjoying lower success rates. Despite the heavy take of wolves in Idaho, it was felt that elk numbers hadn't rebounded sufficiently, and officials authorized nearly year-round wolf seasons in some zones. When that didn't work, they resorted to aerial gunning by game department employees.

They had on occasion gone a step further. In December 2013, game officials hired a professional trapper and sent him deep into

the Frank Church River of No Return Wilderness, a federal pre-
serve along the middle fork of the Salmon River in central Idaho
so remote that it is unreachable by any road. His charge was to
completely eliminate a pair of packs in the area.

If not for a chance meeting between the trapper and a biologist
named Isaac Babcock, who had tracked collared wolves in the area
for years, the plan might have remained a secret. Babcock snapped
a photo of the trapper on horseback heading into the woods leading three mules behind him, carrying the provisions he would need
for the months-long job. The photo and story found their way to
the *Idaho Statesman*, and the backlash was immediate. But for the
color film, the image, as the *New York Times* observed, could have
been captured in the nineteenth century.

On a warm day in the summer of 2015, Rick watched from
the roadside as 755 squared off with a grizzly over an elk carcass.
He was in the Hayden Valley, a broad plain along the Yellowstone
River about twenty-five miles southwest of the Lamar Valley. With
755 was a four-year-old female he had taken up with the previous
fall. She was from the Canyon Pack, which had long controlled
this part of the park. The Canyons were known for their beautiful
white females, and 755's new mate was striking, not quite white
but a pleasing and easy-to-spot pale blonde. As luck would have it,
the longtime Canyon alphas, both ten years old, had recently left
the Hayden and moved to parts unknown in the park's interior,
leaving the territory available.

Rick recognized the grizzly. He was an old male known as
Scarface, and he had haunted this part of the park for years. He'd
taken over the wolves' kill on the banks of the Yellowstone the
day before and had been lying on it more or less continuously ever
since. As Rick looked on, the pair tag-teamed the bear, as Rick had

watched 755 and O-Six do so many times over the years, hazing and harassing him until both wolves managed to get a chance to feed.

The female departed first, heading up out of the river bottom and into a nearby stand of trees, where three pups ran out to greet her. Rick knew there was a fourth in there somewhere, waiting for his mother to come home with dinner. Late in the day, his father headed that way, too. After two and a half years on his own, scavenging off other packs' kills and roaming across the Northern Range, 755 was an alpha again. He had finally found a home.

BACK IN THE LAMAR VALLEY, THE CHAOTIC AFTERMATH OF O-SIX's death gradually stabilized. 776 eventually left, following her new mate back to the Hoodoos' traditional territory near Crandall, where she settled in as that pack's new alpha female. Middle Gray's paramour 856 departed with them, leaving his would-be mate behind. But another Wyoming wolf took his place at Middle Gray's side, and in the spring of 2013, to the watchers' delight, she bore a litter of pups in the old Druid Peak den. The Lamars had a new alpha pair, and the valley would host another chapter in their story.

The Lamar female 820 hadn't been so fortunate. Shortly after 755 was driven from the valley, the pack's other females began persecuting her at every opportunity, pinning her again and again and preventing her from coming in to feed on kills. O-Six's death had caused the pack's breeding-age females to view one another as competitors, and 820's dominant sisters wanted her gone. She became a lone wolf like her father, occasionally pairing up with him for short periods but more often wandering by herself. Eighteen months after O-Six's demise, she was dead, shot after preying on chickens in the yard outside someone's home near Jardine.

Rick was glad to see a new generation of Lamar wolves denning in O-Six's old home, but he often found himself driving south, along the park road that paralleled the Yellowstone River, to check on 755. The old male was now seven, an age that O-Six, the wolf who taught him everything he knew, had never reached. His black coat had turned a rabbit gray. His new family was called the Wapiti Pack, after the Native American word for elk, of which there were plenty in this part of the park. The pack's summer rendezvous was on the far side of the Hayden Valley from the road, and sightings of the pups were infrequent and usually brief.

Still, Rick found that the wait was worth it.

Epilogue

In the spring of 2014, I met someone who knew Steven Turnbull. Although she wouldn't tell me where he lived or give me his phone number, she agreed to call him and give him mine. I didn't have much hope that it would lead to an interview. In the dozens of reports on the death of the famous Yellowstone wolf, Turnbull's name had never surfaced, and he had never spoken to the media. Fourteen months had now passed since he had taken the world's most beloved wolf, yet he was still a blank space in the story, a null, a mystery.

To my surprise, I received a call from him that same night. "Hi, Nate, this is the guy you were looking for today," said a voice, booming and gruff. I offered to let him remain anonymous* if he would agree to talk to me about shooting O-Six. Again, I did not have high hopes. But it seemed I had unwittingly reached out to

---

* We eventually agreed to use the pseudonym Steven Turnbull.

him at the perfect moment. Bob Landis's film about O-Six, titled *She-Wolf*, had just premiered, and Turnbull had watched it. The film, which featured wonderful footage of the Lamar wolves, stayed away from the politics of wolf-hunting, but it had still touched a nerve. Turnbull was ready to tell his side of the story. "I shot her, and I'm not ashamed," he boomed. "I'd do it again!" We arranged to meet the following morning near his cabin in Crandall.

Turnbull was waiting at a snowy pullout along the Chief Joseph Highway, sitting behind the wheel of a large pickup idling against the cold, when I pulled up in my rented Subaru. Looking down on me through the driver's window, he seemed to briefly reconsider the wisdom of his decision. He made me promise once again not to use his name. "I'm from Wyoming," he said. "I found her, and I can find you, too."

Satisfied that we understood each other, he told me to follow him up a snowy road to his cabin. Inside it was cozy and tidy, and once we took off our coats, he became less wary and more hospitable. He offered me some elk jerky he'd made himself earlier in the winter. It was outstanding.

The walls were covered with photos of Turnbull smiling alongside various freshly killed trophies: bear, moose, antelope, and lots of elk, including some truly massive bulls. I noticed a beautiful picture of O-Six in the Lamar Valley, by a local photographer whose name I recognized. On a shelf along one wall was a birdcage with a parakeet inside. His name was Bubba, Turnbull told me, a gift from his girlfriend after his beloved hunting dog had died. "I don't suggest you put your finger in there," he added.

We sat at a small kitchen table. The drawers and cabinets all had antler pulls that looked homemade and skillfully done. Turnbull had a stack of paper he wanted to show me, printouts of stories about O-Six's death that a friend had collected and brought by. "Man, there are some people out there who really hate your guts," his friend had marveled. It was true. In the months after he shot O-Six, Turnbull had been the target of considerable scorn, especially in the comments section of various online reports, where a few anonymous readers suggested creative and cruel ways in which he might be harvested himself.

In those first few weeks, he had begun carrying a pistol with him, he told me, for fear that somebody would find him and force a confrontation. "I don't want trouble," he said. There hadn't been any, but he still seemed flummoxed by what had happened to him, a feeling that was reinforced by the bizarre experience of watching the documentary on O-Six, in which he was represented by a stock image of a hunter with a rifle. Millions of people were passing judgment on something he had done one morning, alone, in one of the remotest places in the Lower 48. "She didn't tell me she was famous before I shot her," he said.

A few days after her death, Mark Bruscino had called to let him know that some wolf advocates wanted a meeting. They were after O-Six's remains, he explained, so that she could be buried in the Lamar Valley. Bruscino hadn't revealed Turnbull's name, but he'd offered to act as a go-between. Turnbull refused. He had no interest in a meeting, and he had no intention of giving up his trophy. "I didn't do anything wrong," he told me time and again as we talked that first morning.

And yet he couldn't help but feel besieged, even though hardly anybody outside Crandall knew that he had been the one who pulled the trigger that day in 2012. Shortly after he shot O-Six, Turnbull had posted a picture of her carcass lying in the back of his truck on the wall at the Painter Outpost. It wasn't especially gory, but she was clearly dead. One day a government trapper who was a regular at the café asked him to take it down. It would only stir up trouble if people realized which wolf it was, he explained. The trapper was an old friend, and Turnbull reluctantly complied.

From time to time he'd overhear a tourist asking about the famous wolf who had been shot in Crandall, but he'd always played dumb.

Turnbull seemed genuinely mystified by the watchers' enthusiasm for individual wolves but was also curious about it. I mentioned that some wolf advocates had held a memorial service for Yellowstone wolves that had been killed in the hunt, including O-Six. He said he'd wished he'd known about it, because he would have gone—not to be disruptive but just to see what it was like.

Turnbull knew about loss. About three months before he shot O-Six, his younger brother had died suddenly of a heart attack. He'd been an outdoorsman, too, and at his funeral a family friend had sung "A Country Boy Can Survive," Hank Williams Jr.'s defiant tribute to rural life. Then, a few days into the furor over O-Six's death, he lost his uncle Wayne, the old hunting guide–turned–delivery driver. Turnbull seemed acutely interested in what people in the park thought of him. "I don't want them thinking I'm the world's biggest asshole," he said. "That's not me."

Then he described for me what happened the day he'd shot O-Six, the details spilling out as though he'd been waiting for someone to come and give him a chance to tell the story. When he reached the part about 755 and the rest of the pack howling over O-Six's body, he suddenly seemed to realize how this scene would play when I relayed it to the watchers back in the park. "It was almost sad," he acknowledged. "I'm a hunter, but I'll admit that."

"Do you want to see it?" he finally asked, after we'd been talking for an hour or so. It took a moment to register what he was referring to; I hadn't imagined that he'd have O-Six's pelt there in the cabin. He stepped into a back room I couldn't see. When he returned, he had an enormous gray wolf skin draped over his arm. He proudly hung it on a hook next to the door so I could see how long it was. Most of his trophies were at his house in town, he explained, but this one was special. He usually kept it hanging on the wall, with the receipt for his wolf tag tacked up above it, so everyone could see he had shot her legally.

He urged me to feel the fur. He'd shot her at the height of winter, and her coat—amazingly soft, like a rabbit's—was as thick as it ever would be. He'd had her tanned professionally and had ensured that every inch of her hide was preserved, including her paws, so that the pelt could be used to create a full mount—the kind of specimen you might see in a museum diorama—if he decided to spend the money to have it done. There was no sign of damage from the collar she had worn; good taxidermists could excise such flaws and seamlessly rejoin the skin, he explained.

"Now, that's a trophy," he said.

When Turnbull noticed me shooting video with my phone, he urged me to stand next to the pelt so people could get a better sense of how big O-Six had been, as he took over filming. Reluctantly I did, holding out one of her legs to show how wide her paws were, examining her long snout, now devoid of teeth. It was impossible not to think of the countless stories I'd heard about what she'd done with those tireless legs and those formidable teeth, the elk she'd taken down single-handedly, the territorial battles she'd won, the pups she'd reared, the loyalty and love and fear she'd inspired, and the enormous and magnificent stage upon which she'd done it all, in front of her thousands of fans. Now she was hanging from a plastic hook in a two-room cabin with an audience of just Turnbull and myself and Bubba, silently looking on from his cage. It felt profane, though I had no idea how to explain to my host why. Instead I stepped quickly out of the frame, took my phone back, and turned off the camera.

. . .

I VISITED HIM SEVERAL MORE TIMES OVER THE COURSE OF THE next two years, and each time he became more open and friendly, which was more or less his default mode with everyone he encountered. I came to understand that he had built his life around his favorite pastime, like a ski bum with a bow and arrow and a rifle instead of a snowboard. Despite how angry it made him the first time he watched it, he had rewatched the O-Six documentary several times, marveling at the scenes of ungulate behavior more than anything else, he told me. A scene in which a herd of bison shunned an elk calf trying to hide in their midst from nearby wolves fascinated him. "I'd never seen anything like that before," he said.

Hunting was an intellectual pursuit for him. You had to know your prey, and you had to take them ethically. He spoke often about the principle of fair chase and what it meant to him. He wanted me to know he'd followed the Lamar wolves' movements for weeks before he found them, driving around Crandall looking for tracks and listening for their howls. "I put in my time to get that wolf," he said.

On one visit, he agreed to take me to the location in the valley where he'd shot O-Six. But when we got close, he seemed strangely reluctant to show me the exact spot, driving by quickly and gesturing vaguely toward the area. It was private property, he said, and though he had permission to hunt there, he didn't feel good about taking me there now.

When I returned later without him, I began to realize why. Crandall was undeniably spectacular, yet the place where he'd found the wolves that morning was disappointingly prosaic. O-Six had died perhaps half a mile from the Chief Joseph Highway, on a piece of ranch property that hosted a modest house, a couple of outbuildings, some man-made stock ponds, and a row of farm equipment. Turnbull had spotted O-Six and 755 between a hayfield and a twenty-five-yard-wide strip of close-cropped grass that served as an airstrip for the landowner's small plane in the summer. O-Six, the queen of a wilderness beyond compare, had been shot more or less in someone's front yard, or what passed for such in Crandall.

Standing near the spot where she died, it occurred to me that no special skill had been required to bring her in, either, other than good marksmanship. Turnbull had parked his truck, walked maybe 150 yards, and sounded his rabbit distress call. The wolves had come right to him, stopping a couple of football field lengths away, a reasonable distance with a modern rifle scope. No doubt to O-Six the man standing in the willows was like any of the thousands of humans she'd encountered in Yellowstone from a similar distance—not a threat. Whether it had been fair chase was debatable, but it was not a good story, and Turnbull seemed to know it. I suddenly understood Louie Cary's wry smile when I'd told him whom I had come to Crandall to find. "The great wolf hunter," he'd said.

Over the course of the two years that followed our first interview, Turnbull's feelings toward wolves seemed to harden somewhat, especially after Judge Jackson returned Wyoming wolves to the endangered species list in 2014. During our final meeting, he told me that for the first time in his life, he'd failed to draw a tag for an elk in the upcoming fall hunt. The elk were simply not there anymore, not like they used to be, and they didn't seem to be coming back.

"I'm against wolves," he told me. "I want to make sure that's clear."

I assured him that it was.

On a beautiful afternoon in June 2015, Yellowstone's wolf-watchers gathered in Silver Gate to celebrate Rick's career. He wasn't retiring, but it had been twenty years since he'd come to Yellowstone, and to his friends it seemed as good a time as any to show their appreciation. They had reserved the cavernous main hall of the Range Rider, a hundred-year-old hotel made from old-growth pine logs that was by far the biggest building in town. At least a hundred people had made the trip to town for the occasion, making it the largest gathering of the far-flung tribe in years.

The lodge was only two hundred yards from Laurie's house, but it was too far to walk in her heels and dress, and she arrived on the back of a four-wheeler, clinging to the driver's shoulder with one hand and holding her hair in place with the other. Inside were rows of chairs filled with all the people Rick had helped to find wolves over the years, the ones for whom a single visit wasn't nearly enough, who had returned to the park time and time again. Some of them he saw only once a year, but he remembered their names and their favorite wolves. Doug McLaughlin was there, of course, along with Jeremy SunderRaj, on summer break after his first year at the University of Montana, and Bob Landis, with his ever-present camera. Landis took a seat in the front row so that he could film the occasion.

As the audience looked on, Marlene Foard, the veteran watcher from Salt Lake City, presented Rick with a quilt with an image of a wolf and a bound collection of letters written by the watchers themselves, each describing a favorite memory of Rick. As Rick stood quietly nearby, looking somewhat uncomfortable, Foard explained the significance of the gifts and spoke briefly about what Rick had meant to her. Finally she handed him the quilt. "Okay, thank you," Rick said, a bit too abruptly, and the crowd tittered knowingly.

The afternoon's highlight would be a story from Rick himself, and he had worked on it for weeks in honor of the occasion. Doug Smith stood up to introduce him, drawing a laugh by recalling the subject of the first meeting he attended when he took over as project director almost twenty years ago. It concerned what to do about a headstrong seasonal ranger named Rick McIntyre. Then he turned serious. After years as Rick's supervisor, he told the watchers, these days he sought him out just to talk sometimes, especially when things weren't going well, because Rick always gave him a boost. "I kind of need Rick," he said. "And I think everybody here needs Rick. He really is the glue that holds us all together."

And the wolves need him, too, he continued, perhaps more than Rick knew. It wasn't just that he had watched more wolves, as Smith put it, "than anybody in the history of humanity." It was the community he had helped build, a confederation of people who cared about wolves, one whose impact was felt far beyond Yellowstone.

For his talk that afternoon, Rick had decided not to speak about O-Six. Her death was still too raw, and he was still processing what her story meant. It was bad enough that he still encountered visitors, two and a half years after her death, who hadn't yet heard the news and wanted to know how many pups she'd had that spring and where they could spot her. "I'm sorry to have to tell you this . . . ," Rick would begin, and watch their faces fall.

When a producer for a well-known radio program asked him about her legacy the previous summer, all Rick had been able to come up with was a story about a kindergarten class from a town near the park that had visited not long after she died. "I know the man who shot that famous wolf," one of the boys announced before Rick could even begin his talk for the small group of kids. "My dad just bought a license to kill a wolf," he added, and Rick, who still found it difficult to even talk about O-Six, braced himself for what was coming next. "But I hope he doesn't," the boy said, and Rick found himself filled with optimism.

Today he wanted to talk instead about O-Six's grandparents,

21 and 42. It was a story he had told many times, but even now, eleven years after their deaths, he was still deepening his under-standing of the significance of their lives. It was a story, he told his audience, of a great romance, like Johnny Cash and June Carter, a comparison his friends had heard him make many times before. But this time he made their tale a story about what wolves feel, how they experience what we call happiness, joy, and a sense of connec-tion to one another.

Rick reminded his audience that 21 had never known his fa-ther. He'd been born during the brief and tragic adventure outside the park by his parents, 9 and 10, an excursion from which 10, the Wolf Project's first official alpha male, never returned, shot by a poacher while the pregnant 9 was digging a hasty den nearby. Yet when 21 and the other pups were returned to the park, they were placed in the same holding pen that 10 had once occupied. As the alpha male, he had scent-marked it thoroughly, a smell the return-ing pups could hardly have missed.

His time in the pen, Rick suggested, meant that the young 21 had met his father, in a way. Rick invited the watchers to imagine what an animal sees in his mind's eye when he smells a familiar scent. Does he see, as the celebrated animal rights advocate Temple Grandin had suggested, a picture of the creature that corresponded to the scent? Did 21 see his father in that pen?

Rick returned to his theme—how a wolf's sensory experience helps create its emotional landscape—again and again, as he told the familiar story of the rise of the Druids under 21, the valiant but gentle warrior, and 42, the matriarch who oversaw the pack's astounding growth. At last he came to the story's sad ending—42 killed by the Mollies, and four months later, the aging 21's lonely climb to the top of Specimen Ridge, where Rick found his body. But why, Rick wondered, had 21 chosen to die on top of Specimen Ridge? Did he want to take one last look at his territory, like some

Scottish clan leader from an earlier era? He'd puzzled over it for a long time, he told the watchers, but he believed he had finally solved the riddle.

The breakthrough had come, he told them, when he was thinking about the story of Hachiko, the dog whose name had become synonymous with loyalty in Japan in the 1930s. Unaware that his master had died, Hachiko faithfully waited at the local train station for him to arrive home from work, as had been his daily custom. He returned every day for over nine years, always expecting to see the man, who never appeared. Suddenly Rick knew why 21 had gone to the top of the mountain: he was looking for 42. She had been by herself, far from the pack, when the Mollies attacked and killed her on Specimen. Four months had passed since she died, but for all 21 knew, she was still alive, wandering in the woods, looking for him.

He had gone to the top of Specimen on the last day of his life, Rick suggested, because that was where he and 42 had gone together countless times—to mark a particular tree that served as a kind of sentry post along the edge of the Druids' territory. Of course, she wasn't there that summer day when 21 visited the spot alone. But her scent was still present, Rick reminded his audience, which would have offered 21 at least a glimmer of hope at finding his missing mate. "Now the question at that moment would be: Can a wolf in the wild experience what we know as joy and happiness?" Rick said, his voice breaking noticeably. "And my answer is yes."

Rick had been speaking for over an hour, and there was not a single person in the room who didn't know how his story ended, but his audience was still rapt, the room crackling with emotion. He brought the story to a close by imagining 21's final moments. After the long climb up the mountain, the old wolf would have needed a rest, so he'd bedded down near the sentry tree in the spot where Rick and Doug Smith would later find him. All the aches and pains of old age and the exhaustion from his long climb would have started to fade, Rick said softly, as he began to die. But even as he faded away, 42's scent would still have been in his nostrils, and in his mind perhaps he savored one final thought—an image really. One last glimpse of the wolf that had meant everything to him.

People had been sniffling in the audience for some time, and a few now cried unabashedly. It had taken twenty years, and it had come almost in spite of himself, but Rick had become a master of his craft. Looking out over the assembled watchers, their faces turned expectantly toward his, it was impossible to deny the essential truth of what Smith had said before Rick began his talk. He was needed.

And therein, maybe, was the meaning of O-Six's death. While she lived, Rick—along with Laurie and Doug and so many others over the years—had told thousands of people about her life, most often on the side of the road in the Lamar Valley but also in media interviews and in countless gatherings like this one. Yet it wasn't until she was dead—until the *New York Times* saw fit to give her an obituary—that Rick realized just how far her story had traveled, how powerful the simple act of storytelling could be. Maybe it didn't matter if he never wrote his book about O-Six; maybe, in a way, he already had.

Sitting with a couple of friends in his cabin after the gathering ended, Rick made an announcement of sorts. Lately he'd been thinking, he said casually, that maybe it wasn't so important that he be in the park every day. After all, he could easily get reports from Laurie or Doug or any number of other watchers to keep him up to date. After fifteen years in the park, including, according to his calculations, over eighty-five thousand wolf sightings, he was beginning to see things differently. Looking back on it, he was proud of his streak of consecutive sightings, but he was also relieved that he was no longer in the midst of it. He was calmer now, less anxious, or at least he was trying to be. If he didn't need to see a wolf every day, then maybe he didn't need to be in the park every day, either.

In late summer he finally did take a break, though not for the reasons he anticipated. After a few weeks of feeling short of breath, he visited the doctor. Two weeks later he was in a hospital in Billings having heart surgery. As he recovered at home, Laurie and Doug kept him up to date on what he was missing in the park.

Every night during his recovery he had the same vivid dream, in which he looked out the window of his hospital room and saw the Lamar wolves running across the hills. Nine days after his surgery, he was back in Yellowstone, watching those same wolves and helping other people do the same. He was driving another donated vehicle these days, this one a silver Toyota SUV decorated with enormous color decals depicting scenes from the park. Stretched across one side was a large photo of O-Six, with the snowy peaks and bucolic fields of the Lamar Valley arrayed behind her. Rick found that visitors loved the image, especially kids, who would flock to the car when he pulled into crowded lots. O-Six could still draw an audience, as good a reason as any to begin telling a story.

ACKNOWLEDGMENTS

I am grateful for the many people who helped me with this project. David Patterson, man of many talents, edited my first book and sold the second one; I am hoping he will actually write the third. At Crown, I want to thank my editor, Amanda Cook, who is alarmingly good at her job and wonderful to work with. I also thank Claire Potter for her careful attention to the manuscript, and Jon Darga for his assistance along the way. Thanks also to publisher Molly Stern for her early words of encouragement, and Vanessa Mobley for her vote of confidence.

In Austin, thanks to my editors at *Texas Monthly*, Jake Silverstein and Brian Sweany, for agreeing to the book leave that helped me get this project under way, and to all my colleagues there—especially John Broders and David Courtney, for two years of jokes about howling, peeing, and scat, which meant so much to me. Former *Texas Monthly* intern Mai Schotz helped with timely and expert transcription.

I am indebted to many people in Yellowstone. Laurie Lyman trusted me with her notes about O-Six, which allowed this story to be told in the manner it deserved, and introduced me to everyone she could in the wolf-watching community. Doug McLaughlin encouraged me at every juncture and provided invaluable insight about both the wolves and the people in this story. Rick McIntyre graciously gave me hours of his time for interviews in his cabin in Silver Gate, along the roadside watching wolves in Lamar Valley, and on the phone. I can honestly say I've never met anyone quite like him, and I thank him for allowing me to tell his story.

I would also like to recognize the following list of watchers who helped Laurie produce her nightly update during O-Six's time in Yellowstone (with apologies for those she may have forgotten): Stacy Allen, Doug McLaughlin, Kirsty Peake, Lynette Johnston, Chloe Fessler, Kathie Lynch, Dianne "Wendy" Busch (my Northern Rockies agent), Richard Brown, Sian Jones, Becky Cox, Bill Hamblin, Gerry Hogston, Jeff MacIntyre, Mark and Carol Rickman, Jim and Joellyn Barton, and Dave and Sherryl Clendenen.

In Crandall, I want to thank Steven Turnbull first and foremost for extending his hospitality and answering my questions. He had nothing to gain and a lot to lose, and I appreciate his taking a chance on me on nothing but a handshake. Louie and Shelley Cary were gracious hosts and invaluable sources on Crandall, its history, and its people.

I also wish to thank, in no particular order: Doug Smith, Dan Stahler, Nathan Varley, Mike Phillips, Jim Garry, Ron Blanchard (my old roommate), Mark Bruscino, Alan McIntyre, Ed Glynn, Mike Eastman, Dan Vermillion, Doug Honnold, Tim Preso, Ed Bangs, Carter Niemeyer, Mark Cooke, Betsy Downey, Lee Meador, and David Quammen.

Finally, I'm grateful to my wife, Karen Poff, who encouraged me to go see wolves in Yellowstone in 2007 just before our kids were born, and for my two wonderful kids, who can't wait to get back to Yellowstone themselves.

SOURCE NOTES

Prologue: December 6, 2012

This account is based on interviews with Steven Turnbull.

Chapter 1: Return of the Wolf

The account of O-Six and her companions running down an elk was drawn from Laurie Lyman's notes for December 12, 2009, supplemented by Rick McIntyre's notes, as well as by my interviews with them.

My descriptions of Rick are drawn from my interviews with him, his friends, colleagues, and family members, and from my own observations of him in action in Lamar Valley, spotting wolves and interacting with visitors. Over the years, Rick has given countless media interviews, though they have been mostly about wolves, not about him. See, for example, Josh Dean, "Pack Man," *Outside*, November 11, 2010, and Brett French, "Silver Gate Man Spends Days Recording Wolf Movements," *Billings Gazette*, September 2, 2008.

Aside from a brief and ill-fated effort to bring wolves back to Michigan in 1974, the wolf reintroduction in Yellowstone and Idaho was unprecedented. The best history of the Yellowstone Wolf Project is Douglas Smith and Gary Ferguson, *Decade of the Wolf*, rev. and updated (Guilford, CT: Lyons Press/Globe Pequot Press, 2005). Carter Niemeyer, *Wolfer: A Memoir* (Boise, ID: Bottlefly Press, 2010), is another great firsthand account by someone integral to the project. Hank Fischer's *Wolf Wars* (Guilford, CT: Falcon Guides, 1995) is an insightful account of the politics of reintroduction by one of the activists who helped make it happen. Bruce Hampton, *The Great American Wolf* (New York: Henry Holt, 1997), is a nice complement to Fischer's account. Renée Askins, *Shadow Mountain: A Memoir of Wolves, a Woman, and the Wild* (New York: Anchor, 2004), written by an activist, is also helpful. Rick Bass, *The Ninemile Wolves* (New York: Houghton Mifflin, 2004), describes the challenges wolves and their advocates faced in Montana prior to reintroduction. For a more critical take on reintroduction, see Cat Urbigkit, *Yellowstone Wolves: A Chronicle of the Animal, the People, and the Politics* (Newark, OH: MacDonald & Woodward Publishing, 2008).

On wolves in general, L. David Mech, *The Wolf: The Ecology and Behavior of an Endangered Species* (Minneapolis: University of Minnesota Press, 1981), and L. David Mech and Luigi Boitani, eds., *Wolves: Behavior, Ecology, and Conservation* (Chicago: University of Chicago Press, 2007), are indispensable, as is Adolph Murie, *The Wolves of Mount McKinley* (1944; reprint Seattle: University of Washington Press, 1985). For an easier but no less thorough read on wolf behavior, see Peter Steinhart, *The Company of Wolves* (New York: Vintage Books, 1995).

Chapter 2: In the Valley of the Druids

The story of Chad McKittrick and the saga of 9 and 10 was expertly recounted in Thomas McNamee, "The Killing of Wolf Number Ten," *Outside*, May 1997, and later in McNamee, *The Killing of Wolf Number Ten: The True Story* (Westport, CT: Prospecta Press, 2014).

The story of 31 and 38 is drawn from Smith and Ferguson, *Decade of the Wolf*, along with interviews with Doug Smith. The account of 21 joining the Druids is drawn from Bob Landis's film *Return of the Wolf* (2000), along with *Decade of the Wolf*. Bob Landis's other Druid films include *Wolf Pack* (2003), *In the Valley of the Wolves* (2007), and *The Rise of Black Wolf* (2010). For more on Landis, see Kevin G. Rhoades, *Wildlife Stalker: Days in the Life of Filmmaker Bob Landis* (Missoula, MT: Five Valleys Press, 2011).

My account of Rick's early days in Yellowstone is based on interviews with Rick and Doug Smith. The story of Cameron Diaz and DMX's visit is told in Smith and Ferguson, *Decade of the Wolf.* On the boom in wolf tourism, see James Brooke, "Yellowstone Wolves Get an Ally in Tourist Trade," *New York Times*, February 11, 1996. Yellowstone became the first place where researchers could regularly observe wolves taking down prey. For decades, in one of the longest-running wolf studies in history, on Michigan's Isle Royale in Lake Superior, the biologist Rolf Peterson studied the interaction of wolves and the moose they preyed upon. Over the course of thirty-five years, Peterson examined countless carcasses, but the island's terrain was so heavily wooded and difficult to traverse that he actually observed a wolf pack killing a moose on only a half-dozen occasions.

On Limpy's ramblings, see Brett Prettyman, "Captor of Wolf Near Morgan Says His Experience Is 'Cooler Than Stink,'" *Salt Lake Tribune*, December 29, 2002, and Brent Israelsen, "Wolf Caught in Utah Heads Home," *Salt Lake Tribune*, December 13, 2002.

Chapter 3: A Star Is Born

This chapter draws on Laurie Lyman's notes between January and March 2010, supplemented by Rick McIntyre's notes from January 27 and February 10, 11, 20, and 23. My interviews with Rick, Laurie, Doug McLaughlin, and other watchers provided additional details.

The Adolph Murie quote is from *Wolves of Mount McKinley* (1985 ed.), pp. 28 and 29. Denali National Park was known as Mount McKinley National Park until 1980.

O-Six's hunting prowess was well documented by Rick McIntyre, Laurie Lyman, and others who saw her take down elk without any assistance on numerous occasions. The elk is in the same family as the white-tailed deer (the only deer most Americans encounter in their lives), but the relationship between the two is akin to that of the Great Dane and the Chihuahua. Near Yellowstone's Mammoth visitor center is a small herd of elk whose bulls are known for attacking cars that get too close during mating season; over the years, many rentals have been returned to the airport in Bozeman with dents in the doors. Wolves risk their lives every time they go hunting, and they hunt several times per week.

The decision to label the wolves reintroduced into the Northern Rockies as an "experimental population," which allowed for more flexibility in how they were managed—including culling on behalf of ranchers—is recounted in Hank Fischer's *Wolf Wars*. In December 1980, as Fish and Wildlife was attempting to build support for wolf reintroduction, a male wolf dispersing from Canada appeared on the central plains of Montana and began killing livestock. Ranchers demanded action, but since wolves were on the endangered species list, there was no legal way to kill him. Over the course of the next year, the Bearpaw Wolf, as he was called, was blamed for dozens of livestock deaths (though most were never confirmed). Animal Damage Control tried unsuccessfully to trap and relocate him, but it had few agents with the relevant experience. Desperate to resolve the public relations nightmare, Fish and Wildlife finally declared the Bearpaw Wolf a wolf-dog hybrid (though there was no evidence for this, and it was later demonstrated to be false), and he was shot dead from a helicopter the next day.

The episode further soured ranchers on reintroduction unless the ability to cull depredating wolves was on the table. Even after the agreement was in place, most ranching interests continued to oppose reintroduction. Yet Fischer and others involved in the early push for reintroduction suspected that some farsighted officials in the Northern Rockies agreed to it because they feared that naturally dispersing wolves would eventually make it to their constituents' ranches anyway, as the Bearpaw Wolf had. Arriving under their own power, they would enjoy the full protection of the Endangered Species Act, so culling would not be an option, and land-use restrictions (e.g., no grazing on national forest land) might be implemented to protect them. Only through reintroduction could wolves be labeled an experimental population, giving ranchers the tools they felt they needed to control depredation. Others have pointed out that the natural dispersal of wolves might have taken another fifty years to repopulate the Rockies, assuming enough survived illegal poaching to ever regain a foothold at all.

On Limpy's death, see Patty Henetz, "Wolf's Death Stirs Fears for Species' Fate," *Salt Lake Tribune*, April 7, 2008.

Chapter 4: Killers

This chapter is based on my interviews with Steven Turnbull and other Crandall residents, chief among them Louie and Shelley Cary at the Hunter Peak Ranch. The history of cattlemen and wolves in the West could be told through the various generations of the Cary family. Louie's grandfather was born in South Texas and once worked on the celebrated XIT ranch in the Panhandle. He was among the first to drive longhorns from Texas north into the Rocky Mountains, the practice (dramatized in Larry McMurtry's novel *Lonesome Dove*) that formed the foundation of the ranching economy as it exists today. The arrival of cattle, in turn, provided the impetus for trapping out the remaining wolves in the West.

Local hunting outfitters Dave Siegel (from the KBarZ) and Mickie Fischer (Crandall Creek Outfitters) provided insight about the decline of big game hunting in Crandall, as did Crandall's local celebrity, Mike Eastman, founder of *Eastman's Hunting Journal*, among other publications.

On the history of Crandall, see John K. Rollinson, "Historical Sketches of Upper Clark's Fork of the Yellowstone and Its Tributaries Within the State of Wyoming," *Annals of Wyoming* 12, no. 3 (1940): 222–24. Nancy Heyl Ruskowsky, *Two Dot Ranch: A Biography of a Place* (Greybull, WY: Pronghorn Press, 2009), provides some insight into the history of the region. On the changes in the area's ranching business, see the excellent Ranchlands Study Team, *Ranchland Dynamics in the Greater Yellowstone Ecosystem: Park County, Wyoming* (Center of the American West, University of Colorado at Boulder, 2003).

On the story of the Robinetts and the Diamond G ranch, see Elisabeth A. Wright, "Wyoming Ranch Becomes a Wolf Testing Ground," Associated Press, April 8, 2001, and Christine Peterson, "Ranchers Find Ways to Live with Wolves Despite Losses," *Casper Star-Tribune*, March 25, 2015. It was Hank Fischer's nonprofit, Defenders of Wildlife, that began compensating ranchers from a private fund in order to maintain support for reintroduction.

The Roman aphorism about dogs and wolves comes from Barry Lopez's classic *Of Wolves and Men* (1978; reprint New York: Scribner, 2004). A dog is a domesticated wolf. (It may also be said that a wolf is essentially an uncommonly large feral dog.) Around thirty-five thousand years ago, most likely either in what is today known as Europe or in Central Asia, wolf packs led by unusually intrepid alphas learned that they could scavenge kills left behind by human hunters, and they began to shadow those tribes that would tolerate them. Early humans were very good at finding game, but wolves were even better; for clans astute enough to exploit this basic fact, the relationship became mutually beneficial. Eventually a few wolves were bold enough to join their newfound companions by the fire, and their descendants, over the millennia, became domestic dogs.

Neanderthals, a hominid species that coexisted—and competed against—early humans, apparently never developed this relationship with wolves, leading some anthropologists to speculate that it gave *Homo sapiens* a competitive advantage against our early rivals, who eventually died out. See Bruce Bower, "'The Invaders' Sees Dogs as Key to Modern Humans' Success," *Science News*, March 21, 2015. Humans might not have become humans, in other words, without wolves.

Of course, after tens of thousands of years of domestication, most dog breeds no longer much resemble their common ancestor. Like dogs, wolves have forty-two teeth, but a wolf's jaws can exert twelve hundred pounds per square inch of pressure—roughly twice that of a German shepherd. Their long canines have an elliptical shape, made to resist breaking along the vector taken by a fleeing animal. And there are other, less obvious differences. The gray wolf lacks some of the dog's genetic traits—tolerance of people chief among them. Wolves have larger brains, and studies of captive wolves have found them to be demonstrably smarter than dogs; they are better able to distinguish quantities, for example. Wolves also show more tolerance than dogs in their social interactions with fellow pack members. The pack mentality—the cornerstone of the wolf's existence—is essentially a relic among dogs. While it has not disappeared altogether, it has lost its usefulness in a milieu where hunting and breeding are largely irrelevant.

The line between the wolf and the dog is thinner than it seems.

Wolf pups raised in captivity will accept humans as pack members, despite their genetic predisposition against it. Likewise our dogs, left to fend for themselves in the wild, would eventually begin behaving like wolves. If everyone in North America disappeared tomorrow and only their pets remained, our thirty-five-thousand-year-old experiment with domesticated wolves would quickly reverse itself. After dogs exhausted the bounty of trash—the source of food for most of the world's dogs today—they would fill a new role in their respective ecosystems. Small breeds like dachshunds and Chihuahuas would survive by eating rodents. Over time larger breeds would form packs, establish territories, and migrate toward areas with bigger game, which they would learn to run down and rip to shreds. They would, in other words, become wolves again, even with nobody around to rename them.

Largely under the radar for decades, the culling of predators by USDA's Animal Damage Control (now known as Wildlife Services) has received some critical media attention in recent years; see, for example, Darryl Fears, "USDA's Wildlife Services Killed 4 Million Animals in 2013," *Washington Post,* June 7, 2014, and Tom Knudson, "The Killing Agency: Wildlife Services' Brutal Methods Leave a Trail of Animal Death," *Sacramento Bee,* April 28, 2012.

Venerated by hunters, elk are considered a nuisance by many western ranchers. Like bison, elk carry brucellosis, and transmissions from elk to cattle have been confirmed in a limited number of cases. But unlike bison, elk have a considerable constituency in their corner, and slaughtering them to protect cattle—common practice with Yellowstone's migratory bison herds—is considered beyond the pale.

Fenced winter feeding grounds—known as elk refuges—dot the Northern Rockies and draw many visitors annually. Mostly unknown to those visitors, they were established as a concession to ranchers, who demanded that elk be kept off of their pastures when, every winter, they came flooding down from the higher elevations into the valleys to avoid the heavy snowfall. U.S. Fish and Wildlife and state wildlife officials, who maintain the refuges, stock them with a steady supply of hay and alfalfa pellets to keep the elk alive until spring, when they happily return to higher elevations.

Some argue that feeding elk in winter has essentially turned them into something akin to cattle, but most hunters and ranchers consider the refuges a win-win. Fewer starving elk in the winter means a larger herd when hunting season comes around in the fall, which makes hunters happy. The refuges keep elk out of cattle pastures, and they also happen to buy a lot of feed from local ranchers, which makes them doubly popular in that community. For more on ranchers' resentment of elk, see Michael Milstein, "'Good' Rancher Goes Berserk with an Assault Rifle," *High Country News*, March 3, 1997.

Chapter 5: The King of Currumpaw

This chapter draws on Laurie Lyman's notes from the spring of 2010, supplemented by Rick's notes from May 9, and by my interviews with them.

O-Six's growing popularity kept Rick busy. He kept careful track of each talk he performed for visitors, whether scheduled or impromptu. During this period, he was averaging 180 per year. Among the thousands of visitors who watched O-Six and her pups at the den that spring, I discovered during my research for this book, were my own aunt and uncle, Alison Blakeslee and Rick Fisher.

For an engaging account of Ernest Thompson Seton's story "Lobo, the King of Currumpaw" and its impact on how wolves were perceived by Americans, see the documentary "The Wolf That Changed America," featured on the PBS show *Nature*, November 22, 2008.

For Rick's tribute to Rags the Digger, see Rick McIntyre, *A Society of Wolves: National Parks and the Battle over the Wolf* (Stillwater, MN: Voyageur Press, 1993), p. 115. Details from Gordon Haber's career are from Gordon Haber and Marybeth Holleman, *Among Wolves: Gordon Haber's Insights into Alaska's Most Misunderstood Animal* (Fairbanks: University of Alaska Press, 2013). Haber died in 2009 when his research plane crashed in the mountains in Denali National Park.

The history of wolf eradication in the United States is from Lopez, *Of Wolves and Men*, which, although published in 1978, is still the definitive take on the fraught history between the two species. The quote on Americans' motivation to kill every last remaining wolf is on p. 166.

Chapter 6: Rebels in the Sage

My account of the hearing is based on the official transcript (*Defenders of Wildlife vs. Ken Salazar*, CV 09-77-M-DWM and CV 09-82-M-DWM), briefs submitted by each side (along with various intervenors), and my interviews with Doug Honnold, Tim Preso, and Ed Bangs. The hearing was extensively covered in the press—for example, Matt Volz, "Today in Missoula: Wolf Case a Test for Endangered Species Nationwide," Associated Press/*Missoulian*, June 15, 2010, which is the source for the "yank that wolf tie" quote.

For background on Judge Molloy, see Ray Ring, "How Green Is Judge Molloy?" *High Country News*, August 25, 2010. Ring and his colleagues at *High Country News* have been following the legal and political fight over wolves for years; see, for example, Hal Herring, "How the Gray Wolf Lost Its Endangered Status—and How Enviros Helped," *High Country News*, June 6, 2011.

On the politics of delisting, see Douglas H. Chadwick, "Wolf Wars," *National Geographic*, March 2010. For a concise scientific argument on why many wolf researchers considered delisting to be premature, see Bradley J. Bergstrom et al., "The Northern Rocky Mountain Gray Wolf Is Not Yet Recovered," *BioScience* 59 (2009): 991–99.

On the Sagebrush Rebellion, see the recently published collection from *High Country News* on antigovernment actions in the West, *Sagebrush Rebellion: Evolution of a Movement* (Kindle ed., 2016). For a more scholarly account, see R. McGreggor Cawley, *Federal Land, Western Anger: The Sagebrush Rebellion and Environmental Politics* (Lawrence: University Press of Kansas, 1993).

The account of the bomb left at a ranger station is from Todd Wilkinson, "The Forest Service Sets Off into Uncharted Territory," *High Country News*, November 8, 1999. The detail about the message written on the bomb appeared in the *Jackson Hole News* on October 21, 1998.

Perhaps no single incident better reflected the continued tensions over land management in the West than the armed standoff between Cliven Bundy and federal authorities in Nevada in 2014. Bundy stopped paying fees he owed for grazing his livestock on federal land after the government restricted his access in an effort to protect desert tortoise habitat. Bundy, whose family had homesteaded in the area since the 1870s, was faced with forcible eviction until dozens of armed anti-government activists came to his defense. See Adam Nagourney, "A Defiant Rancher Savors the Audience That Rallied to His Side," *New York Times*, April 23, 2014.

On the broader issue of antigovernment violence in the West, see Ray Ring and Marshall Swearingen, "BLM, Forest Service Workers Under Attack in the West," *High Country News*, November 1, 2014; Kirk Johnson and Jack Healy, "Protesters in Oregon Seek to End Policy That Shaped West," *New York Times*, January, 5, 2016; and Nancy Langston, "In Oregon, Myth Mixes with Anger," *New York Times*, January 6, 2016.

On the impact of grazing on public lands, see Christine Glaser, Chuck Romaniello, and Karyn Moskowitz, *Costs and Consequences: The Real Cost of Grazing on Public Lands* (Center for Biological Diversity, 2015). The federal government has long been a friend to western ranchers. Unknown to many taxpayers in other parts of the country, cattle are a familiar sight on publicly owned lands in the West. In the big picture, the number of livestock involved is small; less than 3 percent of the nation's beef comes from cattle grazed on public lands. But the grazing allotments are still an essential part of the western livestock business, with around one in five cattle operations using public lands for at least part of the year.

The U.S. Forest Service leases about eight million acres of land for grazing in the Northern Rockies. Grazing fees in the area are cut rate, as they are throughout public lands in the West; the federal government generally charges around 6 to 7 percent of the going rate for comparable privately owned rangeland. It amounts to an enormous subsidy to ranchers, on the order of some $120 million per year. Various efforts over the years to raise the rates, even modestly, have been quietly defeated by western members of Congress.

In the Northern Rockies, most of the operations are in southern Idaho or the vast plains of eastern Montana and Wyoming, not in the mountainous areas where wildlife is most plentiful. Yet the government still spends millions per year to control predators in grazing areas, a service it provides free of charge to ranchers.

Population trends for wolves in the Northern Rockies can be found in the *Rocky Mountain Wolf Recovery Interagency Annual Report* (archived on the website of the U.S. Fish and Wildlife Service), which also reports annual wolf mortality numbers, along with confirmed livestock depredations. Beginning in 2012, the Wyoming Game and Fish Department began publishing an annual report as well, titled *Wyoming Gray Wolf Population Monitoring and Management Annual Report.* The annual reports of the Yellowstone Wolf Project are also a useful reference.

For an opposing view on the notion that legal hunting builds social tolerance for wolves, see Erica Goode, "Study Casts Doubt on Theory That Legal Hunting Reduces Poaching," *New York Times*, May 10, 2016. The account of Carter Niemeyer shooting the Whitehawk Pack is from Ray Ring, "Wolf at the Door," *High Country News*, May 27, 2002.

Chapter 7: Iron Man

This chapter draws on Laurie Lyman's notes for the summer of 2010, supplemented by Rick McIntyre's notes from June 15 and by my interviews with them.

Rick's favorite quote comes from Carveth Read, *The Origin of Man and His Superstitions* (Cambridge: Cambridge University Press, 1920), p. 50. The quote from Smith and Ferguson's *Of Wolves and Men* is on p. 86. Rick drove a pair of donated Nissans over the years. His peculiar driving habits took their toll; it seems that never driving above forty-five miles per hour (the park speed limit) is not good for a Nissan's transmission. The account of how Rick came to own a Swarovski is from my interviews with Doug McLaughlin. My account of Rick's career as a photographer and his decision to end it came from my interviews with him.

The speed of the pronghorn—which wolf pups chase but can never catch—is an evolutionary riddle: Why are they so much faster than any predator in North America, far faster than they have any need to be? The answer is no longer with us: the American cheetah, which once preyed on antelope but, unlike the pronghorn, did not survive the Pleistocene. Pronghorns don't need the speed anymore, but they still flaunt it.

Rick's books include two photo collections, *Denali National Park: An Island in Time* (Legacy, 1986) and *Grizzly Cub: Five Years in the Life of a Bear* (Alaska Northwest Books, 1990); the previously cited 1993 book about reintroduction, *A Society of Wolves*; and a collection of historical documents and articles, *War Against the Wolf: America's Campaign to Exterminate the Wolf* (Stillwater, MN: Voyageur Press, 1995).

Chapter 8: Return to the Lamar Valley

This chapter draws on Laurie Lyman's notes for the fall and winter of 2010, supplemented by Rick McIntyre's notes from October 20 and 27, and December 9, as well as by my interviews.

The quote from Judge Molloy comes from his official ruling. The *New York Times* quote is from an editorial that ran on August 7, 2010. For local reaction to the ruling, see Rocky Barker, "Decision to Relist Wolf Undercuts Moderates," *Idaho Statesman,* August 9, 2010, and Kathy Hedberg, "Idaho County Wants to Join Wolf Fight," *Lewiston Morning Tribune* (Idaho), August 18, 2010.

My account of Tester's conversation with Mike Phillips is from an interview with Phillips. (Tester did not make himself available for interviews for this book.) On Senator Tester's campaign and Congressman Rehberg's challenge, see Susan Davis, "Montana Race Could Tip Balance of Power in U.S. Senate," *USA Today,* April 5, 2012; "About $100 spent for every Montana Senate vote," *USA Today,* December 10, 2012; and Eric Lipton, "Mining Companies Back Friend's Bid for Senate," *New York Times,* December 23, 2011. For Rehberg's take on wolves, see Denny Rehberg, "Listening Is First Step in Crafting Wolf Legislation," *Bozeman Daily Chronicle,* September 13, 2010. For background on Tester, see Timothy Egan, "Fresh Off the Farm in Montana, a Senator-to-Be," *New York Times,* November 13, 2006.

The bill Rehberg signed on to was authored by Texas congressman Chet Edwards. Of course, Edwards had no wolves anywhere near his district, but he told reporters he was acting on behalf of requests from hunters in general. One of a handful of Texas Democrats remaining in Washington, he was in a tough reelection race and needed to shore up his conservative bona fides.

On the wolf's instinctive response to pups soliciting regurgitation, see James Gorman, "The World Is Full of Dogs Without Collars," *New York Times*, April 18, 2016. To test the idea that regurgitation is involuntary, researchers working with captive wolves placed unrelated pups with adults who had just been fed. Though the adult wolves presumably had no stake in the pups' well-being, they still regurgitated on cue when the pups solicited food, then stood back and allowed the strange pups to eat what was essentially their own dinner.

How cold does it get in Yellowstone? On February 9, 1933, the temperature at the ranger station near West Yellowstone hit sixty-six below zero, the second-coldest reading in the history of the Lower 48. (The coldest—seventy below—was also recorded in the Greater Yellowstone area, at Rogers Pass, Montana.)

Chapter 9: Betrayal

This chapter draws on Laurie Lyman's notes between April and December 2011, supplemented by Rick's notes for May 8, August 30, and October 4 and 5. An amateur video of the incident described on October 6, in which the Lamars chased off a grizzly, is available on YouTube at https://www.youtube.com/watch?v=oNa3DLJqiYE.

For the controversy over Tester's rider, see Julie Mianecki, "Gray Wolves, Abortion Funding and Other Policy Changes in the Budget Bill," *Los Angeles Times*, April 15, 2011; Kim Murphy, "Idaho and Montana Prepare for Wolf Hunts," *Los Angeles Times*, April 24, 2011; and Robert Pear, "With a Spending Deal in Hand, Lawmakers Now Turn to the Details," *New York Times*, April 10, 2011. On the significance of the rider for the coming election, see Glenn Hurowitz, "Endangered Wolves Sacrificed in Budget Deal," *Huffington Post*, April 11, 2011. On wolf quotas for the coming fall hunt, see Erin Madison, "Wolf Harvest Down Slightly from Last Year," *Great Falls Tribune*, March 18, 2015.

Numerous studies on the subject of Yellowstone's wolves and trophic cascades were published during this period. See, for example,

William J. Ripple and Robert L. Beschta, "Trophic Cascades in Yellowstone: The First 15 Years After Wolf Reintroduction," *Biological Conservation* 145, no. 1 (2011): 205–13. Data on coyotes and wolves is summarized in Smith and Ferguson, *Decade of the Wolf*, p. 133. On pronghorns, see K. M. Berger, E. M. Gese, and J. Berger, "Indirect Effects and Traditional Trophic Cascades: A Test Involving Wolves, Coyotes, and Pronghorn," *Ecology* 89, no. 3 (March 2008): 818–28. Trophic cascade research began receiving media attention during this period; see Mary Ellen Hannibal, "Why the Beaver Should Thank the Wolf," *New York Times*, September 28, 2012.

Smith's comments on the 2009 hunt appeared in Kim Murphy, "Montana Wolf Hunt Is Stalked by Controversy," *Los Angeles Times*, October 25, 2009. On Dan Ashe's visit to Wyoming governor Matt Mead, see Jeremy Pelzer, "Mead, Top Federal Officials Agree 'In Principle' to Wolf Deal," *Casper Star-Tribune*, July 7, 2011.

Chapter 10: Rampage of the Mollies

This chapter draws on Laurie Lyman's notes between September 2011 and August 2012, supplemented by Rick McIntyre's notes from February 9, April 5, and August 3.

The video of the Mollies attacking a bison was taken by Wolf Project biologist Dan McNulty. It is described in Smith and Ferguson, *Decade of the Wolf*, pp. 74–75.

Chapter 11: "The Worst Possible Thing I Could Tell You"

This chapter draws on Laurie Lyman's notes between August and November 2012.

On Mike Hirsch's successful wolf hunt, see Gib Mathers, "Protected Again: Officials, Hunters Unhappy with Wolf Decision," *Powell Tribune*, September 25, 2014. On the death of 754, see Nate Schweber, "Research Animals Lost in Wolf Hunts Near Yellowstone," *New York Times*, November 28, 2012; it is accompanied by a photo of 754 taken by Doug McLaughlin. My account of the hunter who shot 754 is based on my interviews with Mark Bruscino, Steven Turnbull, Louie Cary, and others in Crandall.

Chapter 12: A Good Day in the Park

This chapter draws on Laurie Lyman's notes between December 2012 and May 2013, and on my interviews with Laurie, Rick, Doug McLaughlin, Doug Smith, Steven Turnbull, and others.

After Nate Schweber's "'Famous' Wolf Is Killed Outside Yellowstone," *New York Times*, December 8, 2012, dozens of reports followed, such as Jeff Hull, "Out of Bounds: The Death of 832F, Yellowstone's Most Famous Wolf," *Outside*, February 13, 2013; Christina Ng, "Yellowstone's 'Famous' Alpha Wolf Shot and Killed," ABC News, December 10, 2012; "Wolf Shooting, Trapping near Yellowstone Park Face New Scrutiny," Associated Press, December 9, 2012; and Matt Williams, "Yellowstone's Popular Alpha Female Wolf Shot Dead by Hunters Outside Park," *Guardian*, December 9, 2012.

Dan Stahler was interviewed on NPR's *Here and Now* on December 11. Doug Smith was interviewed on both NPR's *Morning Edition* and *The World* on December 12. For the report in *Science*, see Virginia Morrell, "Hunters Kill Another Radio-Collared Yellowstone National Park Wolf," *Science*, December 11, 2012.

My account of Doug McLaughlin's guerrilla campaign is from my interview with him. He stressed that he did not coordinate his actions with park service employees.

On the death of 831, see Laura Lundquist, "Gardiner Man Kills Yellowstone Park Wolf," *Bozeman Daily Chronicle*, May 8, 2013, and Laura Lundquist, "Gardiner Man to Turn in Wolf Permit," *Bozeman Daily Chronicle*, May 15, 2013. Hoppe denied baiting 831, and Montana game officials ultimately concluded that he had not done so; see Kathryn Haake and Matthew Brown, "FWP Dismisses Wolf Baiting Claims," Associated Press/*Bozeman Daily Chronicle*, May 14, 2013.

Rick's remarks are from Martin Kidston, "Alpha Male, New Female Partner Likely Come from Rival Yellowstone Wolf Packs," *Missoulian*, February 14, 2013. Rick wrote about O-Six in Richard P. Thiel,

Alison C. Thiel, and Marianne Strozewski, eds., *Wild Wolves We Have Known: Stories of Wolf Biologists' Favorite Wolves* (Minneapolis: International Wolf Center, 2013).

Chapter 13: Enough Is Enough

This chapter draws on Laurie Lyman's notes between February 2014 and June 2015, supplemented by Rick McIntyre's notes from July 19 and 21 and September 23.

Rick visited Crandall, a place he generally avoided, during the government shutdown in October 2013, caused by a standoff over a spending bill between President Obama and congressional Republicans. Yellowstone was closed, prompting Rick and other watchers to head east, looking for wolves.

Media coverage continued during this period. Highlights included Nathan Rott, "Wolves at the Door: Can Two Top Predators Coexist in the American West?" NPR, February 3, 2014, and Elliott D. Woods, "Wolflandia: The Fight over the Most Polarizing Animal in the West," *Outside*, January 2015.

On the impact of the 2013 hunting season, see "Protected No Longer, More Than 550 Gray Wolves Killed This Season by Hunters and Trappers," NBC News, March 6, 2013.

There were dozens of media reports on wolves and trophic cascades in Yellowstone during this period (not to mention a TED Talk). Some researchers, notably David Mech, cautioned against the rush to credit wolves for Yellowstone's rebound, or observed that the habitat remained "broken" in important ways. See Warren Cornwall, "Have Returning Wolves Really Saved Yellowstone?" *High Country News*, December 8, 2014.

The effort to retire national forest grazing leases around Greater Yellowstone was spearheaded by the National Wildlife Federation. By 2015, the program had retired 750,000 acres, greatly reducing conflicts between wolves and ranchers in the area. Another nonprofit, WildEarth Guardians, worked with ranchers to reduce livestock losses through the use of nonlethal deterrence techniques, including fladry (hanging flapping banners on fences to scare predators) and increased human presence (e.g., hiring range riders).

Epilogue

The account of Rick's fete at the Range Rider is from my own notes on the event and from my interviews with those present. Rick told the story about the boy whose father had a wolf permit in "06 Female," *Snap Judgment*, NPR, May 23, 2014. My account of Rick's illness is from my interviews with Rick and his friends.

After the death of O-Six, the mantle of world's most famous wolf fell to a gray female who had been collared by Wyoming game officials near Cody. In October 2014, she showed up at the north rim of the Grand Canyon, the first wolf sighted in the area since the 1940s. Her 750-mile journey made national headlines and inspired conservation groups backing Arizona's troubled wolf recovery program. Twenty years after they were reintroduced to the state, fewer than one hundred wolves were still confined to a modest tract of national forest land two hundred miles south of the Grand Canyon. The heavily wooded high country around the Grand Canyon had excellent potential as wolf habitat, but over the years any wolf attempting to make the journey north had been either captured and returned or shot, to protect the state's cattle industry.

Now a wolf had made it to the area at last, albeit from an unexpected direction. Hundreds of schoolchildren from around the world submitted names for the wolf in a contest organized by conservation groups; the winning entry, offered by a ten-year-old from Oregon, was Echo. "Because she came back to the Grand Canyon, like an echo does," the boy explained.

She didn't wear the name for long. About two months after her surprise appearance made the papers, she wandered into Utah, where a hunter mistook her for a coyote. The headline tells the story: "Grand Canyon Wolf That Made Epic Journey Shot Dead in Utah," *National Geographic*, February 13, 2015.

INDEX

Reader's Guide for *American Wolf*

1. According to the author, why was wolf reintroduction called "the greatest wildlife conservation success story of the last fifty years" (40)? Who were some of its opponents, and do you agree with their points of view? Why or why not? What larger cultural clash is revealed through the retelling of this "success story," and what does each side feel they are fighting for? Has this clash ultimately been resolved?

2. Rick McIntyre considers the Druids to be the "face of the reintroduction" (25) and "American royalty" akin to the Kennedys (45). What is it about the Druids that makes them stand out? What ultimately becomes of this pack, and what does their story reveal about the lives of wolves and the fate of wolf families? What larger story is Blakeslee able to tell through the lives of these particular wolves?

3. Who is O-Six, and why do so many people seem to be especially interested in her? What distinguishes her from the other wolves, and why do you think she becomes so famous? How is she regarded by her own pack and by her peers? What evidence do we have for this? How do we, as readers, become invested in O-Six's story? What makes her such a compelling figure on the page?

4. What does the book reveal about the role of politics in the delisting or relisting of wolves on the endangered species list? Is the listing or delisting ultimately determined by science or by politics? How, for example, did the question of whether wolves should be protected or hunted impact a crucial senate race in recent history? What does the author suggest is the larger "real struggle," and how does the Sagebrush Rebellion illuminate this? What are some of the implied dangers of politicians making these conservation decisions?

5. Although *American Wolf* is a work of nonfiction, the book possesses many qualities of a novel, including the treatment of the wolves as "characters" with their own individual narratives. How does

the author create this sense of animal as protagonist? How do you think this rendering affects the way readers respond to the wolves' stories and the controversial issues contained therein, and how did this characterization affect your own personal response?

6. In contrast, the book reveals that many biologists feel it is "a cardinal sin" to anthropomorphize wolves and other animals (139). Why? Do you agree with them? What would be some of the dangers inherent in assigning human qualities to animals as we study them and seek to understand them?

7. What are some of the main sources of conflict in this book? How did you respond to the various animal conflicts versus the human conflicts? Who did you find yourself siding with and why? Did your stance ever change as the story progressed? How does your stance illuminate the ways we respond to conflict and how we choose to offer empathy or support?

8. What does Rick McIntyre observe about the wolf 21 that is considered unusual in the animal world? What does Rick think is the single most important trait for an "alpha" to have, and why does he consider it an "evolutionary imperative" (44)? Do you agree that each of the alphas represented in the book possess this quality? How important is it that human leaders possess this quality as well? Would you say it is also a natural imperative?

9. Who do you think "the killers" is referencing in the title of chapter 4? Consider how the book creates a dialogue around those who kill and those who are killed. With whom do you sympathize? How, if at all, does the book distinguish between killing out of necessity and instinct and killing by choice? How would you characterize the author's overall treatment of the subject of death?

10. The book draws attention to the abundance of cultural myths surrounding wolves. What are some of the popular stories and myths about wolves with which you are familiar? How are wolves depicted in these stories? Are they cast in a positive or negative light? Is this still how wolves are perceived today, or would you say that our views of wolves have evolved over time?

11. Why do you think the author chose to bookend his story with Steven Turnbull? Were you surprised by Turnbull's action at the end of the story? Does he seem to feel any remorse for what he did? Why or why not? How do others react to what he has done? When the author spends time with Turnbull, how does it affect his view of Turnbull and what Turnbull has done? Would you say that Turnbull is a figure who elicits sympathy? Why or why not? How did you feel after reading the epilogue? Did any of your own views change after reading about the meeting of Turnbull and the author?

12. What was Rick McIntyre's dream? Would you say that he achieved it? What impact did Rick's work have upon the Yellowstone community—and on communities beyond Yellowstone? What story does Rick tell at the gathering to celebrate his career, and what does he feel this story is about? Why does he consider the story a romance? What question does he feel this story should invite about wolves, and what does Rick believe is the answer to this question?

13. What does Blakeslee's book reveal about the art of storytelling? What makes a "good" story and where do we find evidence of this in the tales of O-Six and other inhabitants of the American West? Although many of the main characters of *American Wolf* are animals, what common themes, plots, and devices from the world of literature do we find in the stories found in Blakeslee's book? What does the author say is ultimately "as good a reason as any" (269) for telling a story?

About the Author of This Guide

JE BANACH is a senior member of the Resident Faculty in Fiction at the Yale Writers' Workshop. She has written for PEN, *Vogue*, *ELLE*, *Esquire*, *Granta*, *The Paris Review*, *Electric Literature*, and other venues and was a longtime contributor to Harold Bloom's literary series. She is the author of more than sixty literary guides including guides to works by Maya Angelou, Salman Rushdie, His Holiness the Dalai Lama, and Haruki Murakami.

ABOUT THE AUTHOR

NATE BLAKESLEE is a writer-at-large for *Texas Monthly*. His first book, *Tulia*, won the J. Anthony Lukas Book Prize and the Texas Institute of Letters nonfiction prize, and was a finalist for the PEN/Martha Albrand Award. The *Washington Post* called *Tulia* one of the most important books about wrongful convictions ever written. Blakeslee lives in Austin, Texas, with his family.